EVERYONE**CAN**COOK
everything

ERIC AKIS

EVERYONE**CAN**COOK™
everything

whitecap

Whitecap Books is known for its expertise in the
cookbook market, and has produced some of
the most innovative and familiar titles found in
kitchens across North America. Visit our website
at www.whitecap.ca.

Publisher: Michael Burch
Editor: Theresa Best
Cover and interior design: Michelle Furbacher
Typesetting: Setareh Ashrafologhalai
Proofreading: Eva van Emden
Food photography: Michael Tourigny
Food styling: Eric Akis

Printed in China

**Library and Archives Canada
Cataloguing in Publication**

Akis, Eric, 1961-
    Everyone can cook everything / Eric Akis.

Includes index.

ISBN 978-1-77050-109-6

    1. Cooking. 2. Cookbooks. I. Title.

TX714.A4565 2012   641.5   C2011-908318-3

The publisher acknowledges the financial support
of the Government of Canada through the Canada
Book Fund (CBF) and the Province of British
Columbia through the Book Publishing Tax Credit.

12 13 14 15 16   5 4 3 2 1

EVERYONE**CAN**COOK
everything

ACKNOWLEDGMENTS

This book is the culmination of 10 years of pleasurable work. I, being the author, was obviously front and centre in the process, but my name would not be on the cover of such a beautiful publication if it weren't for the big-time help of some very talented people.

To Michael Burch, owner and publisher of Whitecap Books, thank you for your never-ending support and for including me among your fine group of authors. Thank you Theresa Best, whose last name is appropriate, as she has been one of the best editors I've worked with. Theresa, thank you for being so organized in helping me put together this, my most ambitious of books.

To designer Michelle Furbacher, thank you for creating such an easy to read, well-formatted book and for making everything fit! Thank you to talented photographer Michael Tourigny, for making my recipes look as appetizing as they really are. And to proofreader Eva van Emden, thanks for triple-checking all the facts.

Because this book features recipes and information from my first six *Everyone Can Cook* cookbooks, I need to also thank the folks that helped me create those books. I can't list you all, but some dear to my heart are Robert McCullough, Taryn Boyd, Lesley Cameron, Grace Yaginuma and Elaine Jones. Thank you for being such inspiring people to work with.

And, of course, thanks to my wife, Cheryl Warwick, and son, Tyler, for being the best recipe evaluators in the world and for being so patient with me during the long and challenging process of creating a top-notch cookbook.

INTRODUCTION

Can everyone cook? That's a question I've been frequently asked since publishing the first book in my *Everyone Can Cook* series. I'm still shocked by that query, but it seems prepared-food marketers have been ultra-successful in convincing many that preparing a meal at home requires a culinary school diploma and a whole lot of time.

Hogwash, I say. To me, it's not whether or not you can cook; it's whether or not you have the desire, the confidence and the inspiration. If you have those traits, learning to cook, or improving the cooking skills you already have, can be much easier than you think and be a rewarding and taste-filled experience.

If you lack some or all of those traits, *Everyone Can Cook Everything* will change that.

In 15 years as a food writer, I've published well over 1,000 articles that covered every topic imaginable and were filled with practical advice for the home cook. In nine years as a cookbook author, I've published six previous books that explored a wide range of topics and presented over 750 recipes that work. That's a lot of content and I jammed as much of it as I could into this book.

Now, truth be told, I should have called it *Everyone Can Cook Everything Most Folks Like to Eat*. That title, obviously, was too long and doesn't exactly roll off the tongue. But that is what this book offers: hundreds of recipes, tips and techniques—*everything* you'll need to prepare foods you'll want to cook and eat.

Everyone Can Cook Everything was created from a "best of" selection of my recipes. I updated them, where needed, and logically divided them into chapters covering as many topics as possible, such as soups, salads, vegetarian entrées, meat and baked goods, to name just a few.

In those chapters you'll find a very diverse range of recipes, including those for midweek meals, such as Skillet Mac and Cheese (page 149), and others for weekend mornings, such as Morning Glory Pancakes (page 127). There are special-occasion recipes, such as Beef Tenderloin Steaks with Crab-Stuffed Mushrooms (page 319). In this book you'll also find methods for preparing international favorites, such as Green Thai Curry Shrimp (page 213), and those for making sweet treats, such as Moist and Delicious One-Pan Chocolate Cake (page 383).

The book's many sidebars will guide you on preparing frequently used ingredients, such as Cooking Perfect Pasta (page 139). You'll also find very useful ones on cooking items you may only attempt once a year, such as A Guide to Preparing Roast Turkey (page 272).

To simplify things, the recipes use ingredients found at most supermarkets, are succinctly written, and many include a Note or sidebar that anticipates and answers any questions you may have about a certain ingredient or method.

Eric's Options—included with each recipe—offer suggestions for substituting ingredients or tweaking things to make the recipe more to your liking. As well, following this introduction is a section that will help you stock your pantry and make cooking the recipes in this book an even easier and quicker proposition.

Whether you're a novice or quite an accomplished cook, my goal with *Everyone Can Cook Everything* is to create a book that will be used daily, and for generations. Whether you're young, old or somewhere in between, I believe this book will help you to cook and eat well, and thoroughly enjoy doing both!

Happy cooking!

Eric Akis

STOCKING UP

Creating tasty starters, meals and baked goods is much easier if you're not constantly running to the store for kitchen staples. The following are useful items to have on hand.

ASIAN SAUCES, NOODLES AND RICE
North Americans are fond of Asian-style dishes, and there are a number in this book. Soy sauce, teriyaki sauce, sweet chili sauce, wasabi paste, hot chili sauce, coconut milk and hoisin sauce are items you should stock. Alongside them should be quick-cooking Asian-style noodles, such as egg and rice noodles.

BAKING BASICS
If you have time and the urge to bake, fulfilling that desire will be easier if you keep basic ingredients on hand. Key items include all-purpose flour, whole wheat flour, rolled oats, sugar, brown sugar, baking powder, baking soda, pure vanilla extract, butter, eggs, vegetable shortening, cocoa powder and chocolate chips.

BREADCRUMBS AND CORNMEAL
Keep a bag of breadcrumbs on hand to coat foods before pan-frying or baking and to add body to ground meat mixes. Cornmeal can also be used to coat foods and make tasty baked goods, such as cornbread.

CANNED AND DRIED LEGUMES
Chickpeas, kidney beans, black beans and lentils are budget-friendly canned legumes used in a variety of recipes in this book, including soup, burgers and stew. Keep dried white beans on hand if you want to make a splendid batch of baked beans.

CANNED SEAFOOD
Keep tins of seafood, such as tuna and crab, on your shelf and you'll have an instant ingredient to use in an appetizer, noodle dish or other tasty creation.

CANNED TOMATO PRODUCTS
Diced and crushed tomatoes, tomato sauce and tomato paste are important items to keep on hand for making items such as soups, chili and Italian-style dishes.

CHEESE AND OTHER DAIRY PRODUCTS
Mozzarella, goat, blue, feta, cheddar, Monterey Jack and Parmesan are versatile cheeses to keep in the refrigerator. Yogurt, sour cream, buttermilk, whipping and light cream and, of course, milk are other dairy products used in this book.

CONDIMENTS AND SAUCES
Horseradish, ketchup, barbecue sauce, hot pepper sauce and Worcestershire sauce are condiments and sauces to stock and stir into several recipes in this book.

CURRY PASTES AND POWDER
These two splendid Asian-style ingredients, which come in mild, medium and hot versions, can quickly add a world of flavor to a dish.

DRIED HERBS AND SPICES
Everyone has a drawer full, but here are some used in this book: thyme, tarragon, sage leaves, herbes de Provence, rosemary, paprika, chili powder, ground cumin, cayenne pepper, cinnamon, ground nutmeg, ground cloves and five-spice powder.

FLATBREADS
Flour tortillas are handy and versatile: stuff, roll and bake them to make such things as enchiladas. Other flatbreads to keep on hand include pita and naan bread, which are great to heat and serve with some of the curries and stews in this book.

FRESH PRODUCE
All refrigerators contain some fresh produce, but items making several appearances in this book include garlic, ginger, onions, green onions, celery, carrots, bell peppers, new potatoes, Yukon Gold potatoes, baking potatoes, snap peas, romaine lettuce, salad greens, tomatoes, apples, lemons, limes and oranges.

FROZEN PEAS AND CORN
Use these little frozen gems to add color, texture and taste to a range of dishes, such as chili, stews and soups.

HONEY AND MAPLE SYRUP
Beyond adding sweetness, use these ingredients to balance tart, spicy flavorings in salad dressings, sauces and bastes.

MAYONNAISE
Many people think of mayonnaise as simply a sandwich spread or salad binder, but it also makes a base for quick salad dressings and can be used to coat foods, such as chicken strips, before breading.

MUSTARD
In this book I use regular, smooth Dijon mustard, and coarser in texture, wholegrain Dijon mustard, also called country-style or old-style. Both are versatile ingredients to keep on hand and use in all sorts of creations, such as salad dressings, sauces and roasts. Dry and hot English-style mustards are also great to have at the ready.

NUTS AND DRIED FRUIT
Keep walnuts, pecans, almonds, raisins, dried cranberries, currants and other nuts and dried fruit on hand to use in granola, salads and desserts.

OILS
It's hard to imagine cooking without oils, which contribute moisture and flavor to a range of dishes, from salads to stir-fries, meats, seafood and baked goods. The two main types used in this book are olive oil and vegetable oil.

PASTA
If you're looking for a quick supper, a bag of dried pasta in your cupboard or a package of fresh pasta in your refrigerator will be the answer. Stock various shapes and sizes, such as spaghetti, linguini, macaroni, rotini, penne, tortellini and rigatoni.

PESTO
This delicious ingredient appears several times in this book, adding color and flavor to an assortment of dishes. Almost every supermarket sells prepared pesto that will keep a week or more in your refrigerator. You can also make homemade pesto and freeze it in cubes.

PREPARED STOCKS AND CLAM NECTAR
Some very good prepared vegetable, chicken and beef stocks (also called broth) are available in supermarkets these days. Have them on hand to make soups, stews or braised dishes. Clam nectar, also called clam juice, is also good to keep on hand for making chowder.

RICE
Long-grain white and brown rice, risotto rice, and short-grain sushi rice are used in this book. You'll also find options to use more aromatic rice, such as jasmine and basmati.

VINEGAR
Stock balsamic, cider, rice, raspberry and wine vinegars to flavor salad dressings and other dishes that benefit from an acidic bite.

APPETIZERS

Roasted Red Pepper Hummus, top (page 10),
Fig and Olive Tapanade, bottom (page 9)

FIG and OLIVE TAPENADE

I was inspired to create this recipe after a trip to California's Sonoma Valley, where foods such as tapenade are made with locally grown figs and olives. This Mediterranean-style spread and great summer appetizer is a wonderful combination of sweet figs nicely balanced with salty, sharp olives. Pine nuts, basil and other good things add even richer flavor. I like to serve this tapenade with a creamy cheese, such as brie or goat cheese. The tastes mingle beautifully when combined on a slice of baguette or a cracker.

preparation time • 10 minutes
cooking time • 15 minutes
makes • 2 cups (500 mL)

NOTE
Dried black mission figs are available at many supermarkets and fine food stores in the same aisle as other bagged, dried fruits.

ERIC'S OPTIONS
To make a delicious canapé, spread toasted baguette rounds with a soft and creamy goat cheese. Top the cheese with a spoonful of tapenade. Garnish each canapé with a small, thin slice of pear and a small basil leaf.

1 cup (250 mL) dried black mission figs (see Note)

1 cup (250 mL) pitted kalamata olives

¼ cup (60 mL) pine nuts

¼ cup (60 mL) coarsely chopped basil

¼ cup (60 mL) extra virgin olive oil

2 Tbsp (30 mL) balsamic vinegar

2 medium garlic cloves, chopped

Place the figs in a pot, cover with cold water and bring to a boil over high heat. Remove from the heat and let the figs plump up in the water for 15 minutes. Drain well and place the figs in a food processor. Add the remaining ingredients and pulse until well combined and finely chopped; do not purée. Transfer to a serving bowl, cover and refrigerate for 4 hours or overnight to allow the flavors to meld. (Refrigerated in a tightly sealed jar, the tapenade will keep for at least a week.) Serve the tapenade with slices of baguette or crackers to spread it on.

ROASTED RED PEPPER HUMMUS

This red-hued version of the Greek-style dip is flavored with sweet and smoky-tasting roasted red pepper. Serve it as an appetizer with wedges of pita and raw vegetables, such as cucumber slices, carrot sticks and cauliflower florets.

one 19 oz (540 mL) can chickpeas, drained and rinsed

1 large roasted red pepper, coarsely chopped (see Note)

3–4 Tbsp (45–60 mL) olive oil, plus some for drizzling

3 Tbsp (45 mL) tahini (see Note)

2 Tbsp (30 mL) fresh lemon juice, or to taste

2 garlic cloves, coarsely chopped

2 tsp (10 mL) ground cumin

3 Tbsp (45 mL) chopped fresh basil to taste

salt and freshly ground black pepper to taste

Place all the ingredients in a food processor and pulse until smooth. Spoon into a decorative bowl. The dip can be made a day or two in advance of serving; cover and refrigerate. Drizzle the hummus with a little olive oil before serving. *Pictured on page 8.*

preparation time	•	10 minutes
cooking time	•	none
makes	•	about 2 cups (500 mL)

NOTE
Roasted red peppers and tahini, a paste made from sesame seeds, are available in jars at most supermarkets and Mediterranean-style delis.

ERIC'S OPTIONS
If you want to roast your own red pepper, place a large red bell pepper in a small baking pan lined with parchment paper. Roast at 375°F (190°C) for 30 minutes, turning once or twice, until the skin is blistered. Remove from the oven and cover the pan with foil. Let the pepper sit for 20 minutes. Uncover the pepper and slip the skin off. Cut the pepper in half, remove the seeds and it's ready to use.

MOROCCAN-STYLE BABY CARROT DIP

Many Moroccan dishes are infused with the flavors of lemon, garlic, olive oil and spices such as cumin and cayenne. In this dip, these flavors are tastily blended with sweet-tasting baby carrots, an ingredient that is easy to use because supermarkets sell them already peeled in bags.

1½ lb (750 g) baby carrots (also called mini-carrots)

pinch cayenne pepper

2 tsp (10 mL) ground cumin

1 tsp (5 mL) paprika

2 Tbsp (30 mL) red wine vinegar

2 Tbsp (30 mL) freshly squeezed lemon juice

¼ cup (60 mL) extra virgin olive oil

2 garlic cloves, chopped

2 tsp (10 mL) grated fresh ginger

salt and freshly ground black pepper to taste

sliced black olives and chopped fresh parsley for garnish

preparation time • 10 minutes
cooking time • 12–15 minutes
makes • about 3 cups (750 mL)

ERIC'S OPTIONS

You can substitute the baby carrots with 1½ lb (750 g) of peeled, regular carrots. If you do, add 1 Tbsp (15 mL) of honey to the dip. Regular carrots aren't as sweet as baby carrots and this dip needs sweetness to balance the tartness of the lemon and vinegar. This dip can be made up to a day ahead and stored in the refrigerator. When ready to serve, garnish with sliced olives and chopped parsley.

Boil the carrots in a generous amount of lightly salted water until very tender, about 12 to 15 minutes. Drain well and place in the bowl of a food processor with the cayenne, cumin, paprika, vinegar, lemon juice, oil, garlic, ginger, salt and pepper. Pulse until smooth; thin with a little water if the dip is too thick. Transfer to a serving bowl and refrigerate until well chilled. When ready to serve, garnish with a few black olive slices and a sprinkling of chopped parsley. Serve with crisp raw vegetable sticks and wedges of pita bread.

CUMIN and
LEMON–MARINATED OLIVES

Bold spices, aromatic extra virgin olive oil and a citrusy blast of lemon zest give these olives an addictive flavor.

1 cup (250 mL) whole black olives

1 cup (250 mL) whole green olives

2 garlic cloves, finely chopped

1 tsp (5 mL) ground cumin

¼ tsp (1 mL) fennel seeds

1 Tbsp (15 mL) freshly grated lemon zest

½ tsp (2 mL) crushed chili flakes

2 tsp (10 mL) dried oregano

extra virgin olive oil

preparation time •	5 minutes
cooking time •	none
makes •	about 2¼ cups (560 mL)

ERIC'S OPTIONS
For added color, replace ¼ cup (60 mL) of each type of olive with ½ cup (125 mL) of oil-packed sun-dried tomatoes, drained well and coarsely chopped.

Combine the black and green olives, garlic, cumin, fennel seeds, lemon zest, chili flakes and oregano in a medium bowl. Spoon the mixture into a tall 3-cup (750 mL) jar and add enough olive oil to cover the olives. Seal the jar and refrigerate for 1 to 2 days to allow the flavors to meld. Because the olive oil will solidify when chilled, you'll need to bring the olives to room temperature before serving.

SHRIMP COCKTAIL CANAPÉS

These delicious little canapés featuring the elements found in a shrimp cocktail are handily served on small rounds of rye bread—great for a stand-up party.

preparation time • 20 minutes
cooking time • none
makes • 24 canapés

24 cocktail rye bread rounds (see Note)

½ cup (125 mL) spreadable cream cheese

1½ cups (375 mL) mixed baby salad greens

½ lb (250 g) small cooked, fresh or frozen (thawed) salad shrimp, patted dry

⅓ cup (80 mL) cocktail sauce

24 small parsley sprigs

twirls of lemon zest for garnish (see Note)

Spread a thin layer of cream cheese on each piece of rye bread. Top with a few leaves of the salad greens. Place 2 to 3 shrimp on each canapé. (Can be made to this point several hours in advance. Cover and refrigerate until needed.) Top the shrimp with a small spoonful of the cocktail sauce. Garnish each canapé with a parsley sprig and a few twirls of lemon zest and serve.

NOTE

Ready-to-use rye bread rounds are sold in plastic tubs at most supermarket delicatessens. If unavailable, use a round cookie cutter to cut thin slices of rye bread into 1½-inch (4 cm) rounds, or use a small, sturdy round cracker as the base for these canapés. I used a lemon zester to make the thin twirls of lemon zest garnishing the canapés.

ERIC'S OPTIONS

Use store-bought cocktail sauce or make your own by combining ½ cup (125 mL) ketchup, 1 Tbsp (15 mL) prepared horseradish, ½ tsp (2 mL) hot pepper sauce, 1 tsp (5 mL) Worcestershire sauce and 1 Tbsp (15 mL) fresh lemon juice in a small bowl. Stir in salt and freshly ground black pepper to taste. Chill well before using.

NEW YORK STEAK CANAPÉS
with PESTO and PARMESAN

These meaty little bites have an Italian flair. The toasts for the canapés can be made several hours in advance. Keep covered at room temperature until needed.

sixteen ¼-inch (6 mm) thick slices of baguette

3 Tbsp (45 mL) extra virgin olive oil

⅓ cup (80 mL) freshly grated Parmesan cheese

two 6 oz (175 g) New York (strip loin) steaks

coarse sea salt and freshly ground black pepper to taste

⅓ cup (80 mL) store-bought or homemade pesto (see Pesto recipe on page 359)

small fresh basil leaves for garnish

preparation time	•	20 minutes
cooking time	•	about 12–15 minutes
makes	•	16 canapés

ERIC'S OPTIONS
Use another tender steak, such as ribeye or tenderloin, instead of strip loin. For additional color, taste and texture, top the meat with a few thin strips of roasted red pepper before spooning on the pesto.

Preheat the oven to 350°F (175°C). Place the baguette slices on a parchment paper–lined baking sheet. Lightly brush with 2 Tbsp (30 mL) of the olive oil; sprinkle with the cheese. Bake 5 to 8 minutes or until lightly toasted. Remove from the oven and cool to room temperature. Heat an indoor or outdoor grill to medium high. Brush the steaks with the remaining olive oil and season generously with salt and pepper. Grill to desired doneness; 2 to 3 minutes per side should yield a medium-rare steak. Transfer to a plate and rest 5 minutes to allow the juices to set before thinly slicing. Top each baguette slice with 2 or 3 slices of the meat. Top the meat with 1 tsp (5 mL) of the pesto. Garnish with basil leaves and serve.

TIPS FOR MAKING CANAPÉS

Canapé was originally the French word for "couch." Its meaning broadened in France in the late 18th century when a chef thought the bite-sized pieces of bread that served as the base for appetizers were like couches, but instead of supporting people, they supported savory toppings.

Although cucumber rounds and other vegetable slices are often used, bread, in various forms from pumpernickel rounds to baguette slices to gourmet crackers, is still the preferred base for canapés. When preparing, remember that canapés are meant to be bite-sized, not hefty pieces of bread with large chunks of food on top.

Because canapés are most often served at special occasions, the base and toppings should reflect that. Serve quality bread and vegetable slices topped with smoked salmon, fine cheese, pâté or other decadent ingredients; avoid neon-orange cheese spread on soda crackers topped with sliced garlic sausage. For appealing-looking canapés, the toppings should be cut and placed with care. And lastly, if your topping is overly moist and the base is soft and absorbent, don't make your canapés too far in advance or they will be soggy and less appetizing when you serve them.

SMOKED SALMON TARTARE on CUCUMBER ROUNDS

This is a significant spin on the classic dish beef tartare, in which raw meat is chopped and mixed with tangy flavorings and displayed in patty-like form on a plate. In this version, finely chopped smoked salmon replaces the beef, and the tartare mixture is spooned onto palate-refreshing slices of cucumber, making a decadent appetizer.

preparation time	•	30 minutes
cooking time	•	none
makes	•	20 pieces

ERIC'S OPTIONS
These bites can be made several hours in advance; cover and refrigerate until you're ready to serve. Instead of smoked salmon, use smoked tuna to make the tartare. You can find smoked tuna, which is usually frozen (thaw before using), at specialty seafood stores and some supermarkets.

¼ lb (125 g) cold smoked salmon, finely chopped (see About Cold- and Hot- Smoked Salmon on page 18)

3 Tbsp (45 mL) finely chopped red onion

1 Tbsp (15 mL) capers, finely chopped

1 Tbsp (15 mL) extra virgin olive oil

2 tsp (10 mL) fresh lemon juice

1 tsp (5 mL) Dijon mustard

freshly ground black pepper to taste

2 tsp (10 mL) chopped fresh dill

20 English cucumber slices cut ½ inch (1 cm) thick

Place the salmon, onion, capers, oil, lemon juice, mustard, pepper and dill in a bowl and gently mix to combine. Use a small spoon or melon baller to scoop out some of the center portion of each cucumber slice. Mound 2 tsp (10 mL) of the smoked salmon tartare in the center of each cucumber slice and arrange on a serving tray.

ABOUT COLD- AND HOT-SMOKED SALMON

There are two main types of smoked salmon: cold-smoked and hot-smoked.

Cold-smoked salmon is smoked at temperatures ranging from 70°F to 90°F (21°C to 32°C). Before smoking, the salmon is cured in salt brine, which has preservative and antiseptic properties. Cold-smoking gives the salmon a pleasant, smoky flavor and a silky, luscious texture. This style of smoked salmon is most often used in cold preparations—on bagels, tea sandwiches, canapés, sushi or served on its own with a few simple accompaniments. Cold smoked salmon is sometimes labeled lox, but most guides say "true" lox is brined in a much saltier solution and is not usually smoked.

Hot-smoked salmon is smoked and cooked at temperatures ranging from 120°F to 175°F (49°C to 80°C), depending on the desired flavor intensity and the size of the fish. Salt and other flavorings, such as sugar, spices and herbs, often in the form of brine, are used to boost flavor. Hot-smoked salmon is much firmer in texture than cold-smoked and can be enjoyed on its own as a snack or appetizer. It can also be used in a range of cooked and uncooked dishes, such as pasta, soup, quiche, sandwich fillings, salads and pâté.

SMOKED SALMON PÂTÉ

This delicious pâté can be quickly whipped up in the food processor. To make a simple, but elegant canapé, pipe the pâté on small rounds of rye bread and garnish with sprigs of dill and tiny lemon wedges.

½ lb (250 g) brick cream cheese, at room temperature

4 oz (125 g) cold- or hot-smoked salmon, bones and skin removed, coarsely chopped (see About Cold- and Hot-Smoked Salmon on page 18)

2 Tbsp (30 mL) sour cream

2 tsp (10 mL) chopped fresh dill

1 Tbsp (15 mL) horseradish, or to taste

1 Tbsp (15 mL) lemon juice

salt and white pepper to taste

preparation time	•	5 minutes
cooking time	•	none
makes	•	1¾ cups (435 mL), serves 6–8 as an appetizer

ERIC'S OPTIONS
For a lower-fat pâté use light versions of the cream cheese and sour cream. The pâté won't be as thick, but it will still be very tasty.

Pâté can be made up to a day in advance. Cover and keep refrigerated until needed.

Place the cream cheese, smoked salmon, sour cream, dill, horseradish and lemon juice in a food processor; pulse until a coarse pâté forms. Season with salt and pepper; pulse until smooth. Spoon into a serving bowl and serve with sliced bread and crackers.

CHANTERELLE MUSHROOM CROSTINI

In many wooded parts of North America, autumn rains bring chanterelle mushrooms. They are harvested and find their way to fine food stores and some supermarkets. They have an attractive golden color and are trumpet-shaped, with an intriguing, earthy taste and a pleasing, slightly chewy texture.

preparation time • 20 minutes
cooking time • 18 minutes
makes • 12 crostini

ERIC'S OPTIONS
If chanterelles are unavailable, use another type of mushroom, such as brown or oyster mushrooms.

½ lb (250 g) fresh chanterelle mushrooms

2 Tbsp (30 mL) olive oil

1 garlic clove, minced

¼ cup (60 mL) white wine

1 tsp (5 mL) chopped fresh rosemary to taste

salt and freshly ground black pepper to taste

12 thin slices baguette

¼ lb (125 g) soft goat cheese

balsamic vinegar for drizzling

Trim the tips of the mushroom stems. Clean each mushroom well and then slice them thinly lengthwise. Place the oil in a large skillet over medium-high heat. Add the mushrooms and garlic and cook until tender, about 5 minutes. Add the wine and rosemary and bring to a simmer. Simmer until the wine has almost entirely cooked away. Season with salt and pepper and remove from the heat.

Preheat the oven to 375°F (190°C). Line a baking sheet with parchment paper. Spread the baguette slices with the goat cheese and place on the baking sheet. Top each crostini with some mushrooms. Bake, in the middle of the oven, for 10 minutes, or until the crostini are hot and toasted on the bottom.

Cool the crostini for a few minutes before arranging on a platter. Serve the balsamic vinegar alongside so diners can drizzle the crostini with it.

ABOUT CHANTERELLE MUSHROOMS

Chanterelle mushrooms are esteemed for their fruity aroma and pleasingly chewy texture. There is a similar species of this mushroom, the white chanterelle, which you don't often see for sale.

When purchasing chanterelles, look for evenly colored, firm caps with no dark, soft or slimy spots or cracking. If very fresh, they'll keep well in a paper bag in the refrigerator for several days. Clean chanterelles well before cooking, removing any loose debris or dirt with a small, fine brush or paper towel.

In the fall, you'll find fresh chanterelle mushrooms for sale at farmers' markets, specialty food stores and some supermarkets. They can be expensive, but even a modest amount can make a dish extra special.

Cost is one reason some people pick their own chanterelles. If you are thinking about joining that club, it's essential that you learn all you can about harvesting wild mushrooms before even considering it. Toxic mushrooms grow in the same areas chanterelles do. One of the best ways to learn about wild mushrooms is to join a local mycological group. Such groups will share valuable information and tips on all things related to fungi.

BRANDY-LACED PEPPERCORN PÂTÉ
on BAGUETTE ROUNDS

This divine pâté freezes well when sealed in an airtight container. Thaw it in the refrigerator overnight before using.

½ lb (250 g) butter, at room temperature

1 medium onion, halved and thinly sliced

3 garlic cloves, chopped

1 lb (500 g) chicken livers, trimmed of fat and sinew

½ tsp (2 mL) dried thyme

2 Tbsp (30 mL) green peppercorns

¼ cup (60 mL) brandy

salt and freshly ground black pepper to taste

24–30 lightly toasted baguette rounds

thinly sliced gherkins and parsley sprigs for garnish

preparation time	•	15 minutes
cooking time	•	12–15 minutes
makes	•	about 2 cups (500 mL) pâté

ERIC'S OPTIONS
If you can find them, replace the chicken livers in this recipe with an equal amount of duck livers. Melba toast or good-quality crackers could replace the toasted baguette rounds. For a sweet and spicy taste, top the pâté with red pepper jelly or chutney instead of gherkins.

Melt 3 Tbsp (45 mL) of the butter in a skillet set over medium heat. Add the onion and garlic and cook until tender. Add the chicken livers and thyme and cook until the livers are nicely colored and almost cooked through. (Cut a chicken liver open during cooking to see how they are doing. They should look just slightly pink in the middle. Be careful not to overcook them or the pâté will have a less-appealing look, color and taste.) Add the green peppercorns and brandy. If desired, carefully ignite it with a long match. Cook, stirring, another 2–3 minutes, or until the chicken livers are just cooked through and most of the liquid in the skillet has evaporated. Remove from the heat and allow the chicken livers to cool to room temperature.

Place the skillet ingredients in a food processor. Add the remaining butter and process until smooth. Season with salt and pepper. Spoon the pâté into a bowl, tightly cover, and place in the refrigerator for several hours or overnight to allow the flavors to meld.

Allow the pâté to stand at room temperature for 30 minutes before spreading or piping it on the toasted baguette rounds. Garnish each with a few sliced gherkins and a parsley sprig.

FOR TOASTED BAGUETTE ROUNDS
Cut the baguette into ¼-inch-thick (6 mm) slices. Place the slices in a single layer on a baking tray and bake in a 400°F (200°C) oven for 8 minutes, or until golden and toasted.

COUNTRY-STYLE PÂTÉ with PRUNES and PISTACHIOS

My version of this classic French pâté uses bacon to line the mold instead of sliced pork fat—it's leaner and easier to find, and I enjoy the smoky flavor it gives the pâté.

10–12 bacon slices

1¼ lb (625 g) ground pork

½ lb (250 g) ground veal

¼ cup (60 mL) brandy

¼ cup (60 mL) white wine

½ medium onion, finely chopped

2 garlic cloves, finely chopped

1 large egg

1 tsp (5 mL) dried thyme

2 Tbsp (30 mL) green peppercorns

1 tsp (5 mL) salt

1 tsp (5 mL) freshly ground black pepper

⅛ tsp (0.5 mL) ground cloves

⅛ tsp (0.5 mL) ground allspice

1 cup (250 mL) pitted prunes

one ½-inch (1 cm) thick, 3–4-inch (8–10 cm) round,
    slice of ham, cut into ¼-inch (6 mm) strips

¼ cup (60 mL) unsalted, shelled pistachios

3–4 bay leaves

Continued . . .

preparation time	•	15 minutes
cooking time	•	90 minutes
makes	•	10 servings, about 20 slices

ERIC'S OPTIONS
Instead of prunes, try other dried fruits, such as apricots or cherries, in this recipe. For a darker, richer-looking pâté, use red wine instead of white.

COUNTRY-STYLE PÂTÉ with
PRUNES and PISTACHIOS (*continued*)

Preheat the oven to 325°F (160°C). Line an 11¾- x 2¾- x 3-inch (30 x 7 x 8 cm) pâté mold (sold at specialty kitchenware stores), or an 8½- x 4½- x 2½-inch (21 x 11 x 6 cm) loaf pan, with the bacon, slightly overlapping the slices. Place the pork, veal, brandy, white wine, onion, garlic, egg, thyme, green peppercorns, salt, black pepper, cloves and allspice in a large bowl and mix to combine. Pack ⅓ of the meat mixture into the pâté mold or loaf pan. Arrange ½ the prunes, ham slices and pistachios over top. Add another ⅓ of the meat mixture, packing it in tightly. Layer the remaining prunes, ham and pistachios over top. Pack in the remaining meat mixture. Pull the overhanging bacon slices over the layered mixture, ensuring the bacon ends overlap and completely cover the pâté. Top the bacon with the bay leaves. Cover the pâté with aluminum foil and set in a roasting pan. Pour in cold water to halfway up the sides of the pâté mold or loaf pan. Bake for 1 hour; remove the foil and bake for 30 minutes more or until the pâté reaches 160°F (71°C) when an instant-read meat thermometer is inserted in the center.

Place the pâté mold or loaf pan on a cooling rack and cool to room temperature. Cover and refrigerate the pâté for 1 to 2 days before unmolding to let the pâté's flavor develop. When ready to serve, set the pâté mold or loaf pan into a pan containing 2 to 3 inches (5 to 8 cm) of hot water for a few minutes; this will loosen the pâté from the bottom and sides and make it easier to unmold. To unmold, carefully turn the pâté onto a cutting board. Gently lift the mold or pan to reveal the pâté. Scrape away any excess fat from the outside of the pâté. Chill the pâté for 10 minutes before thinly slicing and arranging on a platter. Serve with slices of baguette, cornichon, olives and Dijon mustard.

CREATING A CHEESE BOARD

One of the easiest and most impressive things to serve at a holiday party is a board of assorted quality cheeses. Here are some tips.

TYPES OF CHEESE TO SERVE
Provide an interesting mix of tastes by serving at least five different types of cheese. Offer different colors, shapes, textures and flavors, from meek and mild to bold and beautiful. Because there is such a vast variety of cheese available, it's a good idea to shop at a specialty store where the staff can offer suggestions and let you sample the cheeses.

But as a guide, try to include a firm cheese (such as aged Gouda-style cheese), a semisoft cheese (such as brie), a blue cheese (such as roquefort), a soft and creamy cheese (such as goat) and one that simply looks interesting (such as cheddar flavored with port). You could also include a homemade cheese log, such as Herbed Goat Cheese Logs (page 29).

HOW MUCH TO BUY
When the cheese board is one of several appetizers, allow 2 to 3 oz (60 to 90 g) per person. When served as a snack or single appetizer with wine, or when served as a post-dinner course, serve a more generous ¼ lb (125 g) per person.

HOW TO SERVE
Unwrap the cheese and place on the cheese board 90 minutes before serving to allow it to warm to room temperature. Cover it loosely to allow the cheese to breathe (just like a good wine) but not dry out. Provide a different knife for each type of cheese, which helps avoid having the flavors intermingle. If you're serving a smaller group sitting around a table, present the cheeses just as you buy them, and let guests help themselves. But if you'll be serving a larger, stand-up crowd, present some cheeses as described above, but cut some cheese in bite-sized pieces or cubes so guests can quickly sample some cheese and move out of the way to make room for others. Serve the cheese with good-quality crackers and/ or baguette slices, nuts, and dried and fresh fruit, such as walnuts, almonds, dried apricots, figs, apples and grapes.

HERBED GOAT CHEESE LOGS

This Mediterranean-inspired appetizer is quick and easy. Set the cheese on a platter with a small serving knife or two, surround it with good crackers or thin slices of baguette, and invite your guests to help themselves. You could also include the log as part of a cheese board.

¾ lb (375 g) soft goat cheese

3–4 canned artichoke hearts, very finely chopped

¼ cup (60 mL) pitted black olives, very finely chopped

8 oil-packed sun-dried tomatoes, drained well and very finely chopped

½–¾ cup (125–185 mL) mixed chopped fresh herbs, such as parsley, basil and oregano

preparation time	•	20 minutes
cooking time	•	none
makes	•	2 logs; 12–16 servings

ERIC'S OPTIONS
Use green olives instead of black, or a mix of green and black olives. For a spicy taste, roll the logs in crushed black peppercorns instead of herbs. For a nutty taste, roll the logs in crushed walnuts.

Place the goat cheese in a bowl and beat until lightened and smooth. Mix in the artichokes, olives and sun-dried tomatoes. Lightly dampen your hands with cold water and divide the goat cheese mixture in half. Shape each half into a log that is 6 inches (15 cm) long and 2 inches (5 cm) in diameter.

Place the mixed herbs on a wide plate and stir until combined. Roll each log in the herbs, coating it well and gently pressing the herbs on to help them adhere. Wrap each log in plastic wrap and refrigerate for 2 hours to firm up. (The logs can be prepared up to a day in advance.)

MINI CHEESE-BALL PUMPKINS

Bite-sized mini cheese balls, when coated in crushed cracker crumbs and pushed down in the center to make a squat shape, are reminiscent of pumpkins. Serve them as is, or set them on thin crackers. You can make these up to a day in advance.

½ lb (250 g) brick cream cheese, softened

1 cup (250 mL) cheddar cheese

¼ cup (60 mL) very finely chopped red onion

¼ cup (60 mL) walnut pieces, very finely chopped

2 tsp (10 mL) hot horseradish

½ tsp (2 mL) Worcestershire sauce

¼ tsp (1 mL) salt, or to taste

½ cup (125 mL) finely crushed orange-colored crackers (see Note)

24 pieces green bell pepper, each ½ inch (1 cm) long and ⅛ inch (3 mm) wide

preparation time •	25 minutes
cooking time •	none
makes •	24–30 pumpkins

NOTE
I use goldfish snack crackers for the coating, but any crisp, orange-colored cracker would work. I crush the crackers in a food processor; 1 cup (250 mL) yielded the perfect amount of crumbs.

ERIC'S OPTIONS
Instead of walnuts, use pecans.

Line 2 baking sheets with parchment paper. Place the cream cheese in a bowl and beat with an electric mixer until lightened. Mix in the cheddar cheese, onion, walnuts, horseradish, Worcestershire and salt. Lightly dampen your hands with cold water. Shape the cheese mixture into ¾-inch (2 cm) balls and set on one of the baking sheets.

Place the cracker crumbs on a wide plate. Coat one of the cheese balls in the crumbs, gently pressing them on to help them adhere and shaping the ball so it has a nice round shape. Set it on the clean baking sheet. Repeat with the remaining cheese balls. Gently push down in the center of each cheese ball to give it a pumpkin shape. Make a stem by inserting a piece of green pepper into each cheese ball. Tent with plastic wrap and refrigerate at least 2 hours before serving.

PROSCIUTTO-WRAPPED SCALLOPS
with PESTO MAYONNAISE

Wrapping scallops in prosciutto offers a more intriguing, Italian-style taste, and is a less fatty alternative to streaky bacon.

preparation time • 20 minutes
cooking time • 8–10 minutes
makes • 4 servings

½ cup (125 mL) mayonnaise

2 Tbsp (30 mL) store-bought or homemade pesto
    (see Pesto recipe on page 359)

salt, white pepper and lemon juice to taste

12 large sea scallops (see About Scallops on page 209)

6 paper-thin slices prosciutto, each cut in half lengthwise
    (see About Prosciutto on page 34)

ERIC'S OPTIONS
You can substitute large peeled shrimp or medium shucked oysters for a delicious alternative to scallops. Cooking time remains the same.

Combine the mayonnaise, pesto, salt, pepper and lemon juice in a small bowl. Cover and set aside in the refrigerator. Preheat the oven to 425°F (220°C). Wrap a half piece of prosciutto around the outer edge of each scallop. Secure with a toothpick, if necessary. Place on a nonstick or parchment paper–lined baking sheet. Bake for 8 to 10 minutes, or until just cooked through. Arrange on appetizer plates or a platter, with a bowl of the mayonnaise alongside for dipping.

Prosciutto, the Italian word for "ham," is today most often used to describe ham that is specifically salt-cured and air-dried. The first salt-cured and air-dried prosciutto, and what many say is still the best, was made in the historic town of Parma, Italy. The practice of making prosciutto di Parma, or Parma ham, has gone on since at least 100 BC.

To make prosciutto di Parma, the ham must come from large, white Landrace and Duroc pigs fed on a diet of cereals, grains and whey from Parmigiano Reggiano cheese production. The pigs can only be born and raised in 11 regions of central northern Italy. After careful trimming and salt-curing, the ham goes through months of hanging and drying. This includes a period when they are exposed to the region's aromatic, flavor-building breezes, which many connoisseurs believe is what gives Parma ham its distinct flavor.

Good-quality prosciutto—albeit made with less exacting standards—is now being made in North America. So, when buying prosciutto, the first decision you have to make is whether to buy Italian or domestic. Cost varies and this factor sways many toward the latter, but I recommend initially buying both to do a taste test and determine which one you prefer.

Prosciutto can be cut into cubes, cooked and used in soups and pasta dishes. But if eating it wrapped around a slice of fruit or on top of a crostini, ask your retailer to slice it paper-thin—thin enough to almost be able to see through it. After slicing, be sure the prosciutto is layered side by side on deli paper, not stacked on top of each other, which makes it impossible to pull apart. For the best taste, buy prosciutto the day you intend to use it. However, if need be, sliced and packaged prosciutto can be stored for up to 2 days in the refrigerator.

CURRY and ALMOND-CRUSTED WINGS

Moist and spice-rich wings richly coated with almonds.

1½ cups (375 mL) ground almonds (see Note)

½ cup (125 mL) Indian-style mild, medium
    or hot curry paste

24 chicken wingettes or drumettes, or a mix
    of both (see Note)

small lime wedges for garnish

Preheat the oven to 425°F (220°C). Line a baking sheet with parchment paper. Place the ground almonds in a shallow dish. Place the curry paste in a medium bowl. Add the wings and toss to thoroughly coat with the curry paste. Set a wing in the ground almonds, turn to coat and then set on the baking sheet. Repeat with the remaining wings. Bake for 25 to 35 minutes, turning once, or until cooked through. When done, if you prefer a crispier, darker almond crust, broil the wings for a few minutes. Arrange the wings on a platter and garnish with the lime wedges.

preparation time	•	15 minutes
cooking time	•	25–35 minutes
makes	•	24 wings

NOTE
Ground almonds are sold in bags or in bulk at most supermarkets. Whole chicken wings in most supermarkets are split and sold as wingettes, the middle portion of the wing near the tip, and drumettes, the meaty section attached to the breast. If your store does not sell them this way, you'll have to do the splitting yourself.

ERIC'S OPTIONS
For a different crust, replace the ground almonds with finely crushed unsalted, roasted cashews.

ABOUT CURRY PASTE

Curry pastes are sold at Asian food stores and in the Asian foods aisle of most supermarkets. This aromatic, full-flavored paste is made by moistening a range of spices and other ingredients with oil and/or other liquids.

Red-hued Indian-style curry pastes are sometimes simply labeled "curry paste" and, like curry powder, is available in mild, medium and hot varieties. There are also regional variations of curry paste, such as Madras curry paste, which features ingredients such as red chilies, coriander and cumin.

Thai-style curry pastes—green, red and yellow—are named after the color of the chilies and other ingredients used to make them. I've used these pastes interchangeably in recipes, and what goes into them can vary from maker to maker, but generally speaking, green curry paste is the spiciest, red curry paste is a little less hot and yellow curry paste, which uses milder chilies, is the mildest.

CAMEMBERT and CRANBERRY PHYLLO BUNDLES

Flaky pastry oozing with a hot, creamy cheese and cranberry filling.

6 sheets phyllo pastry (see Handling and Storing Phyllo Pastry on page 229)

⅓ cup (80 mL) melted butter

½ lb (250 g) Camembert cheese, cut into 24 pieces

⅔ cup (150 mL) canned or homemade cranberry sauce

⅓ cup (80 mL) pecan pieces

preparation time • 20 minutes
cooking time • 15 minutes
makes • 24 bundles

ERIC'S OPTIONS
These bundles can be made several hours in advance, wrapped and refrigerated until ready to bake. They can also be frozen for up to 1 month; freeze solid on the baking sheet before transferring to an airtight container. Don't thaw before baking or they will become soggy and limp. Add a few more minutes to the baking time as you will be cooking from frozen. Instead of Camembert, use brie in the bundles, instead of cranberry sauce, try mango chutney.

Preheat the oven to 375°F (190°C). Lightly butter and layer 3 sheets of the phyllo pastry. Cut the layered sheets into 12 squares. Place a piece of the Camembert and 1 tsp (5 mL) each of the cranberry sauce and pecan pieces in the center of each square. Lift up the corners of one of the squares and press them together to create small bundles. Set on a parchment paper–lined baking sheet. Repeat with the remaining phyllo pastry squares, cranberry sauce and pecans. Brush the outside of each bundle lightly with butter. Repeat with the remaining phyllo pastry sheets, butter and fillings. (Cover the bundles you have already made with plastic wrap until the next batch is done.) Bake in the middle of the oven for 15 minutes or until golden brown. Cool slightly before serving.

SUMPTUOUS SEAFOOD MELTS

Crabmeat, smoked salmon and shrimp combine to give these melts a sumptuous taste.

½ lb (250 g) brick cream cheese, at room temperature

¼ cup (60 mL) mayonnaise

1 garlic clove, finely chopped

½ tsp (2 mL) hot pepper sauce

one 120 g can (about 4 oz) crabmeat, drained well

2 oz (60 g) cold-smoked salmon, coarsely chopped (see About Cold- and Hot-Smoked Salmon on page 18)

2 tsp (10 mL) chopped fresh dill or tarragon, plus some sprigs for garnish

salt, white pepper and freshly squeezed lemon juice to taste

1 baguette, cut into 24 ¼-inch (6 mm) rounds

¼ lb (125 g) cooked salad shrimp

1 cup (250 mL) grated Swiss cheese

preparation time	•	30 minutes
cooking time	•	10–12 minutes
makes	•	24 melts

ERIC'S OPTIONS
These melts, unbaked, can be made several hours in advance and stored in the refrigerator until needed. If you do that, because the melts will be cold, add a few minutes to the baking time.

Preheat the oven to 425°F (220°C). Line a baking sheet with parchment paper. Place the cream cheese in a large bowl and beat with an electric mixer until soft and lightened. Mix in the mayonnaise, garlic and hot pepper sauce and beat until smooth. Stir in the crab, salmon, dill or tarragon, salt, pepper and lemon juice. Spread the seafood mixture on the baguette slices and place on the baking sheet. Decorate the top of each melt with the shrimp and sprinkle with the cheese. Bake for 10 to 12 minutes, or until the cheese is melted and light golden on top. Arrange on a serving platter, garnish each melt with a dill or tarragon sprig and serve immediately.

PISSALADIÈRE

These southern French–style pizzas are great to snack on hot or at room temperature. The vol-au-vent shells (patty shells) used in this recipe are sold in the frozen food section of most supermarkets. When rolled thin, they provide a fine and flaky base for savory toppings.

preparation time • 20 minutes
cooking time • 20–25 minutes
makes • 6 pissaladière, 36 wedges

six 3-inch (8 cm) round vol-au-vent shells (patty shells), thawed

18 thin slices ripe tomato (about 3 medium)

⅓ cup (80 mL) niçoise olives, pitted

¼ lb (125 g) soft goat cheese, crumbled

2 Tbsp (30 mL) extra virgin olive oil, plus some for drizzling

2 tsp (10 mL) herbes de Provence (see Note on page 250)

coarse sea salt and freshly ground black pepper to taste

ERIC'S OPTIONS
Niçoise olives are small, black olives with a rich, somewhat fruity taste grown in the south of France. If unavailable at your supermarket or local deli, substitute any other black olive. Anchovies are a traditional topping for pissaladière. If you like anchovies set the desired amount—chopped or in whole fillets—on top of the pastry when adding the tomatoes.

Line a large baking sheet with parchment paper. Roll the vol-au-vent shells, 1 at a time, on a lightly floured surface into 5-inch (12 cm) wide rounds. Place on the baking sheet. Top the rounds with equal portions of the tomatoes, olives and goat cheese. Drizzle with the olive oil and sprinkle with the herbes de Provence, salt and pepper. Chill in the refrigerator for 15 minutes. Preheat the oven to 375°F (190°C). Bake the pissaladière for 20 to 25 minutes or until puffed and golden. Cool slightly and then cut each pissaladière into 6 wedges and arrange on a platter. Drizzle with additional olive oil if desired and serve warm or at room temperature.

PORK and GINGER GYOZA

Gyoza are Japanese-style dumplings that are great for snacking on. This version is tastily filled with ginger-flavored pork, chives and other Asian accents.

THE DIPPING SAUCE

¼ cup (60 mL) soy sauce

¼ cup (60 mL) rice vinegar

1 tsp (5 mL) chopped fresh ginger

2 tsp (10 mL) sugar, or to taste

1 Tbsp (15 mL) snipped fresh chives

¼ tsp (1 mL) Asian-style hot chili sauce

THE GYOZA

¾ lb (375 g) ground pork

3 Tbsp (45 mL) snipped fresh chives

2 tsp (10 mL) chopped fresh ginger

1 Tbsp (15 mL) soy sauce

¼ tsp (1 mL) freshly ground black pepper

2 tsp (10 mL) sugar

2 tsp (10 mL) sesame oil

2 tsp (10 mL) cornstarch

24 to 30 round Asian-style dumpling wrappers (see Note)

2 Tbsp (30 mL) vegetable oil

Continued . . .

preparation time	•	25 minutes
cooking time	•	about 6–7 minutes
makes	•	about 24–30 gyoza

NOTE
Round Asian-style dumpling wrappers, usually about 3 inches (8 cm) in diameter, can be found, refrigerated, in most Asian markets and supermarkets.

ERIC'S OPTIONS
The gyoza can be made, frozen solid uncooked on a baking sheet, transferred to a freezer bag and kept in the freezer for up to 2 months. Cook from frozen; if you thaw, the gyoza will become soggy and be hard to cook. When cooking frozen gyoza, use medium heat and cook for a few minutes more; the cooler temperature and longer cooking time will allow the frozen gyoza to properly thaw and cook through without burning.

PORK and GINGER
GYOZA (*continued*)

THE DIPPING SAUCE

Combine the sauce ingredients in a small bowl. Cover and refrigerate until the gyoza are ready.

THE GYOZA

Combine the pork, chives, ginger, soy sauce, pepper, sugar, sesame oil and cornstarch in a medium bowl. Line a large baking sheet with parchment paper. Place a few dumpling wrappers on a flat work surface. Brush the edges lightly with cold water. Place 2 tsp (10 mL) of the filling in the center of each wrapper. Fold the dumpling wrapper over the filling to make a half moon and crimp the edges together to seal. Set the gyoza on the baking sheet, ensuring that they do not touch or they will stick together. Repeat with the remaining filling and wrappers.

Preheat the oven to 200°F (95°C). Heat 1 Tbsp (15 mL) of the vegetable oil in a large nonstick skillet set over medium-high heat. When hot, add in half the gyoza. Lightly brown each side for 1 to 2 minutes. Pour in a quarter-cup (60 mL) of cold water; cover and cook until the pork filling the gyoza becomes firm and the water has almost entirely evaporated.

Arrange on a heatproof platter and keep warm in the oven. Cook the next batch as you did the first. When all are cooked, serve the gyoza with the bowl of sauce alongside for dipping.

SOUPS

CAULIFLOWER SOUP with CURRY and COCONUT MILK

Spicy curry and the silky richness of coconut milk turn ordinary-tasting cauliflower into a soup that's a treat down to the last spoonful.

preparation time • 10 minutes
cooking time • 25–30 minute
makes • 4 servings

3 Tbsp (45 mL) vegetable oil

1 medium onion, finely chopped

2 garlic cloves, chopped

1 Tbsp (15 mL) mild curry powder

3 Tbsp (45 mL) all-purpose flour

3 cups (750 mL) chicken or vegetable stock

one 14 oz (398 mL) can regular or light coconut milk

2½ cups (625 mL) small cauliflower florets

¼ cup (60 mL) chopped cilantro

salt to taste

ERIC'S OPTIONS
If you do not care for cilantro, replace it with chopped fresh mint or thinly sliced green onions. Try this soup with small broccoli florets instead of cauliflower.

Heat the oil in a pot over medium heat. Add the onion and garlic and cook for 2 to 3 minutes. Add the curry powder and cook, stirring for 2 to 3 minutes more. Stir in the flour. Slowly whisk in the chicken stock. Stir in the coconut milk, bring to a simmer and cook for 10 minutes. Add the cauliflower and cook for 10 minutes more, or until tender. Stir in the cilantro, season with salt and serve.

ABOUT CANNED COCONUT MILK

To make canned coconut milk, the flesh of the fruit is pressed and a milk-like substance extracted. Water is added to get the desired consistency and so, often, is guar gum. Guar gum is made from the seeds of the guar plant and is used to stabilize and thicken foods.

Despite that stabilizer, coconut milk can still separate in the can, with thick coconut milk rising and setting on top, and a watery mixture sitting on the bottom. This separation is normal and some say a sign of good-quality coconut milk. To make completely fluid again, simply shake the can before opening. Any solids will also liquefy once heated.

Although high in saturated fat, the principal fatty acid in coconut milk, called lauric acid, also found in mothers' milk, is believed to promote brain development and healthy bones. Any leftover coconut milk from a recipe should be poured into a jar or container, refrigerated and used within a few days. Coconut milk can also be frozen for up to a month. After thawing, if you wish to heat the milk, do so slowly to ensure the liquid and fat don't separate.

QUICK TOMATO SOUP
with PESTO and FETA

Rich and herbaceous pesto, creamy feta and tangy tomato combine in this Mediterranean-style soup. Complete this meal in a bowl by serving it with thick slices of focaccia, Italian or olive bread.

preparation time • 15 minutes
cooking time • 20 minutes
makes • 4 servings

2 Tbsp (30 mL) olive oil

1 medium onion, halved and thinly sliced

1 garlic clove, crushed

2 Tbsp (30 mL) tomato paste

2 Tbsp (30 mL) all-purpose flour

2 cups (500 mL) chicken or vegetable stock

one 28 oz (796 mL) can diced tomatoes

½ tsp (2 mL) sugar

3 Tbsp (45 mL) store-bought or homemade pesto
    (see Pesto recipe on page 359)

salt and freshly ground black pepper to taste

1 cup (250 mL) crumbled feta cheese

ERIC'S OPTIONS
Instead of feta, top the soup with another cheese, such as crumbled goat cheese or grated Asiago.
This soup, without the pesto and cheese, freezes well. Thaw in the refrigerator overnight, reheat, stir in the pesto, ladle into bowls and top with the cheese.

Pour the oil into a medium-sized pot and set over medium heat. Add the onion and garlic and cook until tender, about 5 minutes. Stir in the tomato paste and flour and cook for 1 to 2 minutes more. While stirring, slowly pour in the stock. Mix in the diced tomatoes and sugar. Bring the soup to a simmer and cook at a simmer for 10 minutes.

Purée the mixture in a food processor or with a hand-held immersion blender. Return the soup to a simmer and mix in the pesto; season with salt and pepper. Ladle the soup into heated bowls, sprinkle with the feta cheese and serve.

MAKING STOCK

You can buy good-quality, ready-to-use stock, but if you have the time, making your own can give you a richer stock tailored to your own taste, and you will know exactly what goes into it.

For vegetable stock, slice two medium peeled carrots, two medium peeled onions, two celery ribs, two medium tomatoes and ⅓ lb (170 g) white or brown mushrooms and place in a tall stockpot. Add a bay leaf, a few whole black peppercorns and a few sprigs of fresh parsley and thyme (or 1 tsp (5 mL) dried). Add 10 to 12 cups (2.5 to 3 L) of cold water. Bring to a gentle simmer and cook uncovered for 1½ to 2 hours, or until the mixture has a pleasing vegetable flavor. Strain, cool and refrigerate.

For fish, chicken or beef stock, place 2 to 3 pounds (1 to 1.5 kg) of bones in a tall stockpot. Use the same vegetables and herbs as for vegetable stock, but reduce the carrot and onion to 1 each. The tomatoes and mushrooms are optional. To add color to chicken or beef stock, roast the bones and vegetables in a hot oven until golden brown, about 30 minutes, before placing in the stockpot. For fish stock, it is best to use white fish bones as bones from fish such as salmon can give the stock a strong, oily taste. Fish stock cooks quickly, so slice the vegetables thinly to better release the flavor into the stock.

Add enough cold water to completely cover the bones and vegetables, about 10 to 12 cups (2.5 to 3 L) depending on the size and width of the pot. Simmer fish stock for 30 to 45 minutes; chicken stock for 1½ to 2 hours; and beef stock 3 to 4 hours. Skim off any foam that rises to the top as it cooks and add additional water as needed. Before straining, taste the stock to see if it has reached its flavor potential. Remember that the stock isn't seasoned like the store-bought variety; add salt and pepper to a small amount of stock before sampling. Cool to room temperature, cover and refrigerate until needed.

Stock can be stored in the refrigerator for 2 to 3 days. Remove any fat from the surface of the stock before using. Stock also freezes well; divide it into portions you are likely to use in cooking before freezing.

CHICKPEA and SPINACH SOUP

This hearty soup is quick to make because there's minimal chopping. If you use vegetable stock and skip the cheese, this soup is vegan.

preparation time • 15 minutes
cooking time • 16–17 minutes
makes • 4 servings

2 Tbsp (30 mL) olive oil

1 medium onion, diced

½ large red bell pepper, diced

1–2 garlic cloves, crushed

1 tsp (5 mL) dried oregano

2 Tbsp (30 mL) tomato paste

4 cups (1 L) chicken or vegetable stock

one 19 oz (540 mL) can chickpeas (see About Chickpeas on page 181), rinsed and drained well

2 cups (500 mL) fresh spinach leaves, thickly sliced

salt and freshly ground black pepper to taste

freshly grated Parmesan cheese to taste

ERIC'S OPTIONS
Substitute a similar-sized can of white kidney beans for the chickpeas. Instead of spinach, chop and mix 2 cups (500 mL) of Swiss chard into the soup.

Heat the oil in a soup pot over medium heat. Add the onion, bell pepper and garlic and cook for 3 to 4 minutes. Mix in the oregano and tomato paste and cook 2 minutes longer. Add the stock and chickpeas, bring to a simmer and simmer for 10 minutes. Add the spinach and cook until it just starts to wilt, about 1 minute. Season with salt and pepper. Ladle soup into bowls, sprinkle with Parmesan cheese and serve.

ABOUT LEGUMES

Legume is the name given to a wide variety of plant species with edible seedpods that split along both sides when ripe. Some of the more familiar varieties are lentils, soybeans, kidney beans, black-eyed peas, black beans and lima beans.

Legumes are available canned and dried. Dried legumes can be soaked overnight in cold water to speed up the cooking by 10 to 15 minutes. The overnight soak can also help freshen the taste of some varieties, such as split peas. Dried legumes, particularly lentils, can also be cooked from their dried state; just be sure to use a generous amount of water as they will expand and absorb a lot of water as they cook.

The time-pressed will be pleased to know that legumes are also sold fully cooked and canned, making them a convenient ingredient to open and add to a wide variety of recipes, including many in this book.

I always rinse canned legumes in cold water before using to remove the often sodium-rich liquid they are canned in.

SLOW COOKER ROOT VEGETABLE SOUP with BLUE CHEESE

Fairly plain tasting on their own, parsnip, carrot and potato are given a big-time flavor boost when slow-simmered with aromatic spices, fresh ginger and garlic. For added richness, the soup is topped with tangy blue cheese just before serving. Serve this with slices of sourdough bread or Buttermilk Biscuits (page 366).

4½ cups (1.125 L) chicken or vegetable stock

2 Tbsp (30 mL) all-purpose flour

2 garlic cloves, minced

1 medium leek, white and pale green part only, cut in half lengthwise, washed and thinly sliced (see About Leeks on page 54)

1 medium parsnip, peeled, halved lengthwise and sliced

1 medium carrot, peeled, halved lengthwise and sliced

1 medium yam, peeled and cubed (See About Sweet Potatoes and Yams on page 337)

1 Tbsp (15 mL) peeled, chopped fresh ginger (see About Fresh Ginger on page 264)

1 tsp (5 mL) ground cumin

¼ tsp (1 mL) ground coriander

pinch cayenne pepper

pinch ground nutmeg

salt and white pepper to taste

¼ lb (125 g) blue cheese, crumbled

2 Tbsp (30 mL) chopped fresh parsley

Continued . . .

preparation time	•	20 minutes
slow-cooker time	•	6 hours
finishing time	•	10 minutes
makes	•	6 servings

NOTE
This recipe is designed for a slow cooker with 4½ to 6½ quart (4.5 to 6.5 L) capacity.

ERIC'S OPTIONS
If you find blue cheese too strong, simply omit it or use a milder cheese, such as nuggets of soft goat cheese. For even more richness, sprinkle each serving of soup with 1 Tbsp (15 mL) of toasted chopped walnuts or pecan pieces. To toast the nuts, place ½ cup (125 mL) of your nut of choice in a dry skillet and set over medium heat. Heat the nuts, swirling the pan from time to time, until lightly toasted and aromatic, about 3 to 4 minutes.

Slow Cooker Lentil Soup with Herbes de Provence, top (page 55), Slow Cooker Root Vegetable Soup with Blue Cheese, bottom (page 52)

SLOW COOKER ROOT VEGETABLE
SOUP with BLUE CHEESE (*continued*)

Place the stock and flour in your slow cooker and whisk until the flour is completely dissolved. Mix in the garlic, leek, parsnip, carrot, yam, ginger, cumin, coriander, cayenne and nutmeg. Cover and cook on the low setting for 6 hours, or until the vegetables are very tender. Purée the contents of the slow cooker with an immersion blender. (You could also purée the soup in a food processor or blender.) Thin the soup with a bit more stock if you find it too thick. Cover and cook for 10 minutes more, or until the soup is piping hot. Season the soup with salt and white pepper. Top bowls of the soup with crumbled blue cheese and chopped parsley.

ABOUT LEEKS

Despite leeks' family connections—they are related to both garlic and onion and have a taste somewhere between the two—they are fairly mild in flavor and aroma. That quality makes them a more refined ingredient to use in a wide range of dishes, such as a creamy soup, quiche, stew or potato dishes.

When buying leeks, choose unblemished, firm leeks with vibrant-looking green and white portions. Store them in a plastic bag in your refrigerator crisper. Very fresh leeks will last for up to 5 days.

Very small, young leeks, sometimes called baby leeks, can be cooked whole and served as a hot or cold vegetable side dish. Wash them well before using. Supermarkets generally sell medium to large leeks. The multiple layers in the white portion of these larger leeks trap dirt, so it is crucial to wash them before using. Simply trim off the hairy root end and cut the leek in half lengthwise, which exposes the places where dirt can get trapped. Wash away any dirt and dry the leek, and it's ready to be chopped or sliced.

SLOW COOKER LENTIL SOUP
with HERBES de PROVENCE

This hearty, meatless soup is not only easy to make, it's also nutritious thanks to the lentils, which contain protein, fiber, B vitamins and other good things. I like to serve it with slices of warm baguette for dunking.

preparation time • 10 minutes
slow-cooker time • 6 hours
makes • 6–8 servings

3 cups (750 mL) vegetable stock

two 19 oz (540 mL) cans lentils, drained, rinsed and
    drained again

one 14 oz (398 mL) can tomato sauce

2 celery stalks, quartered lengthwise and thinly sliced

2 garlic cloves, minced

1 medium onion, finely diced

1 large carrot, quartered lengthwise and thinly sliced

1½ tsp (7 mL) herbes de Provence (see Note on page 250)

salt and freshly ground black pepper to taste

chopped fresh parsley to taste

NOTE
This recipe is designed for a slow cooker with a 4½ to 6½ quart (4.5 to 6.5 L) capacity.

ERIC'S OPTIONS
If you are a meat-eater, you could use chicken stock instead of vegetable stock. You could also roast or grill two fresh chorizo sausages. Thinly slice them, then add them to the soup at the start of cooking.

Combine the stock, lentils, tomato sauce, celery, garlic, onion, carrot and herbes de Provence in your slow cooker. Cover and cook on the low setting for 6 hours, or until the vegetables are tender. Season the soup with salt and pepper. Sprinkle servings with parsley. *Pictured on page 53.*

HOW SLOW COOKERS WORK

Slow cookers comprise a metal container with a heating element and a ceramic cooking pot. The element heats the pot but does not touch it, preventing food from sticking and burning. The food reaches a food-safe temperature of 85°C to 138°C (185°F to 275°F) depending on the setting. As the food cooks, steam rises, hits the lid and falls back on the food, preventing it from drying out, even after hours of cooking.

AUTUMN VEGETABLE SOUP
with TOASTED HAZELNUTS

Squash and root vegetables come into their own in the fall, when shorter days and crisper nights make us crave hearty fare. This soup, warmed with ginger and topped with crunchy nuts, is just the thing.

2 Tbsp (30 mL) olive oil

1 medium parsnip, peeled and chopped

1 medium carrot, peeled and chopped

½ medium onion, chopped

1½ cups (375 mL) peeled and cubed banana or butternut squash

1 garlic clove, chopped

1 Tbsp (15 mL) chopped fresh ginger

2 Tbsp (30 mL) all-purpose flour

4¼ cups (1.060 L) chicken or vegetable stock

½ tsp (2 mL) dried thyme

pinches ground nutmeg and ground cloves

salt and white pepper to taste

1 cup (250 mL) whole, shelled hazelnuts, toasted, skin removed and coarsely crushed (see Note)

preparation time • 30 minutes
cooking time • about 30 minutes
makes • 6–8 servings

NOTE
1 cup (250 mL) whole, shelled, skin-on hazelnuts weighs about 3½ oz (105 g). To toast hazelnuts and remove the skins, place in a single layer in baking pan. Bake in a 350°F (175°C) for 15 to 20 minutes, or until lightly toasted and the skins start to crack. Transfer to a container, wrap tightly with plastic wrap and let stand 5 minutes. (The trapped steam will cause the skins to pull away from the nuts.) Use your hands to rub as much of the skins off the hazelnuts as you can. Place the nuts in a thick plastic bag and pound with a kitchen hammer to coarsely crush them.

ERIC'S OPTIONS
If you don't care for hazelnuts, substitute sliced almonds and lightly toast them.

Heat the oil in a medium-sized pot over medium heat. Add the parsnip, carrot, onion, squash, garlic and ginger and cook until softened, about 5 minutes. Mix in the flour and cook 2 to 3 minutes more. Slowly, continuing to stir, mix in the stock. Add the thyme, nutmeg and cloves. Bring to a gentle simmer and cook until the vegetables are very tender, about 20 minutes. Purée the soup in a food processor or blender, or in the pot with an immersion blender.

HOW TO STORE NUTS

Nuts, such as walnuts, pecans, almonds and cashews, have a high fat content, making them susceptible to going rancid if improperly stored. To prevent this, pack them in an airtight container and store in the refrigerator or freezer. Store shelled nuts in the refrigerator or freezer for 4 to 6 months, and nuts in the shell for 6 to 8 months. Storage times will be much shorter, of course, if the nuts you've bought weren't very fresh to begin with. Buy what you can use in a reasonable length of time from a retailer that sells a high volume of nuts and is constantly restocking with a fresh supply.

CURRIED CARROT SOUP
with MINTY YOGURT

The humble carrot is the base of this very flavorful soup, accented with aromatic curry and fresh orange juice and topped with tangy yogurt and refreshing mint.

preparation time	•	15 minutes
cooking time	•	25 minutes
makes	•	4 servings

2 Tbsp (30 mL) vegetable oil

3 medium carrots, peeled and sliced

1 medium onion, halved and sliced

2 tsp (10 mL) chopped fresh ginger

2 garlic cloves, chopped

3 Tbsp (45 mL) all-purpose flour

2–3 tsp (10–15 mL) mild curry powder

4 cups (1 L) chicken or vegetable stock

½ cup (125 mL) fresh orange juice

2 tsp (10 mL) grated orange zest

salt and white pepper to taste

⅓ cup (80 mL) yogurt

1 Tbsp (15 mL) chopped fresh mint

small mint sprigs for garnish

ERIC'S OPTIONS
This soup, without the yogurt and mint garnish, freezes well. If you have the time, double the recipe, cool what you don't need to room temperature and freeze in a tightly sealed container. To serve, thaw in the refrigerator overnight. Reheat the next day and top with minty yogurt.

Place the oil in a pot over medium heat. When it's hot, add the carrot, onion, ginger and garlic and cook 3 to 4 minutes. Stir in the flour and curry powder and cook 2 minutes more. While stirring, slowly pour in the stock. Mix in the orange juice and orange zest. Bring the soup to a simmer and cook until the carrots are very tender, about 15 minutes.

Purée the soup in a blender or food processor, or in the pot with an immersion blender. Return the soup to a simmer and season with salt and white pepper. Place the yogurt in a small bowl and mix in the chopped mint. Ladle the soup into bowls, place a spoonful of yogurt in the center of each and garnish with the mint sprigs.

ONION SOUP with CRUMBLED STILTON

The sherry raises this delicious onion soup up a notch, and the blue cheese topping finishes the job!

preparation time • 20 minutes
cooking time • 30 minutes
makes • 6 servings

3 Tbsp (45 mL) butter

4 medium onions, cut in half and thinly sliced

2 garlic cloves, finely chopped

2 Tbsp (30 mL) tomato paste

6 cups (1.5 L) beef stock

1 tsp (5 mL) dried tarragon

1 bay leaf

⅓ cup (80 mL) dry sherry

salt and freshly ground black pepper to taste

¼ lb (125 g) Stilton cheese, crumbled

2 green onions, thinly sliced

ERIC'S OPTIONS

The soup can be made a day or two in advance, cooled to room temperature, covered and refrigerated until needed. Top with the cheese and green onion after reheating. Instead of Stilton, top the soup with another, good-quality type of blue cheese, such as roquefort.

Melt the butter in a pot over medium heat. Add the onions and cook, stirring occasionally, for 10 minutes, or until they are caramelized and sticky. Add the garlic and tomato paste and cook 1 minute more. Add the stock, tarragon and bay leaf and simmer the soup for 20 minutes. Stir in the sherry, salt and pepper. To serve, ladle the soup into warmed bowls and top each serving with the crumbled Stilton and green onions.

CHILLED BEET SOUP

Balsamic vinegar, horseradish and honey give this refreshing soup a brilliant taste and color. Serve it when you're looking for a cool, savory start to a summer meal.

preparation time • 20 minutes
cooking time • 30 minutes
makes • 4 servings

1 lb (500 g) beets, boiled until tender, cooled, peeled and sliced

2½ cups (625 mL) chicken or vegetable stock

1 Tbsp (15 mL) horseradish

2 Tbsp (30 mL) balsamic vinegar

2 Tbsp (30 mL) honey

salt and freshly ground black pepper to taste

sour cream and dill sprigs for garnish

ERIC'S OPTIONS

For a dramatic presentation, bring the bowls of soup to the table in a large, attractive, deep-sided dish filled with ice. For a lower-fat alternative, use thick yogurt instead of sour cream.

Process the beets, stock, horseradish, vinegar, honey, salt and pepper in a blender or food processor until smooth. Refrigerate for at least 2 hours. Taste and adjust the seasoning if necessary. Ladle into well-chilled soup bowls. Garnish each serving with a dollop of sour cream and a dill sprig. Serve immediately.

BOUILLABAISSE

This hearty Mediterranean-style soup makes a fine and filling meal. To maximize flavor and texture, use at least two to three kinds of fish when making it. The possibilities include cod, snapper, halibut, sole and salmon. If desired, top bowls of the soup with Roasted Red Pepper Aioli (page 353).

20–24 medium shrimp (see About Shrimp and Prawns, page 212)

2½ cups (625 mL) fish, chicken or vegetable stock

3 Tbsp (45 mL) olive oil

2 garlic cloves, chopped

2 medium onions, chopped

one 14 oz (398 mL) can diced tomatoes

2 Tbsp (30 mL) tomato paste

½ tsp (2 mL) fennel seeds

¼–½ tsp (1–2 mL) crushed chili flakes

½ tsp (2 mL) saffron threads (see About Saffron, page 161)

3 strips orange peel, about ½ × 3 inches (1 × 8 cm)

½ tsp (2 mL) sugar

3 medium white-skinned potatoes, cut into ½-inch (1 cm) cubes

1½ lb (750 g) boneless fish fillets, cubed

salt and freshly ground black pepper to taste

¾ lb (375 g) cooked king or snow crab legs (thawed if frozen), cut into 2-inch (5 cm) pieces

12–18 baguette slices, brushed with olive oil and broiled until golden

2 Tbsp (30 mL) chopped parsley

preparation time • 40 minutes
cooking time • about 40 minutes
makes • 4–6 servings

ERIC'S OPTIONS
For a less expensive alternative, replace the crab with 18 to 24 mussels or clams, or a mix of both. Add them when you add the shrimp, and cook just until they open.

Rinse the shrimp in cold water and drain well. Peel, leaving the tip of the tail attached. Devein shrimp. Cover the shrimp and refrigerate. Place the shells in a pot with the stock. Add 3 cups (750 mL) of cold water. Bring to a boil, then reduce the heat to a gentle simmer. Cook for 20 minutes. Strain and discard the shells. Set the broth aside.

Heat the oil in a large, wide pot over medium heat. Add the garlic and onion and cook until tender, about 3 to 4 minutes. Add the broth, diced tomatoes, tomato paste, fennel seeds, chili flakes, saffron, orange peel, sugar and potatoes. Bring to a simmer and cook for 10 minutes. Add the cubed fish and cook for 3 to 4 minutes more. Add the peeled shrimp and the lobster pieces and cook 5 minutes longer, until the fish and shellfish are just cooked.

Divide the baguette slices among 4 to 6 large, shallow soup bowls. Spoon the bouillabaisse over top, ensuring that everyone gets a mix of seafood. Sprinkle with parsley and serve immediately.

SHRIMP BISQUE

Here's a luscious seafood soup that's a little less costly than its sister soup, lobster bisque. Serve it on special occasions—such as Wednesday night!

16 medium shrimp (see About Shrimp and Prawns on page 212)

3 Tbsp (45 mL) olive oil

1 garlic clove, thinly sliced

1 small carrot, thinly sliced

1 celery stalk, thinly sliced

1 small onion, thinly sliced

1 tsp (5 mL) dried tarragon

1 bay leaf

1 Tbsp (15 mL) tomato paste

½ cup (125 mL) dry white wine

3½ cups (875 mL) chicken, fish, or vegetable stock

3 Tbsp (45 mL) all-purpose flour

½ cup (125 mL) whipping cream

salt, white pepper and cayenne pepper to taste

¼ cup (60 mL) warm brandy (optional)

1 Tbsp (15 mL) chopped fresh parsley or chives

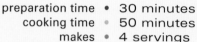

preparation time • 30 minutes
cooking time • 50 minutes
makes • 4 servings

ERIC'S OPTIONS
To elegantly garnish this soup, top each serving with a whole cooked and peeled shrimp. This soup, before the cream is added, can be made a day in advance. When it's needed, reheat and finish as described in the method.

Peel the shrimp, reserving the shells. Devein shrimp. Coarsely chop the meat and set in a bowl and refrigerate until needed.

Heat 2 Tbsp (30 mL) of the oil in a pot over medium heat. Add the prawn shells, garlic, carrot, celery and onion. Cook, stirring occasionally, for 5 to 8 minutes, until the shells are bright red and almost crispy. Add the tarragon, bay leaf, tomato paste, wine and 3 cups (750 mL) of the stock. Gently simmer for 30 to 40 minutes.

Strain the mixture into another pot, then bring it back to a simmer. Mix the flour with the remaining ½ cup (125 mL) of stock until it is smooth. Slowly pour this mixture, whisking continually, into the simmering stock. Gently simmer until the flour has cooked through and the soup has lightly thickened, about 5 minutes. Add the whipping cream and season with salt, pepper and cayenne. Keep the soup warm over medium-low heat. Heat the remaining 1 Tbsp (15 mL) oil in a small skillet over medium-high heat. Add the shrimp pieces and cook until just cooked through, about 1 to 2 minutes. Divide the shrimp and the brandy, if desired, among four heated soup bowls. Pour in the bisque, sprinkle with chopped parsley or chives, and serve.

SUMPTUOUS SEAFOOD CHOWDER

There is so much seafood in this chowder that it easily makes a meal when served with crackers or thick slices from a warm, crusty loaf. Instead of often-used bacon, smoked salmon is used to give this chowder a smoky taste.

½ cup (125 mL) dry white wine

1 lb (500 g) small fresh clams (see How to Buy, Store and Cook Mussels and Clams on page 207)

3 Tbsp (45 mL) butter or vegetable oil

1 medium onion, finely chopped

1 celery rib, finely chopped

2 garlic cloves, chopped

2 Tbsp (30 mL) all-purpose flour

2½ cups (625 mL) fish, chicken or vegetable stock

½ tsp (2 mL) dried thyme

1 bay leaf

2 medium red-skinned potatoes, cut into small cubes

¼ lb (125 g) smoked salmon (see About Cold- and Hot-Smoked Salmon on page 18), chopped

¼ lb (125 g) small cooked shrimp

¼ lb (125 g) fresh, frozen (thawed) or canned crabmeat

1 cup (250 mL) light cream or milk

salt and white pepper to taste

2 Tbsp (30 mL) chopped fresh parsley

preparation time • 25 minutes
cooking time • 20–25 minutes
makes • 4 servings

ERIC'S OPTIONS
Substitute mussels for the clams, or use a combination. If you find this chowder too thick, simply thin with a little more stock, cream or milk. Instead of smoked salmon, try another type of smoked fish in this chowder, such as trout, tuna or dry-smoked (not oil-packed) oysters.

Bring the wine to a boil in a soup pot. Add the clams; cover and cook just until the clams open. Transfer the clams to a plate; strain and reserve the cooking liquid. When the clams are cool, remove the meat from the shells. Discard the shells and reserve the meat. Pour any liquid on the plate into the reserved cooking liquid.

Heat the butter or oil in the same pot over medium heat. Add the onion, celery and garlic and cook until tender, about 5 minutes. Sprinkle in the flour and mix well. Slowly stir in the reserved clam cooking liquid and the stock. Bring to a boil, then reduce the heat to a gentle simmer. Add the thyme, bay leaf, potatoes and smoked salmon and cook until the potatoes are just tender, about 10 to 15 minutes. Add the reserved clam meat, shrimp, crabmeat, and cream or milk. Gently simmer for a few more minutes (do not boil). Season with salt and pepper, pour into bowls and sprinkle with chopped parsley just before serving.

ABOUT CHOWDER

Chowder is derived from the French word chaudière, which means cauldron. Early French settlers who fished off Canada's east coast used these pots on their boats to cook up some of the day's catch into a stew-like mixture that eventually became known as chowder.

It soon became popular on land as well, and was an ideal way to use up household staples. Some early versions were made by combining rendered salt pork with fish or shellfish in simmering water and thickening the mixture with biscuits or bread.

As the soup evolved, potatoes began to replace or supplement the biscuits or bread, milk and cream were used, and bacon was an occasional substitute for the salt pork. Other styles of chowder also began to appear, such as the tomato-based Manhattan chowder, named after the city it was invented in.

HOT and SOUR SOUP with SCALLOP RIBBONS and GINGER

One spoon of this spicy, yet soothing, concoction will quickly lift your spirits inside and out. I like to serve it on cool, damp, dreary days.

4 cups (1 L) fish, chicken or vegetable stock

¼ cup (60 mL) rice vinegar

3 Tbsp (45 mL) light soy sauce

1 Tbsp (15 mL) Asian-style chili sauce, or to taste

2 tsp (10 mL) sugar

4 medium fresh shiitake mushrooms, or 4 medium dried black Chinese mushrooms (soaked in warm water for 20 minutes to soften), stems removed and discarded, caps thinly sliced

1 small carrot, cut into thin, 1-inch-long (2.5 cm) strips

1-inch (2.5 cm) piece peeled fresh ginger, sliced and cut into thin strips

1 garlic clove, chopped

5 large sea scallops (see About Scallops on page 209), very thinly sliced

one 10 oz (300 g) package soft tofu (see About Tofu on page 175), cut into small cubes or strips

2 Tbsp (30 mL) cornstarch dissolved in 3 Tbsp (45 mL) water

2 green onions, cut diagonally into thin strips

preparation time	•	25 minutes
cooking time	•	about 10 minutes
makes	•	4 servings

ERIC'S OPTIONS

Egg is traditionally added to hot and sour soup. If you would like to add it to this version, do so after it has been thickened with the cornstarch. Beat 1 large egg in a bowl. Slowly pour the egg into the soup, gently stirring in a circular motion to create small ribbons of egg. When the egg is just cooked, it's time to serve the soup.

Place the stock, vinegar, soy sauce, chili sauce and sugar in a pot and bring to a boil over high heat. Add the mushrooms, carrot, ginger and garlic, and adjust the heat to a gentle simmer. Cook for 5 minutes, or until the mushrooms and carrots are just tender. Add the scallops and tofu. Slowly stir in the cornstarch mixture. Simmer until the soup is lightly thickened and the scallops are just cooked through, about 2 to 3 minutes. Ladle the soup into bowls, sprinkle with the green onions and serve.

CABBAGE SOUP with SMOKED TURKEY and ROSEMARY

The fully cooked, smoked turkey leg used in this recipe can be found at most supermarkets and butcher shops. Its smoky meat will infuse the broth with a wonderful flavor and help create a soup filling enough to act as a main course.

2 Tbsp (30 mL) butter

1 medium onion, diced

2 garlic cloves, minced

3 cups (750 mL) chopped green cabbage

1 medium carrot, halved and sliced

2 tsp (10 mL) chopped fresh rosemary

1 small smoked turkey leg, meat removed and cubed

1 bay leaf

2 medium potatoes, peeled and cubed

6 cups (1.5 L) chicken stock

salt and freshly ground black pepper to taste

2–3 Tbsp (30–45 mL) chopped fresh parsley
or green onions

preparation time •	20 minutes
cooking time •	35–45 minutes
makes •	6 servings

ERIC'S OPTIONS
Use cubed ham, to taste, instead of the smoked turkey. If you do not have fresh rosemary, use ½–1 tsp (2–5 mL) dried. Savoy cabbage can be substituted for green cabbage.

Melt the butter in a large pot over medium heat. Add the onion, garlic, cabbage and carrot and cook until softened, about 5 minutes. Add the rosemary, turkey, bay leaf, potatoes and stock. Gently simmer the soup for 30 to 40 minutes. Season with salt and pepper. Pour into bowls, sprinkle with parsley or green onions, and serve.

TURKEY, VEGETABLE
and BOW-TIE PASTA SOUP

If you have leftovers from a turkey dinner, this hearty soup is a delicious way to use them up. Served with slices of crusty Italian bread, it makes a nice lunch entrée.

preparation time • 20 minutes
cooking time • about 25 minutes
makes • 6 servings

1 Tbsp (15 mL) vegetable oil

½ medium onion, diced

2 medium celery ribs, quartered lengthwise and thinly sliced

1 medium carrot, peeled and quartered lengthwise

2 Tbsp (30 mL) tomato paste

5 cups (1.25 L) turkey or chicken stock

one 14 oz (398 mL) can diced tomatoes

pinch sugar

1 cup (250 mL) cooked turkey, cut into small cubes

1 cup (250 mL) bow-tie or other bite-sized pasta

2 Tbsp (30 mL) store-bought or homemade pesto
  (see Pesto recipe on page 359)

salt and freshly ground black pepper to taste

ERIC'S OPTIONS
If you don't have turkey leftovers, buy a small piece of boneless, skinless turkey breast cutlet or steak, and roast, steam or fry it until cooked through; cut what you need for the soup. The soup could also be made with cooked, cubed chicken or ham.

Heat the oil in a pot over medium heat. Add the onion, celery and carrot and cook 3 to 4 minutes. Mix in the tomato paste and cook 1 minute more. Add the stock, diced tomatoes, sugar and turkey, bring the soup to a simmer and simmer for 10 minutes. Add the pasta, return the soup to a simmer and cook until the pasta is tender, about 10 minutes. Stir in the pesto, season with salt and pepper, and serve.

SALADS

SPINACH SALAD with STRAWBERRIES and WALNUTS

This colorful salad wonderfully combines bright-green spinach, sweet red berries, rich nuts and creamy cheese. The sweet and tangy flavor of balsamic vinegar in the dressing helps to tame the earthy taste of the spinach, which tends to make even those who don't care for this leafy green a fan of this salad.

2 Tbsp (30 mL) balsamic vinegar

3 Tbsp (45 mL) olive oil

1 tsp (5 mL) Dijon mustard

2 tsp (10 mL) honey

salt and freshly ground black pepper to taste

one 5 oz (150 g) bag or box baby spinach,
    washed and dried

½ lb (250 g) fresh strawberries, hulled and sliced

⅓ cup (80 mL) walnuts

¼ lb (125 g) blue or soft goat cheese,
    pulled into small nuggets

preparation time • 10 minutes
cooking time • 10 minutes
makes • 6 servings

ERIC'S OPTIONS
Instead of just strawberries, toss this salad with a mix of fresh berries, such as sliced strawberries and whole blueberries, raspberries and blackberries. For the baby spinach, substitute baby salad greens or chopped or torn leaf lettuce.

Place the vinegar, oil, mustard, honey, salt and pepper in a salad bowl and whisk to combine. Add the spinach, strawberries, walnuts and cheese, and toss to coat, ensuring some of the strawberries, walnuts and cheese decorate the top, and serve.

SWEET and TANGY SIX-VEGETABLE COLESLAW

I enjoy coleslaw and I like it even better when I make it with a nutritious mix of vegetables, such as the recipe below. Spoon this salad alongside one of the summer entrées in this book, such as Picnic Chicken (page 249), or Slow Cooker Pulled Pork Sandwiches (page 296).

3 Tbsp (45 mL) cider vinegar

1 Tbsp (15 mL) honey

2 tsp (10 mL) Dijon mustard

salt and freshly ground black pepper to taste

2 Tbsp (30 mL) vegetable oil

4 cups (1 L) finely shredded cabbage (about ½ small head)

1 cup (250 mL) coarsely grated carrot

1 cup (250 mL) coarsely grated yellow or green zucchini

6 radishes, halved and thinly sliced

3–4 green onions, thinly sliced

1 small red bell pepper, cut into small cubes

preparation time • 20 minutes
cooking time • none
makes • 8 servings

ERIC'S OPTIONS
Instead of green cabbage, use red cabbage, or try a mix of both green and red cabbage.

Place the vinegar, honey, mustard and salt and pepper in a large bowl. Slowly whisk in the oil. Toss in the remaining ingredients.

ABOUT COLESLAW

The word "coleslaw" is derived from the Dutch word koolsla, which is formed from kool, meaning cabbage, and sla, meaning salad. Dutch immigrants brought this salad to North America and its popularity quickly spread. Opt for cabbage with a tightly packed head and bright, sturdy leaves. It will give you crisp and almost juicy shredded cabbage. No matter how fresh the cabbage is, the longer dressed coleslaw sits, the less crisp it becomes.

CANDIED SALMON, GOAT CHEESE and BLUEBERRY SALAD

This elegant salad is wonderful on a warm summer day, when turning on the stove is the last thing anyone wants to do. Candied salmon is available at some supermarkets and specialty seafood stores. To make it, salmon is brined and then hot-smoked, fully cooking the fish. During the process the fish is soaked or basted with a sweetener, such as brown sugar, honey or maple syrup, giving it a candy-like look and taste.

2 Tbsp (30 mL) balsamic vinegar

3 Tbsp (45 mL) olive oil

1 tsp (5 mL) Dijon mustard

1 tsp (5 mL) honey

salt and freshly ground black pepper to taste

6–8 cups (1.5–2 L) baby salad greens

½ lb (250 g) candied salmon, coarsely flaked

5 oz (150 g) soft goat cheese, crumbled

1 cup (250 mL) fresh blueberries

preparation time	•	10 minutes
cooking time	•	none
makes	•	4 servings

ERIC'S OPTIONS
If you can't find candied salmon, use slices of cold-smoked salmon or coarsely flaked hot-smoked salmon (see About Cold- and Hot-Smoked Salmon on page 18) or trout. Use baby spinach or chopped romaine or leaf lettuce in the salad instead of organic mixed salad greens. For a fruitier taste, make the salad dressing with raspberry vinegar instead of balsamic.

Place the vinegar, oil, mustard, honey, salt and pepper in a large bowl and whisk to combine. Add the salad greens and gently toss to coat. Divide the greens among 4 plates. Arrange the salmon, goat cheese and blueberries on top of the greens and serve.

ROMAINE HEARTS with FOCACCIA CROUTONS and PARMESAN

This caesar-like salad is made with romaine hearts, the crisp, center portion of romaine lettuce, sold in bags in the produce section of most supermarkets. Serve this salad as a starter or light lunch.

preparation time • 20 minutes
cooking time • 8–10 minutes
makes • 4 servings

8 thin slices focaccia bread

½ cup (125 mL) mayonnaise

⅓ cup (80 mL) freshly grated Parmesan cheese, plus some for sprinkling

⅓ cup (80 mL) buttermilk

1 Tbsp (15 mL) fresh lemon juice

1 tsp (5 mL) sugar

1 garlic clove, minced

salt and freshly ground black pepper to taste

splash Tabasco sauce

splash Worcestershire sauce

2 romaine hearts, chopped, washed and dried

4 lemon wedges

ERIC'S OPTIONS
Instead of slicing the focaccia bread, make more traditional croutons by cutting the bread into small cubes. Toast them on the baking sheet as directed for the focaccia slices. Sprinkle the toasted bread cubes over the salad when ready to serve. If you like anchovies, you could mix 1 tsp (5 mL) of anchovy paste into the salad dressing. For a more filling main-course salad, once plated, top each salad with 4 to 5 large grilled shrimp.

Preheat the oven to 350°F (175°C). Line a baking sheet with parchment paper. Set the focaccia slices on the prepared baking sheet. Bake for 8 to 10 minutes, or until lightly toasted. Remove from the oven and set aside. Combine the mayonnaise, Parmesan cheese, buttermilk, lemon juice, sugar, garlic, salt, pepper, Tabasco and Worcestershire sauce in a small bowl. Divide the romaine hearts among 4 salad plates. Drizzle some of the dressing overtop and serve the rest tableside. Set 2 croutons alongside each salad. Garnish each salad with a lemon wedge, sprinkle with a little Parmesan cheese and serve.

BABY GREENS with JULIENNE VEGETABLES and TOMATOES

This eye-catching salad combines tender young greens, sweet tomatoes and a colorful mix of vegetables.

¼ cup (60 mL) olive oil

1½ Tbsp (22 mL) cider vinegar

2 tsp (10 mL) Dijon mustard

honey, salt and freshly ground black pepper to taste

8 cups (2 L) baby mixed salad greens

1 small carrot, cut into thin strips

1 small celery rib, cut into thin strips

½ small yellow bell pepper, cut into thin strips

6 small radishes, cut into thin strips

2 green onions, cut into thin strips

12 cherry tomatoes, each halved

preparation time • 20 minutes
cooking time • none
makes • 4 servings

ERIC'S OPTIONS
Instead of baby greens, use baby spinach or chopped leaf lettuce in this recipe. In place of cherry tomatoes, top each salad with a few thin wedges of on-the-vine tomato. Make a darker, slightly sweeter tasting dressing by using balsamic vinegar instead of the cider vinegar.

Make the dressing by whisking and combining the oil, vinegar, mustard, honey, salt and pepper in a small bowl. Divide and mound the greens on 4 plates. Artfully top with the remaining ingredients. Drizzle the salads with dressing and serve.

TIPS on MAKING SALADS

PREPARING LETTUCE FOR THE SALAD BOWL

Improperly washing and drying lettuce or other greens will give your salad a limp texture and a water-drowned taste. Place trimmed, whole leaves into a large bowl of cold water. Gently swirl to remove any dirt. Allow the leaves to rise to the surface; the dirt will sink to the bottom. If your lettuce was a little limp, leave it in the water for a few minutes to crisp up. Dry the lettuce in a salad spinner or on towels, tearing into pieces or chopping if necessary. Do not use a salad spinner to dry the more delicate leaves, such as butter lettuce, as they can easily bruise.

SALAD DRESSING 101

When making a salad dressing, be generous with flavorings, such as salt, pepper, herbs and spices. A highly flavored dressing can be added more sparingly, thus reducing the amount of oil in the salad. Salads primarily composed of vegetables with a high water content, such as lettuce, are prone to wilting and should be dressed just before serving. Those that are designed to absorb the dressing ingredients, such as potato- or pasta-based salads, will benefit if they are dressed a few hours before serving to allow the flavors to develop. Always consider food safety when preparing, storing and serving salads. Keep salads and dressings with ingredients that could develop bacteria quickly, such as meat, poultry, eggs, fish and dairy products, well chilled. Make sure they are kept refrigerated until serving time, and refrigerate leftovers promptly.

LIGHT and DELICIOUS CAESAR SALAD

Here's a lower-fat—no mayonnaise, no egg, no oil—version of the classic salad. The yogurt in the dressing adds a refreshing tanginess.

¼ baguette, cut into small cubes

3 garlic cloves, minced

2 tsp (10 mL) Dijon mustard

½ tsp (2 mL) sugar

⅓ cup (80 mL) low-fat yogurt

1 tsp (5 mL) anchovy paste (see About Anchovies on page 83)

2 tsp (10 mL) red wine vinegar

2 Tbsp (30 mL) lemon juice

2 tsp (10 mL) Worcestershire sauce

½ tsp (2 mL) hot pepper sauce

salt and freshly ground black pepper to taste

1 medium head romaine lettuce, chopped, washed and dried

¼ cup (60 mL) freshly grated Parmesan cheese

4 lemon slices or wedges

preparation time	• 15 minutes
cooking time	• 8–10 minutes
makes	• 4 servings

ERIC'S OPTIONS
If you love olive or focaccia bread, use either of them to make the croutons instead of baguette. If you do not care for anchovies, simply omit them.

Preheat the oven to 400°F (200°C). Make croutons by placing the baguette cubes on a nonstick or parchment paper–lined baking tray. Bake for 8 to 10 minutes, or until tightly toasted. Place the garlic, mustard, sugar, yogurt, anchovy paste, vinegar, lemon juice, Worcestershire sauce, hot pepper sauce, salt and pepper in a large bowl and whisk well to combine. Toss in the lettuce, croutons and half the cheese. Divide the salad among 4 plates. Sprinkle with the remaining cheese, garnish with the lemon and serve immediately.

ABOUT ANCHOVIES

Small, slivery fish called anchovies are harvested in warm waters around the world, but true anchovies, (*Engraulis encrasicolus*), are only caught in places such as the Mediterranean and southern European coastlines. Because of where they're caught, it's not a surprise that anchovies are a popular ingredient in places such as Portugal, Spain, Italy, Turkey and France.

In some places anchovies can be bought whole and fresh, or salted, but anchovies are most often sold filleted and canned, or turned into a paste and sold in tubes. The best canned anchovies will be packed in olive oil. If you want to reduce their saltiness, rinse the fillets thoroughly in cold water, and then pat dry on paper towel. If you want to remove only the oil, simply pat them dry on paper towel before using. To make it squeezable, anchovy paste is blended with other ingredients, such as butter. Because of that, it's not as strongly flavored as canned anchovies. If substituting one for the other, one canned anchovy fillet will equal about a half-teaspoon of anchovy paste.

Although some completely love the taste of anchovies and will joyfully top a pizza with loads of them, most savvy cooks use them in modest amounts. Anchovies are strong-tasting and just a little can add a rich, but not overwhelming hit of flavor to a salad dressing, sauce, pasta, or sautéed dish.

TOMATO and GOAT CHEESE SALAD

A mix between a salad and an appetizer, this dish is best served on a platter and shared in a casual way with your dinner companions. All you need is sliced baguette to mound the tomatoes and cheese on.

5 oz (150 g) round or log of fresh goat cheese

4–6 vine-ripened tomatoes, thinly sliced (choose a selection of colors if available)

12–16 fresh basil leaves, torn into smaller pieces if large

½ cup (125 mL) black olives

¼ cup (60 mL) extra virgin olive oil

salt and freshly ground black pepper to taste

preparation time	•	15 minutes
cooking time	•	none
makes	•	4–6 servings

ERIC'S OPTIONS
Replace the tomatoes with a selection of sliced, grilled vegetables, such as zucchini, onions, peppers, mushrooms and eggplant. Lightly brush vegetables with olive oil and season with salt and freshly ground black pepper to taste. Grill over medium-high heat until just tender. Cooking times will vary from vegetable to vegetable.

Place the cheese in the center of a serving platter. Arrange the tomatoes in an overlapping pattern around the cheese. Disperse the basil and olives over top. Drizzle the olive oil over the tomatoes and cheese. Sprinkle with salt and pepper. Let stand 10 minutes to allow the flavours to melt, and then serve.

MELON and SEAFOOD SALAD with MINT and CUMIN

A wine, martini or other decorative glass makes an elegant serving vessel for this light and colorful salad.

2 shallots, finely chopped

1 Tbsp (15 mL) lemon juice

1 Tbsp (15 mL) chopped fresh mint

½ tsp (2 mL) ground cumin

salt and white pepper to taste

3 Tbsp (45 mL) olive oil

4 oz (125 g) small cooked salad shrimp, patted dry
(see About Shrimp and Prawns on page 212)

4 oz (125 g) fresh or tinned crabmeat, drained well

1 cup (250 mL) honeydew melon balls

1 cup (250 mL) cantaloupe balls

1 cup (250 mL) seedless watermelon balls

2–3 cups (500–750 mL) baby salad greens

4 mint sprigs for garnish

preparation time • 20 minutes
cooking time • none
makes • 4 appetizer-sized servings

ERIC'S OPTIONS
If you don't have a melon baller, you can cut the fruit into ½-inch (1 cm) cubes instead. For a tropical taste, replace the melon balls with balls or cubes of fresh pineapple, mango and papaya.

In a bowl, whisk together the shallots, lemon juice, mint, cumin, salt, pepper and olive oil. Add the shrimp and crabmeat, and honeydew melon, cantaloupe and watermelon balls, and gently toss to combine. Marinate and refrigerate for 30 minutes. Divide the greens among 4 decorative glasses. Spoon the salad on top. Garnish with mint sprigs and serve.

CHILLED ASPARAGUS with CHERRY TOMATO BASIL VINAIGRETTE

Although asparagus is now available year-round, nothing says "spring" quite like this vegetable. Lightly cooked and paired with bright-red tomatoes, this salad will add a cheerful note to the table for meals such as Easter dinner.

preparation time • 10 minutes
cooking time • 2–3 minutes
makes • 8 servings

2 lb (1 kg) asparagus, tough lower parts of the stems trimmed and discarded (see Buying, Storing and Preparing Asparagus on page 89)

⅓ cup (80 mL) olive oil

1 tsp (5 mL) Dijon mustard

2 Tbsp (30 mL) red wine vinegar

pinch sugar

salt and freshly ground black pepper to taste

10–12 cherry tomatoes, finely chopped

2 Tbsp (30 mL) chopped fresh basil

ERIC'S OPTIONS
If you only require four portions, simply divide the ingredients in half. You can prepare the vinaigrette and cook the asparagus a few hours in advance and refrigerate. When it's almost time to serve, warm the vinaigrette to room temperature before spooning it over the asparagus.

Bring a large pot of water to a boil. Add the asparagus and boil until bright green and crisp/tender, about 2 to 3 minutes. Drain well, then plunge the asparagus into ice-cold water to stop the cooking. Drain well, dry on a kitchen towel and arrange on a platter.

Place the oil, mustard, vinegar, sugar, salt and pepper in a medium bowl and whisk to combine. Mix in the tomatoes and basil. Spoon the vinaigrette over the asparagus. Allow the flavors to meld at room temperature for 15 to 20 minutes before serving.

BUYING, STORING AND PREPARING ASPARAGUS

Fresh asparagus will have tightly closed tips and smooth, straight, firm stems. The cut end of the asparagus should not be dry or gray in color; if it is, the asparagus is either old or was improperly stored. For the best flavor, cook asparagus the day you buy it. If you have to store it, seal it in a plastic bag and place in the refrigerator crisper for up to 3 or 4 days. Asparagus is often grown in sandy soil, so wash it well before you cook it. To prepare it, hold the tip firmly in one hand and use your other hand to bend the spear; the lower, woody part will snap off at its natural breaking point. You can keep the lower part of stem, if it's not too tough, to use in soup.

ROMAINE with ORANGES, FETA and OLIVES

This Mediterranean-style salad bursts with color and flavor. Serve it as a starter or a side dish for grilled fish, pork or poultry.

3 Tbsp (45 mL) orange juice

2 Tbsp (30 mL) red wine vinegar

3 Tbsp (45 mL) olive oil

½ tsp (2 mL) sugar

salt and freshly ground black pepper to taste

3 medium oranges, peeled, halved and sliced

¾ cup (185 mL) crumbled feta cheese
(see About Feta)

20–24 whole black or green olives

2 ripe medium tomatoes, cut into small wedges

6 cups (1.5 L) chopped romaine lettuce

1 small red onion, thinly sliced

preparation time	•	10 minutes
cooking time	•	none
makes	•	4 servings

ERIC'S OPTIONS
Replace the romaine with an equal amount of spinach leaves or baby salad greens. A sprinkling of capers is also nice in this salad. Replace regular oranges with blood oranges when available.

Whisk together the orange juice, vinegar, oil, sugar, salt and pepper in a salad bowl. Add the remaining salad ingredients and gently toss. Divide among plates or serve on a large platter, ensuring some of the oranges, cheese, olives, onions and tomatoes decorate the top.

ABOUT FETA

Traditionally made with sheep's or goat's milk, or a mix of both, feta is now also made with cow's milk. The cheese is prepared by curdling milk with rennet, an enzyme that coagulates the milk and creates curds that separate from the whey. The curds are drained, placed in perforated molds and pressed to create a solid cheese. It's then covered in brine and cured for several weeks, giving it a tangy flavor and the crumbly texture that feta is famous for.

DELUXE POTATO SALAD

Asparagus, wholegrain Dijon mustard, wine vinegar and sour cream are just a few of the ingredients that make this potato salad deluxe. I like to serve it with just about anything cooked on the barbecue, such as steaks, ribs or salmon.

1½ lb (750 g) red-skinned potatoes, cubed

½ cup (125 mL) mayonnaise

2 Tbsp (30 mL) sour cream

2 Tbsp (30 mL) white wine vinegar

2 Tbsp (30 mL) wholegrain Dijon mustard (see Note)

6 blanched asparagus spears, thinly sliced
    (see How to Blanch Vegetables on page 253)

1 small carrot, grated

3 large hard-boiled eggs, chopped (see Perfectly
    Cooked Hard-Boiled Eggs on page 112)

2 green onions, sliced

salt and freshly ground black pepper to taste

preparation time • 10 minutes
cooking time • 10 minutes
makes • 8 servings

NOTE
Coarser wholegrain Dijon mustard, sometimes called country- or old-style, is sold alongside the smooth Dijon at most supermarkets.

ERIC'S OPTIONS
To make a lower-calorie version of this salad, use light versions of mayonnaise and sour cream.

Gently boil the potatoes until just tender, about 10 minutes. Drain well and cool to room temperature. Place the mayonnaise, sour cream, vinegar and mustard in a large bowl and mix to combine. Add the potatoes, asparagus, carrot, egg, green onion, salt and pepper and gently toss to combine. Cover and refrigerate the salad until needed. (Can be made up to a day in advance.)

MOROCCAN-SPICED POTATO and CARROT SALAD

This mildly spiced, invitingly fragrant salad complements Mediterranean and Middle Eastern–style meats, chicken and fish. Try it with Lemony Lamb Chops with Artichokes, Olives and Mint (page 301).

preparation time • 15 minutes
cooking time • 15 minutes
makes • 6 side dish servings

ERIC'S OPTIONS
A nice addition to this salad is ½ cup (125 mL) of whole black or green olives. You can substitute 1 tsp (5 mL) of dried mint for the fresh.

1 lb (500 g) carrots, cut into ½-inch (1 cm) coins

1 lb (500 g) white or red-skinned potatoes, cut into ½-inch (1 cm) cubes

1 lemon, juice of

¼ cup (60 mL) olive oil

1 tsp (5 mL) sugar

2 tsp (10 mL) ground cumin

2 tsp (10 mL) paprika

¼ tsp (1 mL) cayenne pepper

2 garlic cloves, minced

salt and freshly ground black pepper to taste

3 green onions, thinly sliced

3 Tbsp (45 mL) chopped fresh mint

Place the carrots and potatoes in medium pot and cover with cold water. Gently simmer until vegetables are just tender, but still holding their shape, about 8 minutes. Combine the remaining ingredients in a large bowl, mixing well. Drain the carrots and potatoes and, while still hot, toss them with the dressing. Adjust the seasoning with salt and pepper. Serve hot or at room temperature.

THAI-STYLE TUNA NOODLE SALAD

Cooled tuna and rice noodles, enhanced Thai-style with peanuts, lime, chili sauce and other bright flavors. Serve the salad as a main course, pack it for a work lunch or make and bring it to a potluck.

preparation time • 30 minutes
cooking time • 1 minute
makes • 6 servings

1 Tbsp (15 mL) chopped fresh ginger

2 garlic cloves, minced

3 Tbsp (45 mL) light soy sauce

1 Tbsp (15 mL) vegetable oil

1 Tbsp (15 mL) sesame oil

1 Tbsp (15 mL) rice vinegar

1 Tbsp (15 mL) fresh lime juice

sugar to taste

Asian-style chili sauce to taste

½ lb (250 g) package rice noodles

one 6 oz (175 g) can chunk light tuna, drained well

1 small carrot, grated

1 cup (250 mL) grated cucumber or zucchini

1½ cups (375 mL) bean sprouts

2 ripe, medium tomatoes, finely chopped

3 green onions, thinly sliced

⅓ cup (80 mL) chopped cilantro or sliced basil

½ cup (125 mL) roasted, unsalted peanuts, coarsely chopped

ERIC'S OPTIONS
Replace the tuna with cooked seafood, such as salad shrimp or crabmeat or use Chinese-style egg noodles instead of rice noodles. The salad can be made several hours in advance and kept refrigerated until needed.

Place the ginger, garlic, soy sauce, vegetable oil, sesame oil, rice vinegar, lime juice, sugar and chili sauce in a large bowl. Whisk to combine, then set aside.

Cook the rice noodles in boiling water until just tender, about 1 minute. Drain well, cool in ice-cold water and drain well again. Add the noodles to the dressing. Add the tuna, carrot, cucumber or zucchini, bean sprouts, tomatoes and green onions. Gently toss to combine.

Transfer the salad to a serving platter or to individual plates if serving as a main course. Sprinkle with cilantro and peanuts and serve.

MAC and CHEESE SALAD

Here's a creamy and cool version of the always-popular combination of macaroni and cheese.

1½ cups (375 mL) elbow macaroni

½ cup (125 mL) mayonnaise

¼ cup (60 mL) sour cream

2 Tbsp (30 mL) regular or wholegrain Dijon mustard

1 Tbsp (15 mL) finely chopped fresh sage
    (or 1 tsp/5 mL crumbled dried sage)

½ lb (250 g) old cheddar cheese, cut into small cubes

½ medium red bell pepper, finely diced

2–3 green onions, thinly sliced

salt and freshly ground black pepper to taste

preparation time • 20 minutes
cooking time • 7–8 minutes
makes • 8 servings

ERIC'S OPTIONS
For extra protein and a smoky taste, add ⅓ lb (170 g) ham or smoked turkey cut into small cubes. For a lighter salad, use light versions of sour cream and mayonnaise.

Cook the pasta in a large pot of lightly salted boiling water until just tender, about 7 to 8 minutes. While it cooks, place the mayonnaise, sour cream, mustard and sage in a large bowl and whisk to combine. Drain the cooked macaroni well, cool in ice-cold water, drain well again and place in the bowl. Add the remaining ingredients and toss to combine with the mayonnaise. Cover and refrigerate until serving time. (Can be made a few hours before needed.)

WHOLE WHEAT PASTA SALAD
with TUNA and VEGETABLES

This healthy salad is rich in fiber, protein and vitamin C—and it's delicious!

½ lb (250 g) whole wheat penne

¼ cup (60 mL) store-bought or homemade pesto
  (see Pesto recipe on page 359)

3 Tbsp (45 mL) red wine vinegar

1 Tbsp (15 mL) olive oil

½ tsp (2 mL) sugar

salt and freshly ground black pepper to taste

one 6 oz (170 g) can chunk tuna, drained and flaked

12 cherry tomatoes, halved

24–30 snow or snap peas, blanched
  (see How to Blanch Vegetables on page 253)

1 medium carrot, peeled and grated

preparation time • 20 minutes
cooking time • 8–10 minutes
makes • 4 servings

ERIC'S OPTIONS
Instead of penne, use any other bite-sized whole wheat pasta, such as rotini or bow-tie. If you prefer regular pasta, use it instead of whole wheat. Instead of snow or snap peas, use 24 small broccoli florets, blanched. This recipe could easily be doubled.

Bring a large of pot of lightly salted water to a boil. Add the pasta and cook until just tender, about 8 to 10 minutes. Drain the pasta well, cool in ice-cold water and then drain well again. Place the pasta in a bowl, add the remaining ingredients and gently toss to combine. Cover and refrigerate. Toss again just before serving.

SOUTHERN-STYLE BROWN RICE SALAD

Fiber-rich brown rice tossed with black beans, chili powder, lime juice, Tabasco and a colorful mix of fresh vegetables makes a nice side dish for grilled meats, poultry or fish. It's also a great salad to bring to a potluck.

3 cups (750 mL) cooked, chilled brown rice
   (see About Brown Rice on page 99)

one 19 oz (540 mL) can black beans, drained,
   rinsed in cold water, and drained again

8 cherry tomatoes, quartered

½ cup (125 mL) finely diced yellow bell pepper

½ cup (125 mL) grated carrot

3 green onions, thinly sliced

¼ cup (60 mL) chopped fresh cilantro or parsley

¼ cup (60 mL) fresh lime juice

1 Tbsp (15 mL) honey

1 tsp (5 mL) chili powder

1 tsp (5 mL) ground cumin

salt and Tabasco or other hot pepper sauce to taste

3 Tbsp (45 mL) olive oil

preparation time • 25 minutes
cooking time • 30–40 minutes
(to cook rice)
makes • 8 servings

ERIC'S OPTIONS
For a more aromatic salad, use fragrant jasmine or basmati brown rice. If you don't care for the nuttier taste and texture of brown rice, substitute an equal amount of white long-grain rice.

Place all ingredients in a large bowl and gently toss to combine. Cover and refrigerate until serving time. (Can be made up to a day in advance.) Toss the salad again just before serving to reincorporate any liquid ingredients that have sunk to the bottom of the bowl.

ABOUT BROWN RICE

Brown rice has kernels of the grain that, unlike white rice, have only the hull removed. This leaves the tan-colored bran layer intact and preserves the nutritious elements it contains, such as vitamins B and E, calcium, protein, thiamine, niacin, riboflavin and iron. Because of the protective bran layer, brown rice takes about twice as long to cook as white rice and has a chewier texture. Brown rice is available in short-, medium- and long-grain varieties. Asian-style rice varieties such as jasmine and basmati are also available in a brown format. Because the oil-rich bran is still intact, brown rice can go rancid more quickly than white rice. Store brown rice in a tight-sealing container in a cool, dark place or in the refrigerator and buy only what you can use within a month or two. For every 1 cup (250 mL) of brown rice you want to steam, add 2 cups (500 mL) cold water or flavored liquid. Bring to a rapid boil. Cover, reduce the heat to its lowest setting and cook, undisturbed, for 35 minutes, or until the rice is tender. Fluff the rice with a fork and serve, or cool and use in such things as salads. One cup (250 mL) raw rice should yield about 2½ to 3 cups (625 to 750 mL) of cooked rice.

TROPICAL SHRIMP SALAD

This vibrant salad makes a light and inviting summer meal. Or serve it in winter when the snow is falling and you're looking for a taste of the tropics.

1 ripe papaya, halved, seeded, peeled and
    cut into 16 wedges

2 ripe avocados, halved, pitted, peeled and
    each cut into 12 wedges

1 large grapefruit, peel and pith removed,
    halved and thinly sliced crosswise

2 Belgian endives, cored and separated into leaves

¾ lb (375 g) small cooked salad shrimp, patted dry
    (see About Shrimp and Prawns on page 212)

½ cup (125 mL) yogurt

½ cup (125 mL) sour cream

2 Tbsp (30 mL) tarragon or white wine vinegar

1 tsp (5 mL) honey, or to taste

1 Tbsp (15 mL) chopped fresh tarragon

salt and white pepper to taste

preparation time • 30 minutes
cooking time • none
makes • 4 servings

ERIC'S OPTIONS
Replace the papaya with a large ripe mango or 2 smaller ones. If you don't have fresh tarragon, substitute ½ tsp (2 mL) of dried. Cooked scallops, crab or lobster meat can replace the shrimp—or try a combination of cooked seafood.

Arrange the papaya, avocados, grapefruit and endive in a spoke-like fashion on 4 dinner plates. Divide the shrimp into 4 servings and mound in the center of each plate. Combine the remaining ingredients in a bowl, mixing well. Drizzle the dressing on the salads, or serve it alongside.

BREAKFAST AND BRUNCH

SPARKLING LEMON-POMEGRANATE SPRITZERS

Here's a fizzy brunch drink that's fun to serve and good for you, as it's rich in antioxidants and vitamin C from the pomegranate juice and lemon.

2 cups (500 mL) cold water

½ cup (125 mL) granulated sugar

1 cup (250 mL) fresh lemon juice

½ cup (125 mL) pomegranate juice

2 cups (500 mL) sparkling wine or soda water

3 lemon slices, halved

6 fresh mint sprigs

preparation time • 10 minutes
cooking time • a few minute
makes • 6 servings

ERIC'S OPTIONS
For added pizzazz, freeze 2 to 3 blueberries in each slot of your ice cube trays when you're making ice cubes and use these in the drinks.

Place ½ cup (125 mL) of the water and the sugar in a small pot over medium-high heat and bring to a boil. Cook, stirring, until the sugar has completely dissolved and the liquid is clear, about 1 to 2 minutes. Pour into a 4-cup (1 L) container. Mix in the remaining 1½ cups (375 mL) of cold water, lemon juice and pomegranate juice. Cover and refrigerate until needed. (Can be prepared a day or two in advance.)

To serve, assemble 6 tall 8 oz (250 mL) glasses and put 4 to 5 ice cubes in each. Divide the lemon/pomegranate mixture among them and top up each glass with the sparkling wine or soda water. Garnish each drink with a half lemon slice and a mint sprig.

FRUIT COCKTAIL
with SPARKLING WINE

Light, bubbly and colorful—this easy-to-make fruit cocktail is always a hit at brunch. You may wish to have an extra bottle of sparkling wine on hand just in case you need to top up the glasses.

preparation time • 15 minutes
cooking time • none
makes • 6 servings

1 cup (250 mL) fresh or frozen blueberries

1 medium banana, peeled and sliced

1 medium-sized ripe mango, peeled and cubed

12 medium strawberries, hulled and sliced

3 medium kiwis, peeled, halved lengthwise and sliced

one 24 oz (750 mL) bottle sparkling wine

6 mint sprigs for garnish

ERIC'S OPTIONS
To make this drink non-alcoholic, replace the wine with non-alcoholic, sparkling apple cider. You'll find this beverage in the juice aisle of many supermarkets.

Divide the fruit equally among six 6 to 8 oz (175 to 250 mL) decorative glasses. Top with the sparkling wine. Garnish each serving with a mint sprig and serve with a spoon for scooping out the fruit.

SHRIMP BLOODY MARYS

This version of the classic brunch drink offers the tasty addition of shrimp to snack on.

8 large shrimp

6 oz (175 mL) vodka

dash Worcestershire and Tabasco or other hot pepper sauce

freshly ground black pepper to taste

24 oz (750 mL) tomato juice

4 small celery stalks

4 lemon wedges

preparation time • 10 minutes
cooking time • 2–3 minutes
makes • 4 servings

ERIC'S OPTIONS
Make virgin bloody Marys by replacing the vodka with more tomato juice. Make a shrimp Caesar by replacing the tomato juice with clamato juice.

Cook the shrimp in a pot of lightly salted boiling water until just cooked, about 2 to 3 minutes. Drain, place in ice-cold water to chill, and then drain well. Peel the shrimp, leaving the tip of the tail attached. Devein, if desired (see About Shrimp and Prawns on page 212). Fill 4 tall glasses half-full with ice cubes. Divide the vodka among the glasses, and then add the Worcestershire, hot pepper sauce and black pepper. Pour in the tomato juice. Garnish each drink with a celery stalk and lemon wedge. Hook 2 shrimp on the rim of each glass and serve.

YOU-CHOOSE-THE-FRUIT SMOOTHIES

Flavor this energy-filled breakfast smoothie with your favorite fruit or whatever you have on hand. Kiwis, mangoes, bananas, melons, berries or a mixture are all good choices.

2 cups (500 mL) sliced or cubed fresh fruit

1 cup (250 mL) low-fat yogurt

¼ cup (60 mL) orange juice

1 tsp (5 mL) grated fresh ginger

2 tsp (10 mL) honey, or to taste

sliced or whole fresh fruit for garnish (optional)

Place the 2 cups (500 mL) of fruit, yogurt, orange juice, ginger and honey in a food processor or blender. Pulse until smooth. Pour into glasses, garnish with sliced or whole fruit, if desired, and serve.

preparation time	•	5 minutes
cooking time	•	none
makes	•	2 generous servings

ERIC'S OPTIONS
For a richer-tasting smoothie, use full-fat instead of low-fat yogurt. Substitute any other type of juice, such as pineapple or cranberry, for orange juice, and try using maple syrup as a sweetener instead of honey.

HOMEMADE HOT CHOCOLATE MIX

If your kids or you like to wake up with a mug of hot chocolate, this recipe is for you. It's easy to make and you get to control the ingredients that go into it.

1½ cups (375 mL) icing sugar

¾ cup (185 mL) cocoa powder

1 tsp (5 mL) ground cinnamon

1½ cups (375 mL) skim milk powder

2 cups (500 mL) mini-marshmallows (optional)

preparation time	• 10 minutes
cooking time	• none
makes	• 4 cups (1 L) (enough for 12–16 mugs of hot chocolate)

Sift the icing sugar, cocoa and cinnamon into a large bowl. Thoroughly whisk in the skim milk powder. Stir in the mini-marshmallows, if using. Store in an airtight container at cool room temperature; the mix will keep for several weeks.

To make a serving of hot chocolate, spoon ¼ cup (60 mL) to ⅓ cup (80 mL) of the mix into a mug. Add 1 cup (250 mL) of hot water or milk, stir to combine and serve.

ERIC'S OPTIONS
Double the recipe if your house is filled with hot-chocolate fanatics. For sweet and spicy hot chocolate, add ¼ to ½ tsp (1 to 2 mL) of ground cayenne pepper to the mix when stirring in the skim milk powder.

AGED CHEDDAR CHEESE BALL

Everyone loves a good cheese ball. This crowd-pleaser combines tangy, aged cheddar with color-enhancing vegetables. This makes a nice addition to a brunch buffet.

1 lb (500 g) brick cream cheese, at room temperature

3½ cups (875 mL) grated aged cheddar cheese

⅓ cup (80 mL) finely chopped green onion

⅓ cup (80 mL) finely chopped red bell pepper

⅓ cup (80 mL) finely chopped celery

dash Worcestershire and hot pepper sauce

2 Tbsp (30 mL) chopped fresh parsley

preparation time • 20 minutes
cooking time • none
makes • 12–16 servings

ERIC'S OPTIONS
The Aged Cheddar Cheese Ball can be made a day in advance, wrapped and refrigerated until needed. If you like nuts, replace the grated cheese–parsley mixture used to coat the outside of the cheese ball with a cup or so (about 250 mL) of finely chopped walnuts or pecans.

Place the cream cheese in a large bowl and beat with an electric mixer until light and smooth. Use a large spoon and mix in 2½ cups (625 mL) of the cheddar cheese and the green onion, bell pepper, celery, Worcestershire and hot pepper sauce until well combined. With cold water-dampened hands, form the mixture into a ball. In another bowl, combine the remaining cheese and parsley. Still using your hands, coat the outside of the cheese ball, gently pressing on the mixture. Place the cheese ball on a large serving plate; cover and chill in the refrigerator for an hour or two. When ready to serve, uncover and surround with crackers and fruit, such as grapes and sliced apples and pears.

DEVILLED EGGS

To make the 24 devilled eggs this recipe yields, I used 15, not 12 eggs. The extra yolk from the additional 3 eggs serves to bulk up the filling, and the extra hard-cooked egg-white halves provide backup in case the eggs are damaged during boiling or peeling.

15 hard-boiled eggs (see Perfectly Cooked Hard-Boiled Eggs on page 112)

finely shredded head lettuce (optional)

⅓ cup (80 mL) mayonnaise

2–3 tsp (10–15 mL) dried mustard, or to taste

salt to taste

⅛ tsp (0.5 mL) cayenne pepper

½ tsp (2 mL) Worcestershire sauce, or to taste

preparation time • 30 minutes
cooking time • about 9 minutes (to cook the eggs)
makes • 24 devilled eggs

ERIC'S OPTIONS
Make curry-spiced devilled eggs by replacing the mustard with mild curry powder.

Cut the eggs in half lengthwise. Carefully remove the yolks and place in a medium bowl. Arrange 24 of the egg halves on a serving tray lined, if desired, with finely shredded head lettuce. Mash the egg yolks until as smooth as possible. Mix in the mayonnaise and whip until the mixture is creamy and light yellow in color. Mix in the remaining ingredients. Spoon or pipe the filling into the eggs halves. (The eggs can be prepared up to this point several hours in advance and stored in the refrigerator. Carefully tent with plastic wrap before doing so.) Garnish as desired (see Garnishing Devilled Eggs on page 111 for suggestions).

Some choose to simply garnish their devilled eggs with parsley and a sprinkle of paprika. But why not be more creative and make your devilled eggs look and taste like a gourmet treat? Below are some garnishing combinations that fit that theme (the suggested amounts are for each egg):

- a thin slice of cold-smoked salmon topped with ¼ tsp (1 mL) of caviar
- a few small salad shrimp topped with 2 small, blanched fresh asparagus tips
- a trio of thinly sliced spring vegetables: radish, green onion and cucumber
- a slice of black olive, 2 thin strips of roasted red pepper and a small, fresh basil leaf
- 2 thin strips of smoked ham and a sprinkle of fresh snipped chives
- a few capers, a sprinkle of finely chopped red onion and a small, fresh dill sprig.

I've tried many methods for cooking hard-boiled eggs and finally settled on the following technique. It yields perfectly cooked large eggs with golden centers and none of that iron green, gray color that occurs when the eggs are overcooked.

Use room-temperature eggs: cold eggs can crack when shocked by the heat of boiling water. As well, a chilled egg's outer edges will cook more quickly than the colder center, causing the white to overcook and toughen.

Place the eggs in a pot and completely cover with cold water. Bring to a gentle boil over medium-high heat—the surface of the water should be just moving with small bubbles rising and breaking on the surface. Don't rapidly boil the eggs: vigorous boiling may cause the eggs to bounce around and crack or to cook unevenly.

When the water reaches a gentle boil, set a timer for 9 minutes. Most hardboiled egg recipes call for 10 minutes' boiling time, but when eggs are at room temperature, slightly less time is needed.

Immediately after boiling, remove from the heat, drain the eggs well and fill the pot with ice-cold water. Chill for 2 to 3 minutes to just cool the eggs—during this cooling time the eggs will contract from the shell, making them easier to peel. Tap and crack the eggs on the bottom and top of the shell; gently roll between your hands and then peel.

A piping bag is a handy tool for neatly and artfully filling devilled eggs or topping canapés. Below are tips to help those home cooks who struggle when using a piping bag.

Most stores selling cookware stock piping bags in a variety of sizes. Invest in a small, medium and large bag so you'll have the correct size to match the job at hand. The bigger the piping job, the bigger the bag should be, otherwise you'll be refilling the bag too often, which can cause the exterior to get all mucked up and difficult to handle.

After inserting the tip, carefully fill the bag. To do so without getting any of what you'll be piping on the outside of the bag, make a 2-inch (5 cm) cuff, just like on a shirt, at the top of the bag. Slide 1 hand under the cuff and hold the bag. Use your other hand to scoop in what you're piping.

Only half-fill the bag: this will give you more room to gather together the open end and therefore allow greater control when piping.

Unfold the cuff and tightly twist the top portion of the bag until what you are piping just starts to poke out the end. Squeeze from the top with 1 hand and direct the tip with your other hand. After squeezing out 1 portion, gently twist the bag to push the next portion to the tip of the bag and squeeze it out. Repeat until the bag is empty.

MAPLE CRUNCH GRANOLA

Make this nutritious mixture of oats, fruit, nuts and seeds on your day off and you'll have 12 delicious breakfast servings or snacks you can pack for work or school in a bag. Purchase large-flake rolled-oats, not the smaller-flaked, quick-cooking kind.

3 cups (750 mL) large-flake rolled oats

¼ cup (60 mL) dried cranberries

¼ cup (60 mL) raisins or currants

¼ cup (60 mL) slivered almonds

¼ cup (60 mL) sunflower seeds

¼ cup (60 mL) pecan halves, coarsely chopped

¼ cup (60 mL) pumpkin seeds

¼ cup (60 mL) unsweetened coconut flakes

12 dried apricots, sliced

½ tsp (2 mL) ground cinnamon

½ cup (125 mL) maple syrup

¼ cup (60 mL) vegetable oil

Preheat the oven to 325°F (160°C). Line an 11- × 17-inch (28 × 43 cm) or similar-sized baking sheet with parchment paper. Place the oats, cranberries, raisins or currants, almonds, sunflower seeds, pecans, pumpkin seeds, coconut, apricots and cinnamon in a large bowl and toss to combine.

preparation time	•	15 minutes
cooking time	•	25–30 minut
makes	•	about 12 servings, ½ cup (125 r each

ERIC'S OPTIONS

This recipe can be doubled. If desired, substitute other dried fruits, such as blueberries and cherries, and other unsalted nuts, such as walnuts or cashews, for some of those called for in the recipe. Substitute an equal amount of honey for the maple syrup. If you would prefer not to bake and richen the color of the dried fruit, stir the cranberries, raisins or currants, and apricots into the granola after the other ingredients have been baked.

Combine the maple syrup and oil in a small pot. Set over medium heat until warm, but not hot. Pour into the bowl with the dry ingredients and stir well. Spread the mixture on the prepared baking sheet. Bake for 25 to 30 minutes, stirring 2 or 3 times, until the oats and other ingredients are lightly toasted. Cool on a rack to room temperature.

Transfer to an airtight container and store at cool room temperature for up to 3 weeks.

To serve, scoop ½ cup (125 mL) of the granola into a bowl and top with milk, soy beverage or yogurt.

WHY EAT OATS?

If you're looking for a nutritious food, look no further. Oats are low in fat, an excellent source of thiamine and B vitamins and a good source of iron, potassium and other minerals—and they contain vitamin E. They're rich in soluble fiber, believed to help reduce blood cholesterol levels. The bran surrounding the oat kernel is much thinner and paler than other grains, such as wheat. It is not removed during milling, and so retains all its nutritional value.

SPICED GRAPEFRUIT BRÛLÉE

Brûlée is a French cooking technique where a topping of sugar is caramelized under a broiler or with a blowtorch—this is often done with a cup of custard, as in crème brûlée. In this breakfast treat, tangy, nutritious grapefruit is deliciously sweetened with spiced-up, golden brown sugar.

1 large grapefruit, sliced in half

2 Tbsp (30 mL) golden brown sugar

pinch each cinnamon, nutmeg and cloves

preparation time • 5 minutes
cooking time • 2 minutes
makes • 2 servings

ERIC'S OPTIONS
To speed up preparation at breakfast time, combine the sugar and spices and halve and segment the grapefruit the night before.

Set the oven rack 6 inches (15 cm) beneath the broiler. Preheat the broiler. Cut between the segments of the fruit with a grapefruit knife so the flesh will be easier to scoop out after broiling. Place the grapefruit, cut-side up, in a small baking dish. Combine the brown sugar and spices in a small bowl; sprinkle the mixture on top of the grapefruit. Broil the grapefruit for 2 minutes, or until the sugar is bubbly and caramelized.

ABOUT GRAPEFRUIT

When buying grapefruits, choose smooth ones with brightly colored skin. The best grapefruits will feel heavy for their size—an indication they're packed with juice. Grapefruit can be stored for a few days at room temperature. If you've bought a big bag and need to keep them longer, store them in the crisper of your refrigerator for up to 2 weeks. Remove and leave at room temperature overnight for juicier fruit. Grapefruit is low in calories and rich in vitamin C. It also contains folic acid and potassium and is a good source of inositol, a member of the vitamin B complex, which studies have shown may help lower blood cholesterol levels.

ONE-PAN BREAKFAST for FOUR

Make extra boiled potatoes for dinner and save a couple to make this the next morning. It's a quick way to cook a substantial breakfast for four people.

2 Tbsp (30 mL) butter

1 cup (250 mL) cubed ham

2 medium red potatoes, boiled until tender, cooled and cubed

¼ cup (60 mL) finely chopped red bell pepper

8 large eggs

¼ cup (60 mL) milk or water

1 cup (250 mL) grated cheddar cheese

2 green onions, thinly sliced

salt and freshly ground black pepper to taste

preparation time • 20 minutes
cooking time • 6–8 minutes
makes • 4 servings

ERIC'S OPTIONS
Halve the recipe if you're serving two people. If you like mushrooms, clean and slice six of them and add them to the skillet with the ham, potatoes and bell pepper. For a vegetarian version, omit the ham and add a cupful of another vegetable, such as diced zucchini.

Melt the butter in a large nonstick skillet over medium-high heat. Add the ham, potatoes and bell pepper and cook for 3 or 4 minutes, stirring occasionally. Whisk the eggs with the milk until well combined. Stir the cheese, green onions, salt and pepper into the egg mixture and pour into the pan. As the eggs begin to set, gently turn and lift them from the bottom and sides of the skillet, forming large, soft curds. When the eggs are just set, divide among 4 plates and serve immediately with toast.

ABOUT GRATED CHEESE

Before grating cheese, make sure it's well chilled; that makes it firmer and easier to grate. Expect ¼ lb (125 g) of cheese to yield about 1 cup (250 mL) of grated cheese. Grated cheese melts more evenly and quickly than cubes or chunks; add it to sauces at the end of cooking and use just enough heat to melt and mix it in. If heated too long, cheese can toughen and the fat may separate out and rise to the surface.

When I was younger and had little money, I always had eggs on hand to see me through. Inexpensive, easy to prepare, relatively low in calories and very nutritious, they provide high-quality protein, every vitamin except C, iron and other minerals. Some people think brown eggs are superior to white when it comes to nutritional content, but the values are the same.

When preparing eggs, whether by frying, poaching or boiling, don't crank up the heat and rush things. If you cook them in gently simmering water or over medium heat, you'll improve your chances of getting perfectly cooked, tender eggs, not overcooked, rubbery ones.

Check the best-before date before buying eggs and store them in the refrigerator; eggs kept at room temperature lose their quality quickly. Believe it or not, eggshells are porous and the flavor of an egg can be affected if exposed to odorous foods in your refrigerator. Unless your refrigerator has a separate, closed area to store eggs, keep them in the carton you bought them in. It was designed to protect the eggs and maximize their shelf life.

BAKED FRENCH TOAST
with CINNAMON

Serve this to your kids when they have an active day planned at school or on the weekend and you want to make sure they're off to a good start. The preparation can be done the night before; the next morning you can serve a hot breakfast in less than 30 minutes.

preparation time	• 20 minutes
cooking time	• 27–28 minutes
makes	• 4 servings (2 slices each)

3 Tbsp (45 mL) butter, melted

½ cup (125 mL) packed golden brown sugar

½ tsp (2 mL) ground cinnamon

eight 1-inch-thick (2.5 cm) slices French bread

4 large eggs

½ cup (125 mL) milk

½ cup (125 mL) light (10%) cream

¼ cup (60 mL) orange juice

ERIC'S OPTIONS
Make the French toast spicier and even more aromatic by mixing pinches of ground nutmeg and cloves into the brown sugar along with the cinnamon. For fruit-filled French toast, use thick slices of raisin bread instead of French bread. For more fiber, use thick slices of whole wheat bread.

Coat a 9- x 13-inch (3.5 L) baking pan with the melted butter. Combine the sugar and cinnamon in a small bowl and sprinkle half of it evenly into the bottom of the pan. Place the bread slices in a single layer in the pan, squeezing them in to make them fit if necessary. Beat the eggs in a medium bowl until the yolks and whites are thoroughly combined. Mix in the milk, cream and orange juice. Slowly pour this mixture over the bread, ensuring each slice is evenly coated. Sprinkle the top of the bread with the remaining brown sugar mixture. Cover and refrigerate overnight.

The next morning, place the rack in the middle position and preheat the oven to 375°F (190°C). Uncover the dish and bake the French toast for 25 minutes. Turn the oven to broil and broil the French toast for 2 to 3 minutes, or until the top is golden brown. Serve with warm maple syrup.

BAKE and FREEZE
PUMPKIN DATE MUFFINS

These nutritious and delicious muffins freeze beautifully, making them perfect for a large batch. Enjoy some fresh and freeze the rest to warm for a quick midweek breakfast.

4 large eggs

1½ cups (375 mL) packed golden brown sugar

one 14 oz (398 mL) can pumpkin

1½ cups (375 mL) unsweetened applesauce

2 tsp (10 mL) pure vanilla extract

2 cups (500 mL) whole wheat flour

1 cup (250 mL) all-purpose flour

2 tsp (10 mL) ground cinnamon

1 tsp (5 mL) ground ginger

2 tsp (10 mL) baking soda

2 tsp (10 mL) baking powder

1 tsp (5 mL) salt

1 cup (250 mL) chopped dates

1 cup (250 mL) chopped walnuts or pecan pieces

vegetable oil spray

preparation time	•	25–30 minute
cooking time	•	18–20 minute
makes	•	24 medium-sized muffins

ERIC'S OPTIONS
This recipe can be halved. Instead of dates, use another type of dried fruit, such as cranberries or raisins. For a decorative touch, sprinkle the muffins with pumpkin seeds before baking. Instead of muffins, make this recipe into two 9- × 5-inch (2 L) loaves—great to serve at teatime or for dessert. The loaves will take 50 minutes to bake; baking temperature remains the same. Cool before slicing.

Preheat the oven to 375°F (190°C). Whisk the eggs, brown sugar, pumpkin, applesauce and vanilla in a large bowl until the mixture is smooth. In a second bowl, mix together the whole wheat and all-purpose flours with the cinnamon, ginger, baking soda, baking powder and salt using a whisk. Stir the dates and nuts into the dry mixture. Add the dry ingredients to the wet and mix until just combined.

Spray two 12-cup nonstick muffin pans lightly with vegetable oil. Spoon the batter evenly into the cups. Bake the muffins for 18 to 20 minutes. Cool in the pans for 15 minutes. Carefully remove the muffins from the pan (and enjoy some while they're still warm). Freeze leftover muffins in an airtight container after they have cooled to room temperature. To reheat, thaw at room temperature overnight and then warm for a few minutes in a 200°F (95°C) oven.

MAKE-AHEAD
EGGS BENEDICT

Preparing eggs Benedict for a table full of guests can be a challenge if you are trying to poach the eggs, toast the English muffins and make the hollandaise sauce all at the last minute. This recipe allows you to spread out those tasks. You can softly poach the eggs in advance, make the sauce 30 minutes before it's needed and quickly toast the muffins on a baking sheet under the broiler. When you're ready to serve, it's a simple matter of assembling the bacon, eggs and sauce on the muffins and making it all piping hot in the oven.

2 tsp (10 mL) white vinegar

12 large eggs

3 large egg yolks

¼ cup (60 mL) white wine

½ cup (125 mL) butter, melted

white pepper to taste

dash Tabasco sauce, Worcestershire sauce
    and fresh lemon juice

6 English muffins

12 slices Canadian (back) bacon

1 Tbsp (15 mL) finely chopped fresh parsley

preparation time • 40 minutes
cooking time • about
              25 minutes
makes • 6 servings
        (2 eggs each

ERIC'S OPTIONS
To make this with smoked salmon and spinach, replace each slice of back bacon with 1 to 2 slices of smoked salmon. Top each muffin with ¼ cup (60 mL) wilted fresh spinach, drained of excess moisture. Continue with the eggs and hollandaise sauce and bake as described in the recipe.

Bring a large, wide pot of water to a gentle simmer. Add the vinegar. Fill a large bowl with ice-cold water. Swirl the simmering water with a spoon, and then crack 3 to 4 of the eggs into the water. (The movement of the water will help prevent the eggs from touching.) Poach the eggs 2 minutes; the yolks should still be quite soft. With a large, slotted spoon, carefully lift the eggs out of the water and place in the bowl of ice-cold water. This will stop the cooking and cool the eggs. Repeat these steps with the remaining eggs. Carefully lift the eggs out of the cold water and set on a large plate covered with plastic wrap or parchment paper.

(The eggs can be prepared to this point several hours in advance, or even the night before. Cover and refrigerate until needed.)

Place the egg yolks in a heatproof bowl; whisk in the wine. Place the bowl over a pot of simmering water. Vigorously and rapidly whisk until the egg yolks become very light and thickened and feel warm, not hot. (This will occur quite quickly; do not overcook or the egg yolks will scramble.) Remove from the heat and slowly whisk in the melted butter, a few dribbles at a time. When the butter is all incorporated, season the hollandaise with white pepper, Tabasco, Worcestershire and lemon juice. Cover the bowl with plastic wrap and set aside until needed.

Preheat the broiler. Cut or split the English muffins in half and set, cut-side up, on a large baking sheet. Broil the muffins until lightly toasted; remove from the oven and set aside. Preheat the oven to 425°F (220°C). Transfer the muffins to a parchment paper–lined baking sheet. Place a slice of bacon on each muffin half. Set a poached egg on top of the bacon. Top the eggs with the hollandaise sauce. Bake for 12 to 15 minutes, or until the eggs are heated through and the hollandaise sauce is lightly golden. Divide among plates, sprinkle with parsley and serve.

HISTORY OF EGGS BENEDICT

According to a number of sources, eggs Benedict was created at Delmonico's Restaurant around 1894. This Manhattan eatery was the birthplace of many famous dishes, such as Delmonico steak, lobster Newburg and baked Alaska. The story goes that one day, regular lunch customers Mr. and Mrs. LeGrand Benedict wanted to try something new. Mrs. Benedict and the restaurant's maître d' discussed the possibilities, and the dish now known as eggs Benedict was the result of their culinary conversation. With its base of crisp bread topped with succulent, smoky meat and a perfectly poached egg, all covered with a silky sauce, you can understand why it was a hit with the Benedicts and became a classic dish that remains popular today.

BEAUTIFUL BRUNCH
for TWO

Here's a simple yet elegant and colorful way to assemble a special brunch for two.

2–4 croissants

4 slices of fresh papaya or cantaloupe

2 paper-thin slices prosciutto, each cut in half lengthwise

¼ lb (125 g) wedge brie cheese

8 fresh strawberries

small bunch seedless grapes

2 glasses freshly squeezed orange juice

1½ cups (375 mL) sparkling wine (optional)

small bowl raspberry jam or other preserve

cream and sugar

coffee or tea

preparation time	•	20 minutes
cooking time	•	10 minutes to warm the croissant
makes	•	2 servings

ERIC'S OPTIONS
Instead of brie, serve the grapes and strawberries with a bowl of yogurt. Replace the croissants with warm muffins, made at home or bought from a good bakery.

Preheat the oven to 200°F (95°C). Place the croissants on a baking sheet and warm in the oven 10 minutes. Meanwhile, line a large serving tray with a napkin. Wrap each slice of papaya or cantaloupe with a half-slice of prosciutto and arrange on one side of a decorative plate. Place the cheese, strawberries and grapes on the other side of the plate. Place on the tray, along with the orange juice, sparkling wine, jam, cream and sugar. Add the warmed croissants in a napkin-lined basket or plate to the tray, and finish up with 2 coffee cups and a small spoon and knife. Serve the tray of goodies in a comfortable location, such as the bedroom, in front of the fire or on a sunny patio. Pour the tea or coffee. Sip some orange juice and then top up each glass, if desired, with sparkling wine.

MORNING GLORY PANCAKES

Get a glorious start to the day with these pancakes flavored with orange and coconut. The generous amount of baking powder used in the batter ensures they are light and fluffy. Serve them with softened butter and a jug of maple syrup.

3 large eggs

¾ cup (185 mL) 2% milk

¾ cup (185 mL) orange juice

2 tsp (10 mL) finely grated orange zest

1¾ cups (435 mL) all-purpose flour

⅓ cup (80 mL) granulated sugar

2 Tbsp (30 mL) baking powder

½ cup (125 mL) medium, unsweetened coconut flakes

¼ tsp (1 mL) salt

preparation time • 10 minutes
cooking time • 4–5 minutes per batch
makes • about 18 pancakes

ERIC'S OPTIONS

For an extra special touch, serve the pancakes with maple cranberry sauce. Place 1½ cups (375 mL) fresh or frozen cranberries in a pot with 1 cup (250 mL) maple syrup, ¼ cup (60 mL) orange juice, and pinches of ground cinnamon, clove and nutmeg. Gently simmer 20 to 25 minutes, or until the cranberries are tender. Serve warm or at room temperature.

Whisk together the eggs, milk, orange juice and orange zest in a bowl. Combine the flour, sugar, baking powder, coconut and salt in a second bowl. Add the dry ingredients to the wet and stir until just combined. Let rest 5 minutes (it will become bubbly), and give it a few stirs before cooking. Preheat the oven to 200°F (95°C).

Preheat a nonstick griddle to medium or medium-high heat. Lightly coat with oil or cooking spray. With a small ladle, pour 4-inch (10 cm) rounds of batter on the griddle, leaving a 2-inch (5 cm) space between each pancake. Flip the pancakes when the top becomes speckled with bubbles. Continue cooking until the underside is browned and the center of the pancake springs back when touched. Keep warm in the oven until all are done.

PORK and OAT SAUSAGE PATTIES

Savory, hand-formed sausage patties are a great side dish with eggs, French toast or pancakes.

1¼ lb (625 g) ground pork

1 large egg, beaten

½ cup (125 mL) quick-cooking oats

½ tsp (2 mL) dried sage leaves (see Note)

¼ tsp (1 mL) paprika

¾ tsp (4 mL) salt

½ tsp (2 mL) freshly ground black pepper

2 Tbsp (30 mL) vegetable oil

Preheat the oven to 200°F (95°C). Place the pork, egg, oats, sage, paprika, salt and pepper in a bowl and mix until just combined. Moisten your hands with cold water. Divide the pork mixture into 12 equal balls and shape each ball into a ¾-inch-thick (2 cm) patty. Heat the oil in a large skillet over medium or medium-high heat. Cook the patties in batches for 3 to 4 minutes per side, or until entirely cooked through and the juices run clear with no hint of pink. Reserve the cooked patties in the oven while frying up the rest.

preparation time	•	15 minutes
cooking time	•	6–8 minutes per batch
makes	•	12 patties

NOTE
In this book, the dried herb I call sage leaves is dried whole sage leaves, which are crumbled into small but discernible pieces and bottled or sold in bags most often labeled "sage leaves." Do not substitute ground sage, which is a finely ground powder and much more intense in flavor.

ERIC'S OPTIONS
The patties can be mixed and shaped the day before, refrigerated and cooked when needed.

APPLE-GLAZED BREAKFAST SAUSAGES

After browning, the sausages are simmered in apple juice or cider until the liquid cooks down and becomes a sweet glaze.

1 Tbsp (15 mL) vegetable oil

12 pork, turkey or chicken breakfast sausages

⅓ cup (80 mL) apple juice or cider

Heat the oil in a large skillet over medium to medium-high heat. Add the sausages and cook until nicely browned on all sides, about 5 minutes. Discard the excess fat. Add the juice or cider to the skillet, bring to a simmer and cook until the sausages are cooked through and the juice or cider has almost evaporated and nicely glazed the sausages.

preparation time	•	5 minutes
cooking time	•	about 10 minutes
makes	•	4 servings

ERIC'S OPTIONS
To make maple-glazed sausages, omit the apple juice or cider and cook the sausages entirely through in the skillet. Drain the excess fat. Drizzle the sausages with 2 Tbsp (30 mL) maple syrup. Roll the sausages around in the pan to coat them with the syrup and serve.

SWEET BELL PEPPER HASH BROWNS

To save time in the morning the potatoes can be parboiled the night before, cooled on a tray, covered and refrigerated. The red and green peppers give these potatoes a great taste and a festive look.

2 lb (1 kg) white-skinned potatoes

3 Tbsp (45 mL) vegetable oil

½ medium onion, finely chopped

½ red bell pepper, finely chopped

½ green bell pepper, finely chopped

¼ tsp (1 mL) paprika

½ tsp (2 mL) ground cumin

salt and freshly ground black pepper to taste

preparation time • 20 minutes
cooking time • 10–13 minutes
makes • 6–8 servings

ERIC'S OPTIONS
For a meaty taste, add ½ cup (125 mL) finely chopped corned beef to the potatoes when first starting to fry them.

Cut the potatoes, unpeeled, into ½-inch (1 cm) cubes and gently boil until just tender and still holding their shape, about 4 to 5 minutes. Drain the potatoes well. Heat the oil in a very large skillet over medium heat. Add the potatoes, onion, red and green bell pepper, paprika and cumin and cook 6 to 8 minutes, or until the potatoes are nicely crusted and colored. Season with salt and pepper and serve.

NOODLES AND RICE

FETTUCCINI with CHICKEN, PESTO and CHERRY TOMATOES

Pesto imparts a delicious flavor to this simple, quickly made dish.

¾ lb (375 g) fettuccini

2 Tbsp (30 mL) olive oil

2 (each about 8 oz/250 g) boneless, skinless, chicken breasts, thinly sliced

1 cup (250 mL) store-bought or homemade pesto (see Pesto recipe on page 359)

16 cherry tomatoes, halved

salt and freshly ground black pepper to taste

freshly grated Parmesan cheese and olive oil to taste

small fresh basil leaves and toasted pine nuts for garnish (optional)

preparation time • 10 minutes
cooking time • 10 minutes
makes • 4 servings

ERIC'S OPTIONS
For seafood lovers, the chicken in this recipe can be replaced with 20 medium-sized raw, peeled shrimp (see About Shrimp and Prawns on page 212). Add them in place of the chicken, but only cook them for about 2 minutes, or until they are just cooked through.

Cook the pasta in a large pot of boiling, salted water until just tender. While it is cooking, heat the oil in a large skillet over medium-high heat. Add the chicken and season with salt and pepper. Cook, stirring, for 4 to 5 minutes, or until the chicken is just cooked. Stir in the pesto and cherry tomatoes and cook for 1 to 2 minutes more. Reduce the heat to medium-low.

Drain the pasta, reserving ½ cup (125 mL) of the cooking liquid. Add the pasta and reserved liquid to the skillet. Season with salt and pepper. Place the pasta in individual serving bowls or on a large platter. Sprinkle with the Parmesan cheese and drizzle a little olive oil over top. If desired, garnish with basil leaves and toasted pine nuts.

FETTUCCINI with LOBSTER and OYSTER MUSHROOMS

This decadent pasta dish provides cost-effective luxury: one lobster feeds four people.

preparation time • 30 minutes
cooking time • 10 minutes
makes • 4 servings

¾ lb (375 g) fettuccini

2 Tbsp (30 mL) olive oil

2 garlic cloves, minced

½ lb (250 g) oyster mushrooms, sliced
(lower stems removed and discarded)

½ cup (125 mL) dry white wine

½ tsp (2 mL) saffron

1 Tbsp (15 mL) chopped fresh tarragon,
or 1 tsp (5 mL) dried

2 cups (500 mL) whipping cream

1½ lb (750 g) cooked lobster,
meat removed and thinly sliced (see Note)

½ cup (125 mL) frozen peas

salt and freshly ground black pepper to taste

2 green onions, thinly sliced

NOTE
Cooked, whole lobsters are sold at some supermarkets and seafood stores. If you wish to cook your own, see Boiled Lobster or Dungeness Crab (page 198).

ERIC'S OPTIONS
Use ½ lb (250 g) other cooked seafood, such as crabmeat or salad shrimp, instead of the lobster.
Any long pasta, such as linguini or spaghetti can be used instead of fettuccini.

Cook the fettuccini in a large pot of boiling, lightly salted water until just tender. Meanwhile, heat the oil in a large skillet over medium-high heat. Add the garlic and mushrooms and cook until the mushrooms are just tender, about 3 to 4 minutes. Add the wine, saffron and tarragon and cook until the wine is reduced by half. Add the cream and cook until the sauce is slightly thickened. Add the lobster and peas and just heat through, about 2 minutes. Reduce the heat to medium-low. When the pasta is cooked, drain well and mix it into the sauce. Season with salt and pepper. Divide among heated plates or pasta bowls and sprinkle each serving with green onions.

LINGUINI with MIXED PEAS and ARTICHOKES

Cherry tomatoes, fresh basil, artichoke hearts and a vibrant trio of peas give this pasta a springtime feel. Since all the ingredients are now available year-round, you can make this dish and enjoy that feeling even in January.

¾ lb (375 g) linguini

3 Tbsp (45 mL) olive oil

1–2 garlic cloves, chopped

one 14 oz (398 mL) can artichoke hearts, drained and quartered

16–20 snap peas, trimmed

16–20 snow peas, trimmed

1 cup (250 mL) chicken or vegetable stock

½ cup (125 mL) frozen peas

12 cherry tomatoes, halved

⅓ cup (80 mL) freshly grated Parmesan cheese

¼ cup (60 mL) chopped fresh basil

salt and freshly ground black pepper to taste

preparation time •	20 minutes
cooking time •	about 15 minutes
makes •	4 servings

ERIC'S OPTIONS
If desired, provide some additional olive oil and Parmesan cheese for drizzling and sprinkling on the pasta at the table. Instead of linguini, use another noodle, such as spaghetti or fettuccini. Instead of chopped fresh basil and garlic, add 2–3 Tbsp (30–45 mL) of store-bought or homemade pesto (see Pesto recipe on page 359).

Bring a large pot of lightly salted water to a boil. Add the linguini and cook until tender, about 8 to 10 minutes. Meanwhile, heat the olive oil in a large skillet over medium heat and add the garlic, artichokes, snap peas and snow peas. Cook, stirring, for 2 to 3 minutes. Add the stock and bring to a simmer.

Drain the pasta, reserving ½ cup (125 mL) of the cooking liquid. Add the pasta, reserved cooking liquid, frozen peas, cherry tomatoes, Parmesan, basil, salt and pepper to the skillet. Toss to combine, heat through for 1 to 2 minutes and serve.

ROASTED VEGETABLE LASAGNA
with RICOTTA FILLING

Roasting the vegetables gives them a rich, almost sweet taste that nicely offsets the acidity of the tomatoes.

2 medium onions, chopped

1 medium red or yellow bell pepper,
    cut into ½-inch (1 cm) cubes

1 small zucchini, quartered lengthwise and cut into
    ½-inch (1 cm) pieces

4–6 garlic cloves, thinly sliced

12 medium white or brown mushrooms, quartered

2 Tbsp (30 mL) olive oil

1 tsp (5 mL) dried oregano

salt and freshly ground black pepper to taste

one 28 oz (796 mL) can diced tomatoes

one 28 oz (796 mL) can crushed tomatoes

2 Tbsp (30 mL) tomato paste

¼ cup (60 mL) store-bought or homemade pesto
    (see Pesto recipe on page 359)

one 1 lb (500 g) tub ricotta cheese

2 large eggs, beaten

16 dried lasagna noodles, cooked as per package directions

¾ lb (375 g) mozzarella cheese, grated

preparation time • 30–40 minutes
cooking time • 55–60 minutes
makes • 8 servings

ERIC'S OPTIONS
Lasagna can be assembled in advance, wrapped and stored in the refrigerator for up to a day, and baked later. Unbaked lasagna can also be frozen. Thaw it in the refrigerator overnight before baking. Add a few minutes to the baking time, as you'll be starting from cold.

To freeze cooked lasagna, cut it into portions, place in smaller baking dishes, wrap and freeze. Thaw in the refrigerator overnight before reheating in the oven or microwave. You may need to add a little water or tomato sauce to the dish to keep it moist if reheating in the oven.

Preheat the oven to 425°F (220°C). Place the onions, bell pepper, zucchini, garlic and mushrooms in a bowl and toss with the olive oil, oregano, salt and pepper. Place on a large baking sheet and roast for 20 to 30 minutes, or until the vegetables are tender and lightly browned. Remove the vegetables and reduce the oven temperature to 350°F (175°C).

Place the vegetables in a pot and mix in the diced and crushed tomatoes and tomato paste. Bring to a gentle simmer on the stovetop. Cover and cook, stirring occasionally, for 20 minutes. Season with salt and pepper. Combine the pesto, ricotta and eggs in a bowl, mixing well.

To assemble the lasagna, begin by spooning a little of the sauce into the bottom of a 9- × 13-inch (23 × 33 cm) baking dish. Top with 4 noodles. Spoon a third of the remaining sauce over the noodles, and then add a third of the mozzarella cheese. Top with 4 more noodles and then spread the ricotta mixture over top. Add 4 more noodles, and top them with ⅓ of the sauce and cheese. Repeat this step again and it's ready for the oven. Cover loosely with foil and bake for 40 minutes. Remove the foil and cook for 15 to 20 minutes more, or until brown and bubbling. Let rest for 10 minutes to allow the lasagna to set before slicing and serving.

COOKING PERFECT PASTA

To cook ¾ to 1 pound (375 to 500 g) of fresh or dry pasta, the amount most often called for in recipes designed for four, bring 12 cups (3 L) of water to a boil, then add 1 Tbsp (15 mL) of salt. Salt in the cooking water heightens the flavor of pasta, particularly important if you are only tossing it with a few other ingredients, not bathing it in a rich sauce. The generous amount of water prevents the pasta from becoming overly starchy and sticking together as it cooks. (In the past, it was common practice to add a little oil to the pot to prevent this, but it is now thought oil coats the pasta and prevents the sauce from adhering to it.) Cook the pasta al dente—an Italian term which means to cook pasta or any other food until it offers a slight resistance when bitten into. Cooking time varies among the different types and brands of pasta. Check the package label for suggested cooking time. During cooking, taste the pasta to see how it is progressing.

SENSATIONAL SEAFOOD LASAGNA

This lasagna is rich and decadent enough to serve on any special occasion. Serve it with a mixed green or Caesar salad.

2½ cups (625 mL) fish or chicken stock

1½ cups (375 mL) light cream or milk

2 garlic cloves, finely chopped

⅓ cup (80 mL) all-purpose flour

salt and white pepper to taste

pinch ground nutmeg

½ lb (250 g) firm fish fillets, such as salmon or halibut, cut into small cubes

one 1 lb (500 g) tub ricotta cheese

2 large eggs

½ cup (125 mL) chopped fresh basil

½ lb (250 g) cooked salad shrimp, patted dry

1 cup (250 mL) fresh or canned crabmeat, squeezed dry

¾–1 lb (375–500 g) mozzarella cheese, grated

½ cup (125 mL) freshly grated Parmesan cheese

16 dried lasagna noodles, cooked as per package directions

preparation time • 40 minutes
cooking time • 55–60 minute
makes • 8 servings

ERIC'S OPTIONS
For even richer-tasting lasagna, replace the mozzarella cheese with a more complex-tasting Italian-style cheese, such as provolone or Asiago. The lasagna can be made oven-ready in advance or frozen as described in Eric's Options for Roasted Vegetable Lasagna with Ricotta Filling (page 138).

Place 2 cups (500 mL) of the stock in a pot. Add the cream or milk and garlic, and bring to a simmer. Mix the remaining stock with the flour until smooth. Slowly whisk into the stock mixture. Bring back to a simmer and cook until the sauce thickens. Season with the salt, pepper and nutmeg; mix in the cubed fish. Remove from the heat and set aside. (The fish will cook through when baked in the lasagna.)

Combine the ricotta cheese with the eggs and basil. Season with salt and pepper and set aside. Preheat the oven to 350°F (175°F).

To assemble the lasagna, spoon a little sauce into the bottom of a 9- x 13-inch (3.5 L) casserole. Top with 4 noodles, a third of the remaining sauce, and half the shrimp and crab. Sprinkle with a third of the mozzarella and Parmesan cheeses. Top with another layer of noodles and then with the ricotta cheese mixture. Top with another layer of noodles, another third of the sauce, the rest of the shrimp and crab and another third of the cheeses. Top with 4 more noodles and the remaining sauce and cheese. Bake, tented with foil so it does not touch the cheese, for 40 minutes. Uncover and bake for another 15 to 20 minutes, until brown and bubbly. Let the lasagna rest for 5 to 10 minutes before slicing and serving.

VEAL-STUFFED PASTA SHELLS
with OLIVE TOMATO SAUCE

Jumbo pasta shells present well and willingly accept just about any savory filling. In this case the filling is based on veal.

preparation time • 40 minutes
cooking time • 55–60 minutes
makes • 8 servings

THE SAUCE

2 Tbsp (30 mL) olive oil

1 medium onion, finely diced

2 garlic cloves, minced

1 tsp (5 mL) dried basil

1 tsp (5 mL) dried oregano

½ cup (125 mL) coarsely chopped black olives

two 14 oz (398 mL) cans tomato sauce

2 Tbsp (30 mL) tomato paste

1 cup (250 mL) red wine or beef stock

pinch crushed chili flakes (optional)

pinch sugar

salt and freshly ground black pepper to taste

THE STUFFED SHELLS

1 lb (500 g) ground veal

1 large egg

¼ cup (60 mL) breadcrumbs

2 Tbsp (30 mL) freshly grated Parmesan cheese

1 tsp (5 mL) each dried basil and dried oregano

2 garlic cloves, crushed

salt and freshly ground black pepper to taste

16–20 jumbo pasta shells, cooked as per package directions

1½ cups (375 mL) grated mozzarella cheese

Continued . . .

ERIC'S OPTIONS
You can use other ground meats, such as beef, turkey or chicken, instead of the veal. This dish can be prepared in advance, wrapped, stored in the refrigerator for up to a day and baked later. It also freezes well unbaked. Thaw in the refrigerator overnight before baking as directed. Add a few minutes to the baking time as you'll be starting from cold.

THE SAUCE

Heat the oil in a pot over medium heat. Add the onion and garlic and cook until tender, about 3 to 4 minutes. Add the remaining sauce ingredients. Bring to a gentle simmer and cook, stirring occasionally, for 20 minutes, and then remove from the heat.

THE STUFFED SHELLS

Preheat the oven to 375°F (190°C). Combine the veal, egg, breadcrumbs, Parmesan cheese, basil, oregano, garlic, salt and pepper in a bowl. Place about 2 Tbsp (30 mL) of filling into each shell. Spoon the sauce into a 9- x 13-inch (23 x 33 cm) casserole. Place the stuffed shells in the dish. Top each with a little mozzarella cheese. Cover the dish loosely with foil and bake for 30 minutes. Remove the foil and bake for 10 to 15 minutes more, or until the tops of the shells are golden and the sauce is bubbling.

SPINACH TORTELLINI with CREAMY LEMON and LEEK SAUCE

The rich sauce gives this tortellini a gourmet touch. Consider this quick dish when you want to serve something special but are short on time. The recipe can be expanded if you're hosting a larger group.

preparation time • 10 minutes
cooking time • 10–12 minutes
makes • 3–4 servings

one 12 oz (375 g) package spinach tortellini, meat- or cheese- filled

2 Tbsp (30 mL) olive oil

1 small leek, white part only, halved, washed and thinly sliced

1 garlic clove, minced

¼ cup (60 mL) lemon juice

1 tsp (5 mL) finely grated lemon zest

1½ cups (375 mL) whipping cream

¼ cup (60 mL) freshly grated Parmesan cheese, plus more for the table

salt and freshly ground black pepper to taste

ERIC'S OPTIONS
Use any other fresh filled pastas, such as ravioli or agnolotti, instead of tortellini. For an herbaceous taste, stir ¼ cup (60 mL) of fresh basil into the pasta just before serving.

Cook the tortellini in a large of pot of boiling, salted water until tender (check package for suggested cooking time). While it is cooking, heat the oil in a large skillet over medium heat. Add the leek and garlic and cook until softened, about 4 to 5 minutes. Add the lemon juice and zest and cook until the lemon juice has almost evaporated. Add the cream and simmer until the sauce thickens slightly. Drain the cooked tortellini and add it to the skillet, along with the Parmesan cheese, salt and pepper. Mix to combine and simmer for 2 minutes more. Spoon into individual serving bowls or a deep platter.

FREEZER PASTA SAUCE

Make this tasty sauce on a day off and you'll be able to freeze individual packages for topping any type of cooked pasta, whether it's ravioli, linguini or rotini. Any ripe, red tomato is fine, but Roma (also called plum) tomatoes have thick flesh, small seeds and a rich flavor, which makes them especially good for sauce.

12 lb (5.5 kg) ripe, red tomatoes

⅓ cup (80 mL) olive oil

4 medium onions, finely chopped

2 large celery ribs, finely chopped

4–6 garlic cloves, chopped

2 cups (500 mL) chicken or vegetable stock or water

2 tsp (10 mL) sugar

¼ cup (60 mL) tomato paste

salt and freshly ground black pepper to taste

3 bay leaves

1 Tbsp (15 mL) dried oregano

1 Tbsp (15 mL) dried basil

¼–½ tsp (1–2 mL) crushed chili flakes (optional)

preparation time • 30 minutes
cooking time • 40 minutes
makes • about 16 cups

ERIC'S OPTIONS
If you prefer a chunky sauce, don't purée after simmering.

Bring 5 inches (12 cm) of water to a boil in a large, wide pot. Cut the stem section out of each tomato and mark a shallow *x* at the blossom end. Immerse the tomatoes, a few at a time, in the boiling water for 1 minute, or until the skins just start to slip off. Transfer the tomatoes to a large tray with a slotted spoon and repeat with the remaining tomatoes. When the tomatoes are cool enough to handle, peel off and discard the skins.

Cut the tomatoes in half lengthwise. Set a sieve over a bowl. Squeeze the seeds out of the tomatoes into the sieve. Discard the seeds and reserve the liquid in the bowl. Coarsely chop the seeded tomatoes.

Place the oil in a large, heavy-bottomed pot over medium heat. Add the onion, celery and garlic and cook until tender, about 5 minutes. Add the chopped tomatoes, reserved liquid, stock, sugar, tomato paste, salt, pepper, bay leaves, oregano, basil and chili flakes, if using. Bring the mixture to a gentle simmer and cook for 30 minutes, or until it looks like a chunky tomato sauce. Remove and discard the bay leaves, and then purée the sauce in a food processor or with a hand-held immersion blender. Cool to room temperature. Divide among containers, seal tightly, label and freeze for up to 6 months. Thaw before using.

SKILLET MAC and CHEESE

Here's a quick, stovetop way to make macaroni and cheese and still have the heavenly crust of an oven-baked version. I serve it with whole wheat dinner rolls and a platter filled with raw, fresh vegetables, such as celery, carrot and cucumber sticks, broccoli and cauliflower florets, and cherry tomatoes.

2 cups (500 mL) macaroni

2 cups (500 mL) milk

3 Tbsp (45 mL) all-purpose flour

¼ tsp (1 mL) paprika

2 cups (500 mL) grated cheddar cheese

salt and white pepper to taste

preparation time • 10 minutes
cooking time • 9–12 minutes
makes • 4 servings

ERIC'S OPTIONS
To add some protein to this dish, mix in a can (6 oz /175 g) of chunk tuna, drained well and coarsely flaked, or 1½ cups (375 mL) of cubed ham or cooked chicken.

Bring a large pot of lightly salted water to a boil. Add the macaroni and cook until just tender, about 6 to 8 minutes. Meanwhile, place the milk, flour and paprika in a bowl and whisk until lump-free. Pour into a 10- to 12-inch (25 to 30 cm) nonstick ovenproof skillet and set over medium heat. Cook the mixture, whisking frequently, until it gently simmers and begins to thicken, about 5 minutes. Mix in 1½ cups (375 mL) of the cheese; season with salt and white pepper. Cook and stir until the cheese melts; reduce to low heat. Place an oven rack 6 inches (15 cm) beneath the broiler; preheat the broiler.

Drain the cooked macaroni well and mix into the cheese sauce. Stir in a little extra milk if you find the consistency too thick. Remove from the heat. Sprinkle the remaining ½ cup (125 mL) of cheese overtop and place under the broiler until it's nicely browned, about 3 to 4 minutes.

SPAGHETTI and MEATBALLS for EIGHT

This tasty recipe serves eight. If you're a family of four, why not invite another family of four over for an Italian-style dinner party? The kids can help set the table (perhaps with a red-and-white checkered table cloth and matching napkins) and choose the Italian music—can you say Dean Martin?

preparation time • 20 minutes
cooking time • about 25 minutes
makes • 8 servings

2½ lb (1.25 kg) lean ground beef

2 large eggs

½ cup (125 mL) dried breadcrumbs

¼ cup (60 mL) milk

2–3 garlic cloves, chopped

1 tsp (5 mL) dried oregano

1 tsp (5 mL) dried basil

1½ tsp (7 mL) salt

1 tsp (5 mL) freshly ground black pepper

6 cups (1.5 L) marinara sauce (see Note)

1 cup (250 mL) water

2 lb (1 kg) spaghetti

butter or olive oil (optional) for tossing

chunk of Parmesan cheese for grating

NOTE
Marinara sauce is a herb and garlic–flavored tomato-based sauce sold in jars or cans at most supermarkets.

ERIC'S OPTIONS
If you're only feeding four simply cut the recipe in half. Give the meatballs a more complex, richer taste by making them with an equal mix of ground beef, pork and veal. Instead of marinara sauce, use Freezer Pasta Sauce (page 146) in this recipe.

Preheat the oven to 350°F (175°C). Line a large baking sheet with parchment paper. Place the beef, eggs, breadcrumbs, milk, garlic, oregano, basil, salt and pepper in a large bowl and mix until just combined. Moisten your hands with cold water. Roll the meat into 1½-inch (4 cm) balls and set on the baking sheet. Roast the meatballs for 25 minutes, or until cooked through.

While the meatballs cook, place the marinara sauce and water in a large pot over medium to medium-high heat, and bring to a simmer. When the meatballs are cooked, drain well. Add them to the sauce and simmer, partially covered, for 15 to 20 minutes.

While the meatballs simmer, bring a large pot of lightly salted water to a boil. Boil the spaghetti until just tender, about 8 to 10 minutes. Drain well and place in a serving bowl. If desired, to prevent the spaghetti from sticking together, toss with a little butter or olive oil.

Spoon the meatballs and sauce into another serving bowl or serve directly from the pot. Serve with the cheese and provide a grater for diners to top their spaghetti and meatballs with cheese, as desired.

SAFELY STORING AND HANDLING GROUND BEEF

At the supermarket, keep ground beef separate from the other items in your cart to prevent it from dripping on other foods. Once home, place in a sided container and refrigerate for up to a day. If freezing for more than a month, wrap packaged meat with foil to prevent freezer burn.

The safest way to thaw ground beef, still in its original packaging, is in a sided container in the refrigerator. It will take about 12 hours per pound (500 g) to thaw. Never defrost ground beef at room temperature—it will thaw unevenly and thawed portions may be exposed to unsafe, warm temperatures. Do not refreeze raw ground beef. If thawed, cook it and then freeze.

Wash your hands thoroughly before and after handling ground beef. Use hot soapy water to clean all surfaces that come in contact with the raw meat. To kill any disease-causing bacteria, it's important to cook ground beef to 160°F (71°C) or above. Use clean utensils and plates when removing cooked ground beef from the heat source, not ones that have been used to mix or move the raw meat.

GRILLED SIRLOIN NOODLE BOWL

This brothy noodle dish will bring a little warmth on a cool winter day.

preparation time • 20 minutes
cooking time • 5 minutes
makes • 4 servings

2 garlic cloves, minced

2 tsp (10 mL) grated fresh ginger

2 Tbsp (30 mL) soy sauce

¼ tsp (1 mL) crushed chili flakes, or to taste

vegetable oil for the grill

1 lb (500 g) top sirloin steak (about 1 inch/2.5 cm thick)

5 cups (1.25 L) beef stock

1 Tbsp (15 mL) sesame oil

½ lb (250 g) rice noodles (see Note)

4 green onions, thinly sliced

NOTE
Rice noodles, also sometimes called rice vermicelli, can be found in the Asian foods aisle of your supermarket.

ERIC'S OPTIONS
Not a meat eater? Then replace the beef broth with a vegetable-based one and the beef with 2 cups (500 mL) of whole or thinly sliced vegetables, such as snow peas, carrots, red bell peppers, broccoli or baby corn. Stir-fry the vegetables, garlic, ginger and chili flakes in vegetable oil until just tender before mixing in the soy sauce. Top the noodles with the vegetables and pour in the broth.

Mix the garlic, ginger, soy sauce and crushed chili flakes in a bowl. Add the steak and turn to coat both sides with the marinade. Cover and marinate for 20 minutes.

Preheat your grill to high. Lightly oil the grill. Grill the steak 2 to 3 minutes per side, until rare to medium-rare in doneness. Remove and let rest for 5 minutes.

Bring a large pot of water to a boil for the noodles. Combine the broth and sesame oil in a separate pot and bring to a rapid boil. Cook the noodles in boiling water for 1 minute, or until just tender. Drain well and divide them among 4 large soup bowls. Thinly slice the beef and distribute on top of the noodles. Sprinkle with the green onions. Add the broth and serve.

ASIAN-STYLE VEGETABLE NOODLE BOWL

A vegetarian noodle bowl filled with colorful vegetables swimming in a tasty broth.

preparation time • 20 minutes
cooking time • about 10 minutes
makes • 4 servings

3½ cups (875 mL) vegetable stock

1 garlic clove, chopped

1 Tbsp (15 mL) chopped fresh ginger

2 Tbsp (30 mL) soy sauce

1 tsp (5 mL) hot Asian-style chili sauce

1 medium carrot, halved lengthwise and thinly sliced

1 medium red bell pepper, halved and thinly sliced

one 14 oz (398 mL) can cut young corn (see Note)

3 baby bok choy, separated into leaves and coarsely chopped

½ lb (250 g) Chinese-style egg noodles

⅓ cup (80 mL) chopped fresh cilantro or green onion

1 cup (250 mL) bean sprouts

NOTE
Canned young (also called baby) corn is sold in the Asian foods aisle of most supermarkets. It is sold in whole small cobs or cut into pieces, the latter being a convenient, no-slicing-required ingredient to add to a range of dishes.

ERIC'S OPTIONS
Make this a meaty soup by topping it with heated slices of the barbecued pork or duck you can find in Asian markets. If you prefer rice noodles, use them instead of egg noodles.

Bring a large pot of water to a boil. Meanwhile, place the stock, garlic, ginger, soy sauce, chili sauce and carrot in a medium pot and bring to a gentle simmer. Simmer for 5 minutes. Add the bell pepper, corn and bok choy and cook 2 to 3 minutes longer.

While the vegetables are cooking, add the noodles to the boiling water and cook until just tender, about 1 minute. Drain the noodles well and divide them among 4 large soup bowls. Ladle the broth and vegetables over the noodles, top with the cilantro or green onions and bean sprouts and serve steaming hot.

THE EMPEROR'S
FRIED RICE

Tender pork, succulent shrimp, crisp snow peas and crunchy, rich cashews make this version of fried rice a regal one.

preparation time • 25 minutes
cooking time • about
10 minutes
makes • 6–8 servings

3 Tbsp (45 mL) vegetable oil

¾ lb (375 g) pork tenderloin, halved lengthwise and thinly sliced

½ medium onion, finely chopped

½ medium green bell pe pper, finely chopped

16 snow peas, thickly sliced

3 cups (750 mL) cooked long grain white rice, cooled (see Tips for Making Fried Rice on page 157)

⅓ lb (170 g) small cooked salad shrimp, fresh or frozen (and thawed), patted dry (see About Shrimp and Prawns, page 212)

one 14 oz (398 mL) can cut young corn (see Note, page 155)

2 Tbsp (30 mL) soy sauce

freshly ground black pepper to taste

3 green onions, thinly sliced

ERIC'S OPTIONS
If you prefer the taste of chicken, replace the pork tenderloin with ¾ lb (375 g) boneless, skinless chicken breast. Slice and stir-fry it as described for the pork. Instead of cooked white rice, use cooked brown in this recipe.

Heat the oil in a wok or very large skillet over medium-high heat. Add the pork and cook 3 to 4 minutes, or until cooked through. Mix in the onion and bell pepper and cook 1 minute more. Add the snow peas and cook 30 seconds more. Mix in the remaining ingredients and stir-fry 3 to 4 minutes, or until all the ingredients are well heated through. Serve immediately.

Do not use freshly cooked, hot rice to make fried rice because it can overcook during frying, turn mushy and clump together. If you want to make fried rice, plan ahead and cook and cool the rice a day or two beforehand.

To make 3 cups (750 mL) of cooked rice, the amount called for in this book's recipes, place 1¼ cups (310 mL) of long-grain white or jasmine rice in a pot and pour in 1¾ cups (435 mL) cold water. Bring the rice to a boil over high heat, reduce the heat to its lowest setting, cover and steam the rice, undisturbed, for 15 to 18 minutes, or until just tender. Spoon the rice into a wide, shallow dish, fluff with a fork, cool to room temperature, and cover and refrigerate.

Before you fry the rice, allow the cold rice to sit out at room temperature for about 20 minutes. This step will help the grains to separate more easily once you start to fry them.

When frying rice, make sure your wok or skillet is hot. This will ensure the rice actually does fry and takes on the slightly smoky taste good fried rice should have. Use a neutral-tasting oil with a high smoke point (the highest temperature it can reach before it burns), such as peanut, corn or vegetable oil.

HOW TO STIR-FRY

Stir-frying is a cooking technique where small pieces of food are quickly cooked over high heat. Meats and seafood sear on the outside, keeping them moist and tender in the middle. Vegetables retain a brilliant color and a crisp-tender texture. A wok or large skillet is the best tool to use as it offers a wide, hot surface for the foods to be moved around and rapidly cooked. Because of the quick cooking time it's important to have all ingredients chopped and ready to go. Heat the pan and cooking oil before you add the ingredients. If you don't, vegetables meant to be crisp can turn limp and meats may stick to the bottom of the pan. Use peanut or good-quality vegetable oil for stir-frying; they have a neutral flavor and can be heated to high temperatures without burning.

CASHEW FRIED RICE

The cashews that so richly flavor this rice can be expensive. If that's a concern, buy them from a bulk food store or a supermarket that sells bulk foods. That way you can buy only the exact amount required for this recipe with no waste.

2 Tbsp (30 mL) vegetable oil

1 cup (250 mL) finely chopped green cabbage

1 small carrot, quartered lengthwise and thinly sliced

½ medium onion, finely chopped

1 garlic clove, minced

3 cups (750 mL) cooked long-grain white rice, cold
(see Tips for Making Fried Rice on page 157)

¾ cup (185 mL) unsalted roasted cashews

½ cup (125 mL) frozen peas

2 Tbsp (30 mL) soy sauce

2 green onions, thinly sliced

freshly ground black pepper to taste

preparation time • 10 minutes
cooking time • 6–7 minutes
makes • 4 servings

ERIC'S OPTIONS
Instead of cashews, use unsalted roasted peanuts or whole almonds in this recipe. Instead of green cabbage, use 1 cup (250 mL) of finely chopped napa or Chinese cabbage. Instead of cooked white rice, use cooked brown in this recipe.

Place the oil in a wok or large skillet set over medium-high heat. Add the cabbage, carrot, onion and garlic and stir-fry for 2 minutes. Add the rice and stir-fry for 2 to 3 minutes more. Mix in the remaining ingredients and stir-fry for 2 minutes, or until the rice is heated through.

MIXED-VEGETABLE RICE PILAF

This rice dish contains a mix of five vegetables. Some, such as the garlic and onion, are used more for flavoring. Others, such as the carrot, red bell pepper and green peas, also add flavor but are included more for their attractive color.

1 Tbsp (15 mL) vegetable oil

½ small onion, finely chopped

1 cup (250 mL) long-grain white rice

1 garlic clove, minced

¼ tsp (1 mL) dried oregano

1¾ cups (435 mL) chicken or vegetable stock

½ small red bell pepper, finely diced

⅓ cup (80 mL) grated carrot

salt and white pepper to taste

⅓ cup (80 mL) frozen peas

preparation time • 10 minutes
cooking time • 20–23 minutes
makes • 4 servings

ERIC'S OPTIONS
Instead of white rice, use brown rice and increase the stock by ¼ cup (60 mL). After the rice comes to a boil, cover it and reduce the heat to its lowest setting. Cook the brown rice, undisturbed, for 35 minutes, or until tender.

Heat the oil in a small to medium-sized pot set over medium to medium-high heat. Add the onion and cook until tender, about 3 minutes. Mix in the rice, garlic and oregano and cook for 2 minutes more. Mix in the stock, red pepper, grated carrot and salt and pepper and bring to a boil. Cover, reduce the heat to its lowest setting and cook, undisturbed, for 15 to 18 minutes, or until the rice is tender. Fluff the rice with a fork, mix in the peas and heat them through for a minute or so, then serve.

SAFFRON RICE
with PARSLEY

Golden-hued rice flecked with bright green parsley. Serve this classy rice alongside one of the more decadent entrées in this book, such as Cornish Hen with Raspberry Ginger Glaze (page 259), or Slow Cooker Beef Daube (page 320).

½ tsp (2 mL) loosely packed saffron threads, crumbled

1 Tbsp (15 mL) olive oil

1 medium shallot, finely chopped

1 cup (250 mL) long-grain white rice

1½ cups (375 mL) chicken or vegetable stock

salt and white pepper to taste

2 Tbsp (30 mL) chopped fresh parsley

preparation time • 5 minutes
cooking time • 27–30 minutes
makes • 4 servings

ERIC'S OPTIONS
Instead of parsley, accent the rice with another type of fresh herb, such as snipped chives.

Steep the saffron in 2 Tbsp (30 mL) of boiling water for 10 minutes. Heat the oil in a small to medium-sized pot set over medium to medium-high heat. Add the shallot and cook for 1 minute. Add the rice and cook, stirring, for 1 minute. Add the steeped saffron and its liquid, stock, and salt and pepper. Bring to a rapid boil, then cover, reduce the heat to its lowest setting and cook, undisturbed, for 15 to 18 minutes, or until the rice is tender. Fluff the rice with a fork, mix in the parsley and serve.

ABOUT SAFFRON

Saffron is dried stigmas of a small flower called the purple crocus (*Crocus sativus*). It is also the world's most expensive spice. More than fourteen thousand stigmas are required to make 1 ounce (30 g) of saffron. Luckily, a little goes a long way in turning the rice in this recipe into an attractive, golden-hued side dish flecked with vibrant green parsley. If you don't use saffron very often, it's actually fairly affordable. You can usually buy it in small containers, enough for three to four recipes, for around $10.

SAFFRON RISOTTO

As the rice cooks in the stock and is stirred frequently, its starches release into the liquid. This creates an almost creamy sauce around the rice that in this case turns a lovely golden color thanks to the saffron. This risotto is the perfect side dish to serve with Slow Cooker Osso Bucco with Gremolata (page 298).

½ tsp (2 mL) loosely packed saffron threads
    (see About Saffron on page 161), crumbled

6 cups (1.5 L) chicken stock

3 Tbsp (45 mL) olive oil

½ medium onion, finely chopped

1½ cups (375 mL) risotto rice

½ cup (125 mL) dry white wine

½ cup (125 mL) freshly grated Parmesan cheese

2 Tbsp (30 mL) chopped fresh parsley

salt and freshly ground pepper to taste

preparation time • 5 minutes
cooking time • 40 minutes
makes • 4–6 servings

ERIC'S OPTIONS
If you don't wish to use or don't have any saffron, prepare this recipe without it to make risotto bianco, or white risotto.

Steep the saffron in 2 Tbsp (30 mL) of boiling water for 10 minutes. Place the stock in a pot and bring to just below a simmer over medium-high heat. When there, reduce the heat to its lowest setting and keep the stock warm on the stove.

Heat the oil in a medium-sized pot set over medium to medium-high heat. Add the onion and cook until tender, about 3 minutes. Add the rice and cook, stirring, until it has a nutty, toasted aroma, about 2 minutes. Add the wine and the saffron and its liquid. Adjust the heat to bring to a gentle simmer. Cook until the wine is almost fully absorbed by the rice.

Add 1 cup (250 mL) of the stock, stir and cook until it is almost fully absorbed by the rice. Add the remaining stock ½ to 1 cup (125 to 250 mL) at a time, cooking and stirring until it is almost fully absorbed by the rice before adding the next portion. Continue doing this until the rice is tender. You may not need all the stock.

When done, the rice should be al dente, tender with some bite. The texture of the risotto should be a creamy mass with enough body to stand up slightly when scooped into a bowl or plate.

When the rice is tender, remove it from the heat and stir in the Parmesan cheese, parsley and salt and pepper. Cover and let sit for a few minutes before serving.

RICE FOR RISOTTO

The best types of rice to use for risotto are stubby, short- or medium-grained varieties. They have a high starch content and absorb less liquid so that when cooked, the rice maintains a nice texture, and the almost creamy sauce that risotto is famous for is created around it. You'll find these types of rice for sale at many supermarkets. Sometimes they are simply labeled "risotto rice." You'll also find specific varieties of rice, particularly in specialty food stores, that are excellent for making risotto: arborio, carnaroli or vialone nano, for example.

EXOTIC MUSHROOM RISOTTO

If you'd like to sample some of the more interesting-looking fresh mushrooms available these days, this dish is a good choice. Brown (also called cremini), oyster, shiitake, portobello, chanterelle and morel are some of the mushrooms you can use in this risotto. I used a mix of the first three. If serving the risotto as a main course, just add some crusty Italian bread and a salad of mixed baby greens dressed with simple vinaigrette to complete the meal. As a side dish, try it with Garlic-Stuffed Chicken Legs with Pan Gravy (page 244).

preparation time • 20 minutes
cooking time • 25–30 minute
makes • 4 servings as
a main cours
6 as a side d

ERIC'S OPTIONS
To make the risotto even richer, drizzle it with a little truffle oil at the table. Truffle oil, which is made by infusing good-quality olive oil with the flavor of white or black truffles, is available at Italian-style markets and most fancy food stores.

6 cups (1.5 L) chicken or vegetable stock

3 Tbsp (45 mL) butter or olive oil

1 medium onion, finely chopped

2–3 garlic cloves, minced

1½ cups (375 mL) risotto rice (see Rice for Risotto on page 163)

½ cup (125 mL) white wine

2 Tbsp (30 mL) butter or olive oil

1 lb (500 g) assorted fresh mushrooms, sliced

salt and freshly ground black pepper to taste

2 Tbsp (30 mL) chopped Italian parsley

½ cup (125 mL) freshly grated Parmigiano-Reggiano cheese

Place the stock in a pot and bring to a gentle simmer. Heat the 3 Tbsp (45 mL) of butter or oil in another pot over medium heat. Add the onion and garlic and cook, stirring, until tender, about 2 to 3 minutes. Add the rice and cook, stirring, for 3 to 4 minutes, until the rice has a slightly nutty, toasted aroma. Add the wine, adjust the heat so the mixture gently simmers, and cook until the wine is almost fully absorbed. Add 1 cup (250 mL) of the hot stock, stirring and cooking until it is almost fully absorbed.

Add the remaining stock ½ cup (125 mL) at a time, cooking and stirring until the liquid is almost absorbed each time. You may not need all the stock.

While the rice is cooking, heat the remaining 2 Tbsp (30 mL) butter or oil in a large skillet over medium-high heat. Add the mushrooms and cook until they are tender and the moisture is gone. Season with salt and pepper and set aside. When the rice is tender and creamy, remove it from the heat and stir in the parsley, cheese and mushrooms. Taste for seasoning and adjust, if necessary. Top with additional cheese at the table, if desired.

ABOUT PARSLEY

Parsley is an underrated herb that attracted an undeserved reputation for being run-of-the-mill. However, chefs seem to be rediscovering its value. And why not? A little of it freshly chopped and mixed into, or sprinkled over, soups, stews, casseroles, poached fish and many other dishes will instantly add flavor and appearance.

The two main types of parsley are curly-leaf parsley and flat-leaf (also called Italian) parsley. You can easily tell the two apart from the shape of the leaves. There is not a great difference in taste between the two; both are described as very slightly peppery and palate-refreshing.

To store parsley, wrap it in a slightly dampened paper towel, set it in a plastic bag and refrigerate for up to a week. Parsley needs to be washed well just before using as its leaves are prone to collecting dirt.

Parsley is so much more than a pretty garnish. It contains vitamins A and C as well as calcium and iron.

SPANISH-STYLE BROWN RICE

This is a homemade version of the spiced rice dish served in many Mexican restaurants in Canada and the United States. What sets this apart is that, instead of white rice, nutritious, almost nutty-tasting brown rice is used to make it.

preparation time • 10 minutes
cooking time • 40 minutes
makes • 6 servings

3 Tbsp (45 mL) olive oil

1 medium green bell pepper, finely chopped

½ medium onion, finely chopped

2 garlic cloves, minced

1½ cups (375 mL) long grain brown rice
    (see About Brown Rice on page 99)

1½ tsp (7 mL) ground cumin

1½ tsp (7 mL) chili powder

⅛ tsp (0.5 mL) cayenne pepper

3 cups (750 mL) chicken or vegetable stock

ERIC'S OPTIONS
If you would prefer to use long-grain white rice to make this dish, reduce the amount of stock to 2¾ cups (685 mL). After the rice comes to a boil, cover it and reduce the heat to its lowest setting. Cook the rice, undisturbed, for only 15 to 18 minutes, or until tender.

Pour the oil into a medium-sized pot and set over medium to medium-high heat. Add the bell pepper, onion and garlic and cook for 3 minutes. Add the rice, cumin, chili powder and cayenne and cook for 2 minutes more. Pour in the stock, increase the heat to high and bring to a rapid boil. Cover, reduce the heat to its lowest setting and cook, undisturbed, for 35 minutes, or until the rice is tender. Fluff the rice with a fork and serve.

VEGETARIAN ENTRÉES

ASPARAGUS, ROASTED PEPPER and MUSHROOM STRUDEL

Serve this savory strudel when you're looking for an attractive, non-meat dish to anchor a celebratory meal. I served it at Easter one year and it was a hit. This is one of the most challenging recipes in the book, in that carefully sealing the filling into the pastry requires a deft touch. Tzatziki Sauce (page 360) and any of the leafy salads in the book are good accompaniments.

2 Tbsp (30 mL) olive oil

1 lb (500 g) brown or white mushrooms, sliced

3 green onions, finely chopped

¼ cup (60 mL) breadcrumbs

1 large egg, beaten

2 garlic cloves, crushed

salt and freshly ground black pepper to taste

5 sheets phyllo pastry (see Handling and Storing Phyllo Pastry on page 229)

¼ cup (60 mL) melted butter or olive oil

2 lb (1 kg) asparagus, trimmed and blanched (see Buying, Storing and Preparing Asparagus on page 89; see How to Blanch Vegetables on page 253)

salt and freshly ground black pepper to taste

⅓ cup (80 mL) freshly grated Parmesan cheese

3 roasted red peppers, halved and patted dry

preparation time	•	30–40 minute
cooking time	•	25–30 minute
makes	•	4–6 servings

ERIC'S OPTIONS
You can use store-bought or homemade roasted red peppers in this dish.

Heat the oil in a skillet over medium-high heat. Add the mushrooms and cook until they are tender and their moisture has evaporated. Cool to room temperature. Mix with the onions, breadcrumbs, egg, garlic, and salt and pepper.

Preheat the oven to 375°F (190°C). Lay a sheet of phyllo pastry on a parchment paper–lined baking tray and brush with butter or oil. Top with another sheet and brush again. Repeat the process until all the sheets are used.

Arrange the asparagus in the middle of the bottom third of the pastry (see photos). Sprinkle with salt, pepper and the Parmesan cheese. Top with the roasted peppers and then the mushroom mixture. Fold the sides of the pastry slightly over the filling and carefully fold the filling over and enclose in the pastry. Brush the top with a little melted butter or oil. Make small cuts, about 2 inches (5 cm) apart, in the top of the pastry to make it easier to cut when baked.

Bake for 25 to 30 minutes. Let rest for 10 minutes before slicing with a sharp, serrated knife.

CREOLE-STYLE STUFFED EGGPLANT

Serve steamed rice and a simple green salad with this satisfying, Louisiana-style dish.

2 medium eggplants, (about 1 lb (500 g) each)

2 Tbsp (30 mL) lemon juice

2 Tbsp (30 mL) olive oil

1 medium onion, finely chopped

2 celery ribs, finely chopped

1 medium green bell pepper, finely chopped

2 garlic cloves, crushed

½ tsp (2 mL) cayenne pepper, or to taste

1½ cups (375 mL) chopped fresh tomatoes

cold water

2 Tbsp (30 mL) chopped fresh basil or oregano

2 Tbsp (30 mL) chopped fresh parsley

½ cup (125 mL) breadcrumbs

salt and freshly ground black pepper to taste

1½ cups (375 mL) grated white cheddar or
    Monterey Jack cheese

preparation time • 30–40 minut•
cooking time • 40–45 minut•
makes • 4 servings

ERIC'S OPTIONS

If you don't have fresh tomatoes on hand, you can use an equal amount of diced canned tomatoes. Substitute 1 tsp (5 mL) dried basil or oregano for the fresh. Add the dried herbs when you add the tomatoes.

Preheat the oven to 375°F (190°C). Trim the stem of each eggplant and then cut in half lengthwise. With a sharp knife, score the flesh side. Use a small spoon to scoop out the flesh, leaving a shell about ¼ inch (5 mm) thick. Set the hollowed-out eggplant halves, cavity side up, in a lightly oiled baking dish. Brush the exposed flesh with the lemon juice. Set the eggplant aside.

Chop the scooped-out eggplant flesh into pieces. Heat the oil in a large skillet over medium heat. Add the onion, celery, green pepper and garlic and cook until tender, about 4 to 5 minutes. Add the eggplant to the skillet with the cayenne and tomatoes. Add just enough water to keep the mixture moist, and gently simmer until the eggplant is tender. Stir in the herbs, breadcrumbs, salt and pepper. Stuff the eggplant shells with the mixture and top with the cheese. Bake for 30 to 40 minutes, until the shells are tender but not collapsed and the top is golden brown.

BROCCOLI and CHEDDAR-STUFFED POTATOES

This recipe is a little fussy. You have to bake the potatoes, cool them a bit, remove the flesh, mash it, mix it with the flavorings, stuff the mixture back into the potato shells and bake them again. After one bite of these cheesy, broccoli-flecked spuds, though, I'm always glad I made the effort.

4 medium baking potatoes, washed and dried

5 oz (150 g) piece broccoli crown, cut into 6 florets (see Note)

¼ cup (60 mL) milk

2 Tbsp (30 mL) melted butter

2 Tbsp (30 mL) sour cream

3½ oz (100 g) cheddar cheese, grated

2 green onions, thinly sliced

salt and white pepper to taste

preparation time • 30 minutes
cooking time • 90 minutes
makes • 4 servings

NOTE
A broccoli crown is the top portion of the vegetable with the stem removed. It's sold in that form at most supermarkets.

ERIC'S OPTIONS
Asparagus is a delicious substitute for broccoli in the stuffed potatoes. Snap off and discard the tough stem-end of 8 asparagus spears. Thinly slice the spears and cook in boiling water for 30 seconds. Cool in cold water, drain well and mix into the potatoes when asked to add the broccoli in the method.

Preheat the oven to 375°F (190°C). Prick each potato a few times with a fork. Bake for 65 minutes, or until quite tender. While the potatoes bake, cook the broccoli in boiling water for 2 minutes. Cool in ice-cold water, drain well and chop coarsely.

When the potatoes are done, leave the oven on. Let the potatoes cool until safe enough to handle but still quite warm. Cut off the top third of each potato. Carefully scoop out as much potato flesh as you can from the top and bottom pieces of potato and place it in a bowl. Discard the top pieces of potato skin; place the bottom, hollowed-out potato shells in a baking dish. Mash the potato flesh until smooth, then beat in the milk, butter and sour cream. Mix in the broccoli, three-quarters of the cheese, and the green onions, salt and pepper. Pack and mound the mixture into the potato shells and sprinkle the remaining cheese overtop. Bake for 25 minutes, or until golden brown.

PAN-SEARED TOFU with BABY BOK CHOY and CURRY SAUCE

Nutrient-rich tofu and bok choy are accented with a flavorful, easily made sauce.

one 1 lb (500 g) package firm tofu (see Note)

2 Tbsp (30 mL) vegetable oil

8 baby bok choy, washed well and trimmed

one 14 oz (398 mL) can coconut milk

1 tsp (5 mL) cornstarch

1 Tbsp (15 mL) Indian-style curry paste
(see About Curry Paste on page 36)

2 Tbsp (30 mL) freshly squeezed lime juice

2 Tbsp (30 mL) brown sugar

2 tsp (10 mL) chopped fresh ginger

salt to taste

preparation time	•	10 minutes
cooking time	•	6–7 minutes
makes	•	4 servings

NOTE
Tofu package sizes can vary from brand to brand. Don't worry about the exact weight as specified in this recipe, it could be a little more, or less.

ERIC'S OPTIONS
To make this lower in calories and saturated fat, use light coconut milk instead of regular.

Preheat the oven to 200°F (95°C). Drain the tofu well and cut it into 8 slices. Carefully pat the slices dry with paper towel. Heat the oil in a large nonstick skillet over medium-high heat. Add the tofu and sear for 1 minute on each side. Transfer the tofu to a large platter and place in the oven.

Drain the excess oil from the skillet and add a quarter-cup (60 mL) of water. Add the bok choy to the skillet, cover and steam for 1 minute. Arrange the bok choy on the platter with the tofu. Add the remaining ingredients to the skillet and whisk to combine. Bring to a boil and cook for 2 minutes. Pour the sauce over the tofu and bok choy and serve.

ABOUT TOFU

Tofu is like pasta. Unadorned, it's about as plain a food as you'll get. But if you dress it up it can soak up a lot of flavor and be the backdrop for many tasty creations.

Tofu is made by soaking, cooking, grinding and pressing dried soybeans to extract a milky-looking liquid. That liquid is coagulated and turned into curds. Similar to cheesemaking, those curds are placed in molds, pressed and shaped and the resulting product is tofu.

The more liquid that's pressed out during processing, the firmer the tofu becomes. In stores you see several styles of tofu that reflect that, such as soft, medium and firm. You will also see flavored tofu and silken tofu, which is almost silky in texture and processed a little differently than pressed tofu.

What you're preparing will determine what type of tofu to use. For example, for a blended drink, easy-to-whirl soft tofu would be the best choice. For a rough-and-tumble stir-fry, a firmer tofu that will hold together would be your best.

CURRIED VEGETABLE STEW

You can tailor this stew to the level of heat you like simply by choosing mild, medium or hot curry paste. Serve with chutney, yogurt, steamed rice, and pappadums or naan.

2 Tbsp (30 mL) vegetable oil

1 large red bell pepper, seeded and cubed

1 medium onion, halved and thinly sliced

2 garlic cloves, finely chopped

1 Tbsp (15 mL) chopped fresh ginger

2 Tbsp (30 mL) Indian-style curry paste
(see About Curry Paste on page 36)

2 medium carrots, cut into ½-inch-thick (1 cm) coins

one 14 oz (398 mL) can coconut milk

½ cup (125 mL) vegetable stock

¼ lb (125 g) green beans, trimmed and
cut into 1-inch (2.5 cm) pieces

½ small head cauliflower, cut into small florets

¼ cup (60 mL) chopped cilantro

salt to taste

preparation time • 20 minutes
cooking time • 20 minutes
makes • 3–4 servings

ERIC'S OPTIONS
Just about any vegetable will work in this curry. Feel free to substitute any that you have on hand or that appeal to you more, such as broccoli florets for the cauliflower, or snap peas for the green beans. Before cooking, evaluate their cooking time to decide when they should be added during the cooking process.

Heat the oil in a wide pot over medium-high heat. Add the red pepper and onion and cook until just tender, about 3 to 4 minutes. Stir in the garlic, ginger and curry paste and cook 2 minutes more. Stir in the carrots, coconut milk and stock. Reduce the heat to a gentle simmer and cook, stirring occasionally, until the carrots are almost tender, about 10 minutes. Add the green beans and cauliflower and cook until the sauce thickens slightly and the vegetables are tender. Add more stock if the curry becomes too thick before the vegetables are cooked. Stir in the cilantro and salt.

NO-FUSS VEGETARIAN BAKED BEANS

I call these no-fuss baked beans because canned beans are used, rather than dried beans. This reduces the cooking time by at least two hours. If you mix all the ingredients together in the morning or the night before, you can get the beans in the oven and on the table in one hour.

1 medium onion, chopped

one 14 oz (398 mL) can tomato sauce

1 cup (250 mL) vegetable stock or beer

½ cup (125 mL) barbecue sauce

¼ cup (60 mL) maple syrup

2 Tbsp (30 mL) molasses

1 Tbsp (15 mL) Dijon mustard

2 tsp (10 mL) Worcestershire sauce

1 bay leaf

three 14 oz (398 mL) cans of great northern
     or white kidney beans, drained well

salt and freshly ground black pepper to taste

preparation time • 15 minutes
cooking time • 60 minutes
makes • 6 servings

ERIC'S OPTIONS
If you're a meat-eater, add 1 cup (250 mL) of cubed ham or Canadian bacon to the beans before you bake them.

Preheat the oven to 350°F (175°C). Place all the ingredients in a wide ovenproof pot and stir to combine. Cover and bake for 60 minutes, or until bubbling and delicious. Adjust the seasoning and serve.

CHICKPEA
BURGERS

If you're not already vegetarian, these delicious, moist, filling, meat-free burgers just may convince you! Serve them with your choice of toppings, such as tomato, cucumber, lettuce or Tzatziki Sauce (see page 360).

one 19 oz (540 mL) can chickpeas
  (see About Chickpeas on page 181)

2 Tbsp (30 mL) tahini (see Note)

1 large egg, beaten

⅓ cup (80 mL) grated onion

⅓ cup (80 mL) grated carrot

3 Tbsp (45 mL) chopped fresh cilantro

1 Tbsp (15 mL) mild curry powder

½ tsp (2 mL) salt

¾ cup (185 mL) dried breadcrumbs

3 Tbsp (45 mL) vegetable oil

4 hamburger buns

Drain the chickpeas, rinse in cold water, and drain well again. Place in a food processor, along with the tahini and egg. Pulse until almost smooth, but still a little coarse in texture. Transfer the mixture to a bowl and mix in the onion, carrot, cilantro, curry powder and salt.

preparation time	•	25 minutes
cooking time	•	6–8 minutes
makes	•	4 servings

NOTE
Tahini is a Middle Eastern–style paste made from ground sesame seeds. You can find it at most supermarkets and delis.

ERIC'S OPTIONS
These burgers can be formed and coated with the crumbs up to 1 day in advance. Cover and store in the refrigerator until ready to cook.

Place the breadcrumbs in a shallow dish. Moisten your hands with cold water and form one quarter of the mixture (it will be quite moist) into a ¾-inch-thick (2 cm) patty. Coat the patty completely with the breadcrumbs, pressing on the crumbs to help them adhere. pressing onthe crumbs to help them adhere. Set the coated patty on a separate plate lined with parchment paper. Repeat with the remaining mixture. Cover and refrigerate the patties for 20 minutes to firm them up.

Heat the oil in a large nonstick skillet over medium heat. Add the chickpea burgers and cook for 3 to 4 minutes per side, or until completely heated through. Serve them in the buns with assorted toppings.

ABOUT CHICKPEAS

Chickpeas, also called garbanzo beans, are the seeds of a plant native to Turkey, but which also flourishes in other parts of the Mediterranean and the Middle East. When people think of chickpeas, they often think of the well-known dip called hummus, but chickpeas are used in a number of other dishes, from salads to soups (see Chickpea and Spinach Soup on page 50) to stews (see Slow Cooker Chickpea Vegetable Stew with Apricots and Raisins on page 188). Chickpeas are an excellent source of protein, potassium and fiber and contain calcium and vitamin B6. Another good thing about them is that they're much easier to digest than other beans and are less likely to cause flatulence.

GREEN BEAN STIR-FRY

This simple colorful vegetable dish will make a light supper when served over steamed rice. You could also serve it with Cashew Fried Rice (page 159).

1 Tbsp (15 mL) vegetable oil

½ lb (250 g) green beans, trimmed

one 8 oz (228 mL) can sliced water chestnuts, drained well

1 medium red bell pepper, cubed

3 Tbsp (45 mL) teriyaki sauce

2 Tbsp (30 mL) orange juice

Heat the oil in a large skillet over medium-high heat. Add the beans, water chestnuts and bell pepper and stir-fry for 2 minutes. Add the teriyaki sauce and orange juice and cook until it forms a slightly thickened sauce, about 2 minutes. Serve immediately.

preparation time • 5 minutes
cooking time • 5 minutes
makes • 4 servings

ERIC'S OPTIONS
For an even more colorful dish, use a mix of wax and green beans. If you like things spicy, add 1 tsp (5 mL) of Asian-style chili sauce with the teriyaki sauce. Replace the beans with ¾ lb (375 g) fresh asparagus; trim and discard the lower stalks, slice the spears into 2 inch (5 cm) pieces and cook as you would the green beans.

TEMPURA VEGETABLES

A light and wispy tempura batter delicately coats the vegetables. Make a meal by serving the vegetables with steamed rice and Sweet and Tangy Six-Vegetable Coleslaw (page 76).

preparation time	•	20 minutes
cooking time	•	3–4 minutes
makes	•	6–8 servings

ERIC'S OPTIONS
Try deep-frying other vegetables, such as cauliflower florets or thin slices of zucchini, Japanese eggplant or carrot.

¾ cup (185 mL) teriyaki sauce

1 tsp (5 mL) grated ginger

1 green onion, finely chopped

1 Tbsp (15 mL) sesame seeds

vegetable oil for deep-frying

1 cup (250 mL) ice-cold soda water

1 egg yolk

1 cup (250 mL) all-purpose flour

8 broccoli florets

8 thin slices of yam (see About Sweet Potatoes and Yams on page 337)

8 small, whole fresh white mushrooms

8 onion wedges

Make a dipping sauce for the vegetables by combining the teriyaki sauce, ginger, green onion and sesame seeds in a small bowl. Cover and store in the refrigerator until needed. Preheat the oven to 200°F (95°C). Set a wire rack over a baking sheet. Heat the oil in a deep-fat fryer to 350°F (175°C). Place the water and egg yolk in a medium bowl and whisk to combine. Whisk in the flour until lump-free and a thin batter forms. Working in batches, dip the vegetables into the batter, draining away the excess. Deep-fry the battered vegetables until light golden in color and crispy, about 3 to 4 minutes. Set the deep-fried vegetables on the wire rack; keep warm in the oven until the rest of the vegetables are deep-fried. Arrange the tempura vegetables on a platter and serve with the dipping sauce.

BAKED ACORN SQUASH with BROWN RICE and MUSHROOMS

Acorn squash, when it's halved lengthwise and the seeds are removed, makes an edible vessel that's perfect for stuffing and baking. In this case, the stuffing is a tasty mix of mushrooms, rice and vegetables that is a meal in itself. This makes a nice vegetarian entrée for a festive meal, such as Thanksgiving dinner.

2 medium acorn squashes

2 Tbsp (30 mL) olive oil

2 shallots, chopped

1 garlic clove, chopped

¼ lb (125 g) shiitake mushrooms,
stems removed and discarded, caps sliced

¼ lb (125 g) oyster mushrooms, lower stems
trimmed and discarded, top portion sliced

¼ lb (125 g) brown mushrooms, sliced

¼ cup (60 mL) finely chopped red bell pepper

¼ cup (60 mL) grated carrots

2 green onions, thinly sliced

1 Tbsp (15 mL) chopped fresh sage

2 cups (500 mL) cooked brown rice, chilled
(see About Brown Rice page 99)

⅓ cup (80 mL) vegetable stock

salt and freshly ground black pepper to taste

preparation time	•	30 minutes
cooking time	•	about 65 minutes
makes	•	4 servings

ERIC'S OPTIONS
The squash can be readied up to a day in advance. After stuffing, cool the squash to room temperature, cover, refrigerate and bake when needed. Add 10 minutes or so to the baking time as they will be quite cold.

Preheat the oven to 350°F (175°C). Cut each squash in half lengthwise. Scoop out the seeds and discard. Trim a little from the uncut side of each squash so it will sit flat. Place squash halves, cavity side down, on a parchment paper–lined baking sheet. Cover and bake for 35 to 45 minutes, or until the flesh just begins to soften.

Meanwhile, prepare the filling by placing the olive oil in a large skillet over medium heat. Add the shallots, garlic, mushrooms, bell pepper and carrots and cook until the mushrooms are very tender, about 5 to 6 minutes. Place the mixture in a medium-sized bowl and mix in the green onions, sage, rice, stock, salt and pepper. Turn the squash halves, cavity side up, on the baking sheet and mound the mushroom mixture into them. Cover and bake 20 minutes, or until the squash is tender and the filling is heated through.

VEGETARIAN TOURTIÈRE

Pickled beets, pickles, mustard pickles, chutneys and relishes—homemade if you have them—are items that go great with this meatless tourtière.

2 Tbsp (30 mL) vegetable oil

1 medium onion, finely diced

2 garlic cloves, chopped

two 12 oz (340 g) pouches Yves Veggie
   Ground Round Original (see Note)

2 Tbsp (30 mL) all-purpose flour

1¼ cups (310 mL) vegetable stock

1¼ cups (310 mL) water

1 tsp (5 mL) dried thyme

½ tsp (2 mL) ground cloves

1½ tsp (7 mL) ground cinnamon

1 cup (250 mL) small potato cubes,
   cooked until just tender

1 Tbsp (15 mL) chopped fresh parsley

salt and freshly ground black pepper to taste

one 9-inch (23 cm) deep-dish double crust
   pie shell (see Eric's Options)

oil or beaten egg

preparation time • 30 minutes
cooking time • 50 minutes
makes • 6–8 servings

NOTE
Yves Veggie Ground Round Original, sold at most supermarkets, looks and tastes similar to beef but is made with ingredients such as soy and wheat protein. If you cannot find it, substitute any similar vegetarian product sold in your area.

ERIC'S OPTIONS
You can use a store-bought or homemade pie crust—see Flaky Pie Dough (page 375). Allowing the filling to sit in the refrigerator overnight gives the flavors a chance to meld and become richer. However, if time is short, you can skip this step and assemble and bake the tourtière as soon as the filling has cooled. Unbaked tourtière freezes well. Thaw the tourtière in the refrigerator overnight before baking.

Heat the oil in a pot over medium heat. Add the onion and garlic and cook until tender, about 3 to 4 minutes. Add the Veggie Ground Round and stir to break it up. Mix in the flour until well combined. Pour in the stock and water. Add the thyme, cloves and cinnamon. Cook, stirring, until the liquid has almost evaporated. Stir in the potatoes, parsley, salt and pepper. Remove from the heat, cool to room temperature and refrigerate overnight.

Preheat the oven to 425°F (220°C). Place the filling in the bottom crust. Brush the sides with a little water or beaten egg. Place the top crust on and crimp the edges to seal. Cut out a small circle in the center to allow steam to escape. Decorate the top of the tourtière with extra pastry if desired. Brush the top crust with a little oil or beaten egg. Bake for 20 minutes, then reduce the heat to 350°F (175°C) and bake 30 minutes more. Allow the tourtière to set for about 10 minutes before slicing.

SLOW COOKER CHICKPEA STEW
with APRICOTS and RAISINS

This vegetarian stew is flavored North African style with ingredients such as cumin, lemon and apricots. I like to serve it over hot couscous (see Eric's Options).

preparation time • 20 minutes
slow-cooker time • 6 hours
makes • 4 servings

one 19 oz (540 mL) can chickpeas, drained, rinsed in cold water and drained again

one 14 oz (398 mL) can diced tomatoes

one 14 oz (398 mL) can tomato sauce

1 cup (250 mL) vegetable stock

2 Tbsp (30 mL) olive oil

1 medium onion, diced

1 medium carrot, quartered lengthwise and sliced

1 small zucchini, quartered lengthwise and sliced

2 garlic cloves, minced

8–10 dried apricots, thinly sliced

¼ cup (60 mL) raisins

2 tsp (10 mL) grated lemon zest

1 tsp (5 mL) ground cumin

¼ tsp (1 mL) cayenne pepper

2 Tbsp (30 mL) chopped fresh mint, cilantro or parsley

salt and freshly ground black pepper to taste

NOTE
This recipe is designed for a slow cooker with 4½ to 6½ quart (4.5 to 6.5 L) capacity.

ERIC'S OPTIONS
To serve the stew on a bed of couscous, place 3 cups (750 mL) of vegetable stock, 1 Tbsp (15 mL) olive oil and 1 minced garlic clove in a medium-sized pot and bring to a boil. Mix in 1¾ cups (435 mL) of couscous. Cover the pot with its lid, turn off the heat and let the couscous stand for 5 minutes. Fluff the couscous with a fork to separate the grains and then serve.

Combine the chickpeas, diced tomatoes, tomato sauce, stock, olive oil, onion, carrot, zucchini, garlic, apricots, raisins, lemon zest, cumin and cayenne in your slow cooker. Cover and cook on the low setting for 6 hours, or until the vegetables are tender. Stir in the mint. Season with salt and pepper and serve.

SLOW COOKER ROMANO BEAN STEW
with ARUGULA and GOAT CHEESE

This Mediterranean-style bean dish is both colorful and flavorful with its spicy, emerald-green arugula, sweet, rich, red cherry tomatoes and tangy goat cheese. I like to serve it with slices of focaccia or olive bread.

preparation time	•	20 minutes
slow-cooker time	•	5–6 hours
finishing time	•	3–4 minutes
makes	•	6 servings

two 19 oz (540 mL) cans romano beans, drained, rinsed in cold water and drained again

1 cup (250 mL) vegetable stock

½ cup (125 mL) dry white wine

18 cherry tomatoes, halved

1 medium green bell pepper, diced

½ medium onion, diced

crushed chili flakes to taste

2 Tbsp (30 mL) olive oil

3 Tbsp (45 mL) store-bought or homemade pesto (see Pesto recipe page 359)

3–4 cups (750 mL–1 L) baby arugula

salt and freshly ground black pepper to taste

6 oz (175 g) soft goat cheese, crumbled

NOTE
This recipe is designed for a slow cooker with 4½ to 6½ quart (4.5 to 6.5 L) capacity.

ERIC'S OPTIONS
If you can't find romano beans, use white kidney beans in this recipe instead. Instead of goat cheese, try crumbled feta cheese.

Place the beans, stock, wine, tomatoes, bell pepper, onion, chili flakes and olive oil in your slow cooker and mix to combine. Cover and cook on the low setting for 5 to 6 hours, or until the tomatoes are quite soft. Mix in the pesto, arugula and salt and pepper. Cover and cook for 3 to 4 minutes more, or just until the arugula is wilted. Top the servings of beans with crumbled goat cheese.

PUMPKIN CHILI with POBLANO PEPPERS and CORN

You can dress up bowls of this vegetarian chili with a dollop of sour cream or yogurt, and add a sprinkling of shredded Monterey Jack cheese and sliced green onion or chopped cilantro.

preparation time • 30 minutes
cooking time • 35 minutes
makes • 6–8 servings

2 Tbsp (30 mL) olive oil

1 medium onion, diced

2 fresh poblano peppers, seeds removed and diced (see Eric's Options)

1 large garlic clove, minced

4 cups (1 L) peeled, cubed fresh pumpkin

one 28 oz (796 mL) can diced tomatoes

2 cups (500 mL) tomato sauce

1 cup (250 mL) beer or vegetable stock

one 19 oz (540 mL) can black beans, drained and rinsed

1 cup (250 mL) frozen corn kernels

2 tsp (10 mL) chili powder

1 tsp (5 mL) ground cumin

1 tsp (5 mL) dried oregano

salt and freshly ground black pepper to taste

ERIC'S OPTIONS
Dark-green, fresh poblano peppers, which have a mildly spicy flavor, are available in the produce section of most supermarkets. If you can't find them, use 1 large green bell pepper in the chili and, if desired, add a splash or two of hot pepper sauce. To make squash chili, replace the pumpkin with cubes of butternut or banana squash. Cooking time and technique remains the same.

Place the oil in a large pot over medium to medium-high heat. Add the onion, poblano peppers and garlic and cook 3 to 4 minutes. Add the remaining ingredients and bring to a gentle simmer. Reduce the heat and simmer, partially covered, for 30 minutes, or until the pumpkin is tender and the chili thickens. (Don't completely cover the chili when simmering. The steam must escape, not hit the top of the lid and fall back in the pot, which will cause the chili to be watery.)

Adjust the seasoning if necessary and serve.

FISH AND SEAFOOD

ROASTED LOBSTER TAILS

This is a restaurant-style way of preparing and cooking lobster tails, in which the meat is pulled out of the shell when raw, artfully set on top of the shell, basted with flavored butter, and roasted.

preparation time • 20 minutes
cooking time • 8–10 minutes
makes • 6 servings

six 5–6 oz (150–175 g) frozen lobster tails, thawed and patted dry

3 Tbsp (45 mL) melted butter

1 Tbsp (15 mL) fresh lemon juice

2 tsp (10 mL) chopped fresh parsley

1 garlic clove, crushed

pinch paprika and cayenne pepper

ERIC'S OPTIONS
The lobster tails can be made oven-ready several hours in advance; cover and refrigerate until you're ready to roast them. Add 1 minute to the cooking time as the lobster will be quite cold. For added richness, serve each lobster tail with a small dish of melted butter for dipping. Create a "surf and turf" dinner by serving each lobster tail with a small, grilled or pan-seared beef tenderloin steak.

Preheat the oven to 425°F (220°C). Line a baking sheet with parchment paper. Place 1 of the lobster tails on a work surface. With a sharp knife, make a lengthwise cut down the middle of the top shell, cutting three quarters of the way into the flesh, but not through the bottom part of the shell. Spread the cut side of the shell open. Carefully pull out the tail meat. Close the shell and set on the baking sheet. Fan the meat, cut-side up, on top of the shell. Repeat with the remaining lobster tails. Whisk the remaining ingredients in a small bowl. Brush the mixture on the lobster meat. Roast the lobster tails 8 to 10 minutes, or until just cooked through.

CORNMEAL-CRUSTED CRAB CAKES

Fresh, frozen or canned crabmeat can be used in this recipe. When using frozen and canned, ensure you squeeze out as much moisture as you as you can, otherwise your crab cakes will have a watered-down taste. Make a main course of these by serving them with a salad, such as Baby Greens with Julienne Vegetables and Cherry Tomatoes (page 80).

½ cup (125 mL) mayonnaise

cayenne, salt and lime juice to taste

2 cups (500 mL) crabmeat

1 large egg, beaten

2 Tbsp (30 mL) all-purpose flour

3 Tbsp (45 mL) mayonnaise

3 green onions, finely chopped

¼ cup (60 mL) very finely chopped red bell pepper

2 Tbsp (30 mL) chopped fresh cilantro or parsley

1 Tbsp (15 mL) lime juice

salt and hot pepper sauce, such as Tabasco, to taste

1 cup (250 mL) cornmeal

3 Tbsp (45 mL) vegetable oil

lime wedges and cilantro or parsley sprigs

preparation time • 20 minutes
cooking time • 6–8 minutes
makes • 8 crab cakes—serves 4 as a starter or main course

ERIC'S OPTIONS
Bread or cracker crumbs can replace the cornmeal. For spicier crab cakes, add 1 Tbsp (15 mL) finely chopped fresh jalapeño pepper to the mix before shaping into cakes. Instead of cayenne-flavored mayonnaise, serve with Tartar Sauce (page 217).

Place the ½ cup (125 mL) of mayonnaise, cayenne, salt and lime juice in a bowl and mix well to combine. Cover and refrigerate until needed. Line a tray with plastic wrap or parchment paper. Place the crabmeat, egg, flour, 3 Tbsp (45 mL) of mayonnaise, green onion, bell pepper, cilantro or parsley, lime juice, salt and hot pepper sauce in a bowl and mix well to combine. (The mixture will be very moist, which will ensure moist crab cakes!)

Place the cornmeal in a shallow dish. Dampen your hands lightly with water and shape ¼ cup (60 mL) of the crab mixture into a ball. Set it on the cornmeal. Sprinkle the top and sides with cornmeal and then gently form into a cake about 3 inches (8 cm) wide and ½ inch (1 cm) thick. Place on the prepared tray. Repeat with the remaining crab mixture. You should get 8 crab cakes.

Heat the oil in a large non-stick skillet over medium heat. Cook the crab cakes for 3 to 4 minutes per side. Drain the crab cakes on paper towels and then place on serving plates. Serve with a dollop of the flavored mayonnaise and garnish with lime wedges and cilantro or parsley sprigs.

BOILED LOBSTER or DUNGENESS CRAB

When being purchased, live lobster and crab should struggle vigorously when pulled from their holding tanks. If they are slow-moving, don't buy them. Live lobster and crab should be purchased the day you intend to cook them.

You never want to overcook lobster or crab or your investment will turn to rubber. Once the lobster or crab is in the pot and the water returns to a boil, I allow 4 minutes for the first pound (500 g) and about 3 minutes for each additional pound (500 g). The lobster or crab starts cook the moment it is in the pot and the water returns to a boil, and I factor that into the cooking time.

¼ cup (60 mL) sea salt

two 1½ lb (750 g) live lobsters or Dungeness crabs

lemon wedges to taste

Bring 1½ gallons (6 litres) of water to a rapid boil in a large pot. Add the salt. Add the lobsters or crabs, return to a boil. Set a timer and cook 6 minutes, or until just cooked through. Carefully remove them from the pot, holding them above the water to allow them to drain, and place on dinner plates. Serve with lemon wedges and, if desired, bowls of warm melted butter.

preparation time • 5 minutes
cooking time • about 10 minutes
makes • 2 servings

ERIC'S OPTIONS

For each additional lobster or crab you wish to cook, use an additional 2 cups (500 mL) water and 2 Tbsp (30 mL) salt. To make it easier to place the live lobster or crab in the pot, place on a tray in the freezer, or submerge in crushed ice, for 15 minutes or so before cooking. This more or less puts it to sleep, making it easier to slip it into the pot. Add an extra minute to the cooking time, as the lobster or crab will be quite cold.

Instead of boiling the lobster or crab, it can be steamed. Place in a large, wide stainless steel or bamboo steamer set over boiling water. Cover and cook for 5–6 minutes, until just cooked through.

Some cooks prefer to clean their crab before boiling; noting that cooking them with their innards negatively affects flavor. Most fishmongers will clean the crab for you; just ask! If you go this route cooking time, once the crab is added and the water returns to a boil, will be about 5 minutes.

BEER and CHILI-STEAMED MUSSELS

Ice cold lager, naturally, is the perfect drink to pair with these spicy, beer-steamed mussels. For a more rounded meal, serve the mussels on steamed rice or Asian-style noodles, accompanied with steamed or stir-fried vegetables.

36 fresh mussels

1 Tbsp (15 mL) vegetable oil

2 garlic cloves, chopped

2 tsp (10 mL) chopped fresh ginger

2–3 tsp (10–15 mL) Asian-style chili sauce, or to taste

½ cup (125 mL) lager

2 Tbsp (30 mL) soy sauce

2 Tbsp (30 mL) chopped green onions

preparation time	•	5 minutes
cooking time	•	about 5 minutes
makes	•	2 servings

ERIC'S OPTIONS
If you like its pungent taste, instead of green onion, sprinkle the mussels with chopped fresh cilantro. Make this dish with clams instead of mussels.

Rinse the mussels in cold water, pull away any beard-like material from their shells, and then drain well. Heat the oil in a pot set over medium-high heat. Add the garlic, ginger and chili sauce and cook until fragrant, about 30 seconds. Add the lager and soy sauce and bring to a boil. Add the mussels, cover the pot and cook just until the mussels open. Transfer the mussels to 2 bowls, discarding any that are not open. Spoon the cooking liquid over top and sprinkle with green onions.

CALIFORNIA ROLLS

This straightforward recipe is designed for novice sushi-makers wanting to learn the craft. The recipe can be expanded if you're feeding a larger group. It can also be used to make other types of sushi (see Eric's Options).

THE RICE

1¾ cups (435 mL) sushi rice

3 Tbsp (45 mL) rice vinegar

1½ Tbsp (22 mL) sugar

1½ tsp (7 mL) salt

2½ cups (625 mL) cold water

THE ROLLS

3 nori sheets (see Note)

3 Tbsp (45 mL) mayonnaise

¾ cup (185 mL) crabmeat

1 small, ripe, peeled avocado, cut into thin wedges

wasabi, soy sauce and pickled ginger to taste

preparation time	•	30–40 minut
cooking time	•	about 20 minutes
makes	•	24 pieces

NOTE
Sushi rice, nori (seaweed sushi wrapper), wasabi and pickled ginger are available at most supermarkets and Asian food stores. The sushi roller is a bamboo mat that can be found at kitchenware stores and Asian food stores.

ERIC'S OPTIONS
To make shrimp and avocado rolls, replace the crabmeat with salad shrimp. To make spicy tuna rolls, replace crabmeat and avocado with a row of green onion and thin slices of raw tuna tossed with spicy Asian-style chili sauce. To make salmon and cucumber rolls, replace the crabmeat and avocado with a row of thinly cut cucumber strips and thin slices of raw salmon.

THE RICE

Rinse the rice under cold running water, rubbing the grains together until the water runs clear. Cover the rice with cold water and soak for 30 minutes. While the rice is soaking, combine the vinegar, sugar and salt in a pot. Bring to a boil and stir to dissolve the sugar, about 30 seconds. Remove from the heat, cool to room temperature and set aside.

Drain the soaked rice well and place in a pot with the 2½ cups (625 mL) cold water. Bring to a boil over high heat. Turn the heat to its lowest setting and cover the pot. Cook for 15 minutes, or until the rice is tender.

Spoon the rice into a large, shallow-sided pan, spreading it out in a thin layer to help it cool quickly. Stir in the vinegar mixture. When the rice has cooled to room temperature it is ready to use.

THE ROLLS

Cover a sushi roller (see Note) with plastic wrap. Place a sheet of nori on the plastic wrap. Moisten your hands with cold water, and then spread a third of the rice on the nori, leaving a 1-inch (2.5 cm) strip at the top of the nori. Spread a thin line of mayonnaise on the rice about a third of the way up. Top with a third of the crabmeat and avocado wedges. (If preparing the sushi rolls in advance, rub the avocado wedges with a little lemon juice to prevent them from browning.) Roll up the nori and filling in jelly-roll fashion, squeezing on the bamboo roller to compact the rice and filling as you go. Cut the roll into 8 pieces. Repeat with the remaining nori, rice and filling ingredients. Serve with wasabi for spicing up the sushi, soy sauce for dipping and pickled ginger for cleansing your palate.

ICED OYSTERS with DILL and RED PEPPER VINAIGRETTE

A tangy, green and red–flecked vinaigrette tops these small, slurping-size raw oysters.

preparation time • 30 minutes
cooking time • none
makes • 6–8 servings

2 Tbsp (30 mL) white wine vinegar

1 tsp (5 mL) Dijon mustard

⅓ cup (80 mL) olive oil

2 Tbsp (30 mL) finely chopped red bell pepper

1 tsp (5 mL) chopped fresh dill

½ tsp (2 mL) hot pepper sauce

pinch sugar

salt and freshly ground black pepper to taste

24 small, fresh oysters, scrubbed well

ERIC'S OPTIONS

You can make and refrigerate the vinaigrette several hours before serving. Oysters always taste best when shucked and served immediately, but you can shuck them 1 to 2 hours before serving, place on a baking sheet, cover and refrigerate until you're ready to put them on a serving tray and top with the vinaigrette. You may wish to do this if your shucking skills aren't great and you want to get the kitchen and yourself cleaned up before guests arrive.

Place the vinegar and mustard in a medium bowl and whisk to combine. Slowly whisk in the oil. Mix in the red pepper, dill, hot sauce, sugar, salt and pepper. Refrigerate until needed.

Place an oyster on a slightly damp kitchen towel, cupped side down with the hinged end facing you. Hold it in place with another kitchen towel. Insert the point of your oyster knife into the hinge of the shells. Work the knife in ¼ inch (6 mm), and then twist it to pry the shell open. Slide the knife across the top shell and remove the shell. Slide the knife under the oyster to detach it from the bottom shell. Remove any shell fragments. Place the oyster on a serving tray filled with crushed ice. Repeat with the remaining oysters. Spoon some vinaigrette on each oyster and serve.

HOW TO BUY, STORE AND SHUCK OYSTERS

When buying the oysters, opt for those with tightly closed shells. In the store, if you're able to hold the oysters, they should feel heavy for their size, a sign the meat is plump and surrounded with flavorful juice.

It's best to use oysters soon after purchase, but if needed, you could store them a day or two. To do so, place them in a shallow container, cover with a damp cloth and refrigerate until needed. Do not store oysters submerged in tap water.

To shuck oysters, first scrub well in cold water. Place an oyster, cupped-side down, with the narrow end facing you, on a slightly damp kitchen towel. With your non-shucking hand, protected with another kitchen towel or rubber glove, hold it in place. Insert the point of your thin-bladed oyster knife into the hinge of the shells, gently working the knife into the oyster about ½ inch (1 cm). Twist the knife to pry the shell open. Slide the knife across the top shell of the oyster and remove and discard it. Slide the knife under the oyster to detach it from the bottom shell. Remove any shell fragments and the oyster is ready to use.

BAKED OYSTERS with SPINACH and PARMESAN

Rich-tasting oysters marry well with equally rich flavors. In this recipe spinach, cream and Parmesan cheese do the work deliciously.

¼ cup (60 mL) dry white wine

4 cups (1 L) stemmed spinach leaves, packed

1 garlic clove, finely chopped

½ cup (125 mL) whipping cream

salt and white pepper to taste

12 medium oysters, shucked and left in the half shell (see How to Buy, Store and Shuck Oysters on page 204)

⅓–½ cup (80–125 mL) freshly grated Parmesan cheese

Preheat the oven to 450°F (230°C). Bring the wine to a boil in a large, wide skillet over medium-high heat. Add the spinach and cook until it just wilts and the wine and liquid from the spinach evaporate. Add the garlic and whipping cream and cook until the cream thickens slightly. Remove from the heat; season with salt and white pepper.

Place the oysters on a large baking sheet or roasting pan. Top each with a spoonful of the spinach mixture and sprinkle with Parmesan cheese. Bake for 10 to 12 minutes, until nicely browned and bubbling. Carefully lift the oysters onto 4 appetizer plates. Serve immediately.

preparation time • 20 minutes
cooking time • 10–12 minutes
makes • 4 servings

ERIC'S OPTIONS
To help prevent the creamy spinach mixture from spilling out of the oyster shells during cooking, spread a thick layer of coarse sea salt on the baking sheet or roasting pan and nestle the shells into the salt until level.

CLAMS STEAMED with PANCETTA, TOMATOES and WINE

Pancetta is Italian-style bacon cured with salt and spices, but not smoked. One of its uses in Italian cooking is to flavor sauces, such as this colorful, fresh tomato and herb–flecked one. You can buy pancetta at Italian food stores and some supermarkets.

1 Tbsp (15 mL) olive oil

¼ lb (125 g) pancetta, finely chopped

½ medium onion, finely chopped

3 garlic cloves, chopped

½ cup (125 mL) dry white wine

3 ripe, medium tomatoes, halved, seeds
    removed and chopped

2–3 Tbsp (30–45 mL) chopped fresh basil
    or oregano

pinch sugar

freshly ground black pepper to taste

2 lbs (1 kg) fresh clams, rinsed in cold water

Heat the oil in a pot over medium-high heat. Add the pancetta and cook until crispy. Drain off all but 2 Tbsp (30 mL) of the oil and rendered fat from the pan. Add the onion and garlic and cook until tender, about 3 to 4 minutes. Add the wine, tomatoes, basil or oregano, sugar and pepper. Simmer for 5 minutes. Add the clams, cover the pot and cook until the clams just open. Divide the clams and sauce among bowls and serve.

preparation time • 15 minutes
cooking time • 10 minutes
makes • 2–3 servings

ERIC'S OPTIONS
For a Spanish-style sauce, use 1 grilled, cooled and finely chopped chorizo sausage instead of the pancetta. Add it to the pot with the tomatoes. Increase the olive oil to 2 Tbsp (30 mL) to replace the fat from the pancetta. Instead of clams, use an equal weight of mussels in this recipe.

HOW TO BUY, STORE AND COOK MUSSELS AND CLAMS

When purchasing fresh, in-the-shell mussels or clams, ask the retailer to let you have a good look at them. Very fresh mussels and clams will have tightly closed shells, or shells that close tightly when squeezed or tapped. If a shell doesn't close, or if it's cracked, it means the mussel or clam is dead and should not be purchased.

For the freshest taste, buy mussels or clams the day you'll cook them. However, if they're very fresh, they could be stored for up to a day in the refrigerator. To refrigerate mussels or clams, first remove them from their store packaging, set them in a bowl and cover them with a damp cloth. Do not submerge them in tap water.

When you're ready to cook, rinse the mussels or clams thoroughly in cold water. Pull off any beard-like material attached to mussel shells. Examine the mussels and clams again and discard any that do not close tightly when squeezed or tapped.

Whether steamed or simmered in a sauce, the moment a mussel or clam opens it is cooked. If a mussel or clam doesn't open, it's another indication that it's dead and should not be eaten.

PAN-SEARED SCALLOPS on GINGER-SPIKED MANGO SAUCE

This combination of mango, lime and ginger brings one of my favorite molluscs to delicious new heights. Make a meal by serving with steamed rice and green vegetables.

preparation time • 10 minutes
cooking time • 10 minutes
makes • 4 servings

THE MANGO SAUCE

1 medium, ripe mango, peeled and coarsely chopped

2 tsp (10 ml) freshly grated ginger

2 Tbsp (30 ml) fresh lime juice

2 tsp (10 ml) brown sugar, or to taste

pinch crushed chili flakes

¼ cup (60 ml) water

THE SCALLOPS

20 large sea scallops

1 tsp (5 mL) ground cumin

salt and white pepper to taste

2 Tbsp (30 mL) olive oil

2 Tbsp (30 mL) fresh lime juice

4 cilantro sprigs and lime slices for garnish

ERIC'S OPTIONS

For curried mango sauce, omit the crushed chili flakes from the sauce and add curry paste (see About Curry Paste on page 36) or powder to taste before simmering the sauce.

THE MANGO SAUCE

Purée the ingredients in a food processor or blender. Transfer to a pot and simmer over medium heat for 10 minutes. Keep warm over low heat until the scallops are cooked.

THE SCALLOPS

Season the scallops with the cumin, salt and pepper. Heat the oil in a skillet over high heat. Cook the scallops for 1 to 2 minutes per side, or until just cooked through. Sprinkle with lime juice and remove from the heat. Spoon the mango sauce on 4 plates. Arrange the scallops on top. Garnish and serve.

ABOUT SCALLOPS

There are many species of scallops, but the ones noted below are those you most frequently see.

Almost sweet-tasting bay scallops, harvested off North America's east coast, are quite small. Their meat is about ½ inch (1 cm) in diameter. Very mild-tasting, very tiny—about the size of a dime—calico scallops are sometimes sold as bay scallops, even though they are harvested in deep waters.

The meat of fine-tasting Icelandic scallops is about the same size or slightly larger than bay scallops. Ironically, because of a decline in stocks, they likely weren't harvested in waters off Iceland, but off places such as the east coast of Canada.

Sea scallops, such as those harvested off Nova Scotia or those farmed on Canada's west coast, are much larger than bay scallops. They average 1½ inches (4 cm) in diameter. Their flavor is slightly sweet, rich and concentrated.

Scallops, no matter what the type, are usually sold shucked, as they do not live long in the shell once out of the water. To maintain that "just harvested" taste, scallops are often quickly frozen minutes after harvesting and being shucked.

In supermarkets across the country, what you'll most often find for sale are frozen scallops, or scallops thawed from frozen. If you've bought fresh or thawed-from-frozen scallops, they are perishable and it's best to eat them within a day of purchase.

If there is excess moisture on the scallops, pat them dry with a paper towel before cooking. If the scallops are wet before cooking they won't brown up nicely if you plan to pan-fry, grill or broil them. Scallops cook up in just minutes (see When Is Fish or Shellfish Cooked? on page 223). Overcook them and they will become tough and stringy.

SPANISH-STYLE SHRIMP
with ROASTED PEPPER SAUCE

I tested this recipe at a cooking class and, once plated, the shrimp vanished within minutes to the sound of yum, yum, yum! Serves six to eight as an appetizer, four as a main course.

THE SAUCE

1 large red bell pepper

½ cup (125 mL) mayonnaise

1–2 Tbsp (15–30 mL) lemon juice

2 Tbsp (30 mL) chopped parsley

salt and freshly ground black pepper to taste

THE SHRIMP

2 Tbsp (30 mL) olive oil

½ tsp (2 mL) dried oregano

¼ tsp (1 mL) paprika

½ lemon, juice of

2 garlic cloves, chopped

pinch crushed chili flakes

24 large shrimp, peeled and deveined, with tail portion left intact (see About Shrimp and Prawns on page 212)

salt and freshly ground black pepper to taste

lemon wedges for garnish

preparation time	•	20 minutes
cooking time	•	about 30 minutes
makes	•	24 prawns

ERIC'S OPTIONS
If time is tight, use a storebought roasted red pepper (sold in jars) in the sauce instead of roasting your own.

If serving shrimp as a main course, accompany with a steamed green vegetable and Spanish-Style Brown Rice (page 166).

THE SAUCE

Preheat the oven to 400°F (200°C). Place the red pepper in a small, parchment paper–lined baking pan and place in the oven. Roast, turning once or twice, until the pepper begins to slightly char and blister, about 25 to 30 minutes. Set on a plate, cover with a tent of aluminum foil and cool for 30 minutes. Once cooled, peel the pepper; the skin should just slip off. Cut in half, remove and discard the seeds, and then coarsely chop. Place in the bowl of a food processor along with the mayonnaise, lemon juice, parsley, salt and pepper; pulse until smooth and well combined. Transfer to a bowl, cover and store in the refrigerator until the shrimp are ready.

THE SHRIMP

Combine the oil, oregano, paprika, lemon juice, garlic and chili flakes in a medium bowl. Add the shrimp and toss well to thoroughly coat. Cover and marinate at room temperature for 20 minutes. Heat a very large skillet over medium-high heat. Add the shrimp and its marinade to the skillet and cook for 2 minutes per side or until the shrimp are bright pink and just cooked through. Arrange on a platter with the bowl of roasted red pepper sauce for dipping; garnish with lemon wedges and serve.

ABOUT SHRIMP and PRAWNS

On the west coast of Canada and in a few other parts of the world, the term prawn is used to describe large shrimp. However, in the rest of North America the term shrimp is used to describe the species, no matter what the size. To keep things consistent, in this book I've used the term shrimp throughout.

Shrimp are priced and categorized according to size. This is determined by the number they yield per pound, once the head is removed. Jumbo have 11–15 per pound, extra large 16–20, large 21–30, medium 31–35 and small 36–45.

Unless they come from nearby waters, the raw shrimp sold at supermarkets are previously frozen. Although there are variations in texture and flavor, the different sizes can be substituted for one another.

Whether or not to remove the dark intestinal vein, a technique called deveining, depends on the size of the shrimp. In general, small and medium-sized shrimp do not need deveining except for aesthetic purposes. However, the veins of larger ones often contain grit and should be removed. If cooking larger shrimp with the shell on, something you may wish to do to protect the flesh if grilling, make a lengthwise slit along the back of the shell with kitchen scissors to expose the flesh. With a paring knife, make a shallow slit down the center of the flesh. Pull out the dark vein, or rinse it out with cold water. Pat the shrimp dry and it's ready to use. To peel and then devein, hold the tail of the shrimp or prawn in one hand, slip the thumb of your other hand under the shell between its swimmerets (its little legs), and then pull off the shell, leaving the tip of the tail intact. Remove the vein as described above. If you don't wish to peel and devein the prawns, purchase them already peeled and deveined, a product sold some supermarkets and seafood stores.

Very small, cooked salad shrimp are sold fresh or frozen. If you bought the latter, pat them dry before using. Any excess moisture can dilute the taste of the dish you're making.

Raw and fresh-cooked shrimp are highly perishable. Once home, remove them from the packaging and place in a bowl; cover and refrigerate until needed. Use within one day of purchase.

GREEN THAI CURRY SHRIMP

Creamy coconut milk, hot green Thai curry paste and tart lime juice are a few of the ingredients that make this spicy shrimp dish addictive.

preparation time • 10 minutes
cooking time • 10 minutes
makes • 4 servings

one 14 oz (398 mL) can coconut milk

1 Tbsp (15 mL) chopped fresh ginger

2 garlic cloves, chopped

2 limes, juice of

3 Tbsp (45 mL) packed brown sugar

2 tsp (10 mL) green Thai curry paste
(see About Curry Paste on page 36)

24 large shrimp, peeled and deveined, with tail portion left intact (see About Shrimp and Prawns on page 212)

¼ cup (60 mL) chopped fresh cilantro

salt to taste

ERIC'S OPTIONS
To make this dish more or less spicy, simply increase or decrease the amount of green Thai curry paste. Try using large scallops or 1-inch (2.5 cm) cubes of salmon fillet instead of shrimp. Cooking time will be about the same, or try a mix of seafood.

Place the coconut milk, ginger, garlic, lime juice, brown sugar and curry paste in a pot and bring to a simmer over medium heat. Gently simmer for 5 minutes, stirring occasionally. Add the shrimp and cook for 3 to 4 minutes, or until cooked through. Stir in the cilantro and salt and serve.

SHRIMP BAKED in CHAMPAGNE BUTTER SAUCE

If you're looking for a simple yet ultradelicious way to prepare shrimp, it's hard to go wrong with this dish. The shrimp is topped with a quick-to-make, buttery, sparkling wine mixture and cooked briefly. All you have to do is wait for your guest to say "Mmm, yummy!"

12 large shrimp, peeled and deveined, with tail portion left intact (see About Shrimp and Prawns on page 212)

1/3 cup (80 mL) champagne or sparkling white wine

3 Tbsp (45 mL) melted butter

1 tsp (5 mL) fresh lemon juice

1 small garlic clove, minced

pinch cayenne pepper

salt and freshly ground black pepper to taste

2 tsp (10 mL) chopped fresh parsley

preparation time • 20 minutes
cooking time • 10–12 minute
makes • 2 servings

ERIC'S OPTIONS
Make shrimp and scallop in champagne butter sauce by replacing 6 of the shrimp with 6 large scallops. Cooking time remains the same.

Preheat the oven to 425°F (220°C). Place the shrimp in a shallow baking dish large enough to hold them in a single layer, with about a half-inch (1 cm) space between each of them. Combine the champagne, butter, lemon juice, garlic and cayenne in a small bowl. Pour the mixture over the shrimp; season lightly with salt and pepper. Bake 10 to 12 minutes, or until the shrimp have turned pink and are slightly firm to the touch. Divide the shrimp and sauce between 2 heated plates, sprinkle with parsley and serve.

OVEN-BAKED
FISH and CHIPS

No deep-fryer, no problem. Use this recipe the next time you have a craving for fish and chips. Serve with lemon slices, Tartar Sauce (page 217) and Sweet and Tangy Six-Vegetable Coleslaw (page 76).

3 medium baking potatoes

3 Tbsp (45 mL) vegetable oil

seasoning salt to taste

four 5 to 6 oz (150 to 175 g) fish fillets, such as cod, haddock, basa, snapper, halibut or salmon

preparation time	•	10 minutes
cooking time	•	30–35 minut•
makes	•	4 servings

ERIC'S OPTIONS
If you are watching your salt intake, consider replacing the seasoning salt with a mix of your own seasonings, such as freshly ground pepper, lemon pepper, paprika, garlic granules and dried herbs.

Preheat the oven to 425°F (220°C). Cut the potatoes in half lengthwise. Cut each half into 4 to 6 wedges. Place the wedges in a bowl and toss with the oil and seasoning salt. Arrange the potatoes in a single layer on a large nonstick or parchment paper–lined baking sheet. Bake for 15 minutes, turn the potatoes over and bake for 5 minutes more. Sprinkle the fish with seasoning salt. Make a spot for each piece of fish among the potatoes. Continue baking until the fish is cooked through, about 10 to 15 minutes more.

BUYING FRESH FISH

Fresh fish should smell sweet and sea-like. If it smells "fishy" it is past its prime and should be avoided. If you're too shy to smell what you hope to buy, ask your retailer when it came in. A reputable fishmonger will let you know which catch is the freshest. You can also visually check seafood for freshness. Fresh fish will have firm flesh that glistens; it should not look dull, soft or look like it's falling apart. It's best to buy fresh fish the day you'll cook it, but if very fresh you could store it in the coldest part of refrigerator for one day.

TARTAR SAUCE

There are a range of commercial tartar sauces sold in stores these days, but they never come close to matching the fresh and lively taste of homemade. Serve this sauce alongside simply prepared seafood or on seafood burgers.

⅔ cup (150 mL) mayonnaise

2 Tbsp (30 mL) finely chopped dill pickle

1 green onion, finely chopped

1 Tbsp (15 mL) drained capers, coarsely chopped

1 Tbsp (15 mL) chopped fresh parsley

1 tsp (5 mL) lemon juice

1 tsp (5 mL) Dijon mustard

1 tsp (5 mL) chopped fresh tarragon, or pinch dried

salt and white pepper to taste

hot pepper sauce

preparation time • 5 minutes
cooking time • none
makes • about 1 cup (250 mL)

ERIC'S OPTIONS
For a less sharp sauce, use sweet mixed pickles instead of dill pickles. If you don't have tarragon or don't care for its licorice-like taste, use dill or parsley instead.

Combine all the ingredients in a bowl and mix well. Chill before serving. This sauce will last a week in the refrigerator if kept in a tightly sealed container.

SEAFOOD SAMPLER

When you need a dish to impress a date or your spouse, try this. It's simple to make, but fancy in appearance and taste.

preparation time • 20 minutes
cooking time • about 15 minutes
makes • 2 servings

two 3 to 4 oz (90 to 100 g) fish fillets, such as salmon, halibut, cod, haddock or sole

4 large sea scallops

4 large shrimp, peeled, with tail portion intact

one 4 oz (125 g) lobster tail, split in half lengthwise

¼ cup (60 mL) dry white wine

2 Tbsp (30 mL) butter

1 Tbsp (15 mL) chopped fresh tarragon, or ½ tsp (2 mL) dried

1 garlic clove, minced

pinch paprika and cayenne pepper

freshly ground pepper to taste

1 Tbsp (15 mL) lemon juice

lemon wedges to garnish

ERIC'S OPTIONS

This dish can be made oven-ready hours in advance. You could put the wine, butter and flavorings in the pot, cover and refrigerate until ready to heat and pour over the seafood. You could also put the seafood in the baking dish and cover and refrigerate until ready to top with the wine mixture, and bake.

Preheat the oven to 450°F (230°C). Place the fish, scallops, shrimp and lobster, cut-side up, in a single layer in a shallow baking dish. Place the wine, butter, tarragon, garlic, paprika, cayenne, salt, pepper and lemon juice in a small pot. Set over medium heat and simmer just until the butter is melted. Drizzle this mixture over the seafood. Bake for 11 to 13 minutes, or until the seafood is just cooked. Serve straight out of the baking dish, or arrange on plates, spooning the pan juices over top. Garnish with lemon wedges.

BARBECUED WHOLE SALMON
with GARLIC, LEMON and HERBS

The inviting aroma from the generous amount of garlic used in this dish may cause your neighbours to peer over the backyard fence and ask, "What time is dinner?"

preparation time • 20 minutes
cooking time • 26–30 minutes
makes • 4–6 servings

one 3–4 lb (1.5–2.0 kg) whole salmon, rinsed and patted dry

½ cup (125 mL) dry white wine

3 Tbsp (45 mL) extra virgin olive oil

salt and freshly ground black pepper to taste

4–6 garlic cloves, thinly sliced

a few sprigs dill, parsley and tarragon

1 small lemon, sliced

ERIC'S OPTIONS
If it's pouring outside, the salmon can also be baked in a 400°F (200°C) oven for 30 minutes, or until cooked through.

Preheat the barbecue to medium. With a sharp knife, cut off and discard the head, fins and tail of the salmon. Arrange 3 sheets of foil so they are slightly overlapping and are large enough to entirely encase the salmon. Place the salmon on the foil. Combine the wine and oil in a bowl. Brush some of the mixture inside the cavity of the salmon and season with salt and pepper. Stuff the cavity with the garlic, herb sprigs and lemon. Brush the outside of the salmon with the remaining wine/oil mixture and season with salt and pepper. Fold the foil over the salmon, ensuring there is a tight seal. Grill for 13 to 15 minutes per side, or until cooked through. The thickest part of the flesh should register 140°F (60°C) on an instant-read thermometer.

BAKED SALMON with CREAMY SHRIMP SAUCE

Decadently delicious, this seafood dish will feed a table full of guests and cooks up in less than 20 minutes.

preparation time • 20 minutes
cooking time • 15–18 minute
makes • 8 servings

eight 5 oz (150 g) salmon fillets

3 Tbsp (45 mL) melted butter

salt and white pepper to taste

½ cup (125 mL) white wine

2 garlic cloves, crushed

1 tsp (5 mL) dried tarragon

½ tsp (2 mL) paprika

2 cups (500 mL) whipping cream

½ lb (250 g) small cooked salad shrimp

2 green onions, thinly sliced

ERIC'S OPTIONS
Halibut fillets are equally good in this recipe. Vary the sauce by replacing the shrimp with an equal amount of crabmeat, or use a mix of shrimp and crab.

Preheat the oven to 350°F (175°C). Line a baking sheet with parchment paper. Arrange the salmon in a single layer skin side down. Brush the fish with the melted butter; season with salt and pepper. Bake the salmon for 15 to 18 minutes, or until cooked through.

While the fish bakes, place the wine, garlic, tarragon and paprika in a medium-sized pot and bring to a simmer. Simmer until the wine has reduced by half. Add the cream and bring back to a simmer. Continue cooking until the mixture lightly thickens. Stir in the shrimp and heat them through for a few minutes. Season the sauce with salt and pepper. Keep the sauce warm over low heat. When the salmon is cooked, place on individual serving plates and top with the sauce. Sprinkle with green onions and serve.

CEDAR PLANK SALMON

Cooking salmon on a cedar plank gives the fish an inviting, slightly smoky taste and makes for an impressive presentation. Untreated cedar planks are available at many supermarkets and barbecue supply and seafood stores.

2 Tbsp (30 mL) olive oil

½ lemon, juice of

1 Tbsp (15 mL) brown sugar

1 Tbsp (15 mL) chopped fresh dill or parsley

salt and black pepper to taste

four 6 oz (175 g) salmon fillets, skin on (see Removing Salmon Pin Bones on page 224)

lemon slices

Presoak an untreated cedar plank by submerging it in cold water for 2 hours. Place the oil, lemon juice, sugar, dill or parsley, salt and pepper in a bowl and mix well. Add the salmon and turn to coat. Marinate salmon 30 minutes.

Remove the plank from the water and dry the side the fish will be placed on. If you have a two-burner barbecue, turn one side off and lower the other to medium-low. Set the fish on the plank and place on the unlit side of the barbecue. (If you have a one-burner barbecue, set to its lowest setting.) Close the lid and cook for 15 to 20 minutes, or until the fish is cooked through. Keep a spray bottle handy just in case the board ignites on the bottom. Set the plank on a serving tray and garnish with lemon slices.

preparation time	•	10 minutes
cooking time	•	15–20 minute
makes	•	4 servings

ERIC'S OPTIONS
Use an equal amount of maple syrup or honey instead of brown sugar. For pepper-crusted cedar plank salmon, coat the fish with a generous amount of coarsely cracked black pepper before cooking.

WHEN IS FISH OR SHELLFISH COOKED?

When cooked, fish and shellfish should feel slightly firm, not hard, a sign you have overcooked it, and not soft, a sign it's not cooked through. When cooked, the flesh will also lose its translucency and become opaque. When fish is cooked it will also slightly separate into flakes. With some oily fish, such as salmon, white deposits of fat will seep out between the flakes when it's cooked.

For fish, the old fisherman's rule of thumb for cooking time is to allow 10 minutes per inch of thickness. This seems to hold true if you are pan-frying or grilling fish over medium to medium-high heat. When baking fish, though, you may need to add a few minutes as the vessel you are cooking the fish in needs to reach oven temperature before the fish really starts cooking.

MAPLE WHISKY-GLAZED SALMON

Maple syrup, whisky and salmon give this rich recipe a taste of Canada. Serve it with small new potatoes and seasonal vegetables.

four 6 oz (175 g) salmon fillets or steaks

salt and freshly ground black pepper to taste

3 Tbsp (45 mL) maple syrup

2 Tbsp (30 mL) Canadian whisky

1 Tbsp (15 mL) Dijon mustard

½ lemon, juice of

2 tsp (10 mL) chopped fresh dill

dill sprigs and lemon wedges for garnish

preparation time • 5 minutes
cooking time • 12–15 minute
makes • 4 servings

ERIC'S OPTIONS
Feel free to adjust the level of sweetness or spiciness of the glaze. For example, if you prefer it less sweet, cut back a little on the maple syrup and add a little extra lemon. If you want it spicy, increase the amount of Dijon mustard. Bourbon can be used instead of whisky. Trout fillets can replace the salmon.

Preheat the oven to 425°F (220°C). Place the salmon in a shallow baking dish. Season with salt and pepper. Combine the maple syrup, whisky, mustard, lemon juice and chopped dill in a bowl. Mix well and spoon over the fish. Bake for 12 to 15 minutes, or until the fish begins to flake slightly. Divide the salmon among 4 plates and spoon the pan juices over top. Garnish with dill sprigs and lemon wedges.

REMOVING SALMON PIN BONES

Unless your seafood retailer has removed them, salmon fillets have small pin bones embedded in the flesh. To remove them before cooking, lay the fillet on a work surface and run your finger down the upper middle of the flesh. The bones should pop up. Grab the ends of the bones with tweezers or needle-nose pliers, then tug to pull them out. If you want to avoid this task, buy tail-end fillet portions, which have no pin bones.

TEX-MEX SALMON BURGERS

Rich-tasting salmon pairs well with bold and complex flavors like the spices found in this colorful burger.

four ¼ lb (125 g) salmon fillets

2 Tbsp (30 mL) olive oil

1 tsp (5 mL) chili powder

1 tsp (5 mL) ground cumin

¼ tsp (1 mL) cayenne pepper

½ tsp (2 mL) dried oregano

salt and freshly ground black pepper to taste

4 kaiser buns, cut in half

¼ cup (60 mL) mayonnaise

4 lettuce leaves

½ cup (125 mL) tomato salsa, store-bought or homemade

1 small, ripe avocado, peeled and sliced into thin wedges

1 lime, juice of

preparation time • 15 minutes
cooking time • 6–8 minutes
makes • 4 servings

ERIC'S OPTIONS
Substitute other firm fish fillets, such as halibut or tuna, for the salmon. For added spice, top the fish with thin slices of fresh or canned jalapeño peppers just before serving.

Brush the salmon with the olive oil; sprinkle with chili powder, cumin, cayenne pepper, oregano, salt and pepper. Cover and let the salmon marinate at room temperature for 20 minutes.

Preheat a nonstick or lightly oiled grill to medium-high. Grill the salmon for 3 to 4 minutes per side, or until just cooked through. Spread the buns with the mayonnaise and top with lettuce. Add the salmon and top with a spoonful of the salsa and a few wedges of avocado. Drizzle with lime juice, set on top of the bun and serve.

HALIBUT and SPINACH WRAPPED in PHYLLO PARCELS

Baking fish in phyllo pastry keeps it moist. It also creates a crispy exterior that's hard to resist, particularly when paired with the rich and creamy sauce featured in this dish.

THE FISH

one 10 oz (300 g) package frozen chopped spinach, thawed

1 Tbsp (15 mL) butter

1 shallot, finely chopped

1 garlic clove, crushed

4 sheets phyllo pastry (see Handling and Storing Phyllo Pastry on page 229)

2–3 Tbsp (30–45 mL) melted butter

two 6 oz (175 g) halibut fillets

salt and white pepper to taste

THE SAUCE

1 Tbsp (15 mL) butter

1 shallot, finely chopped

2 Tbsp (30 mL) lemon juice

¾ cup (185 mL) whipping cream

2 Tbsp (30 mL) capers

1 Tbsp (15 mL) snipped chives or chopped fresh tarragon or parsley

salt and white pepper taste

Continued . . .

preparation time	•	30 minutes
cooking time	•	20–25 minutes
makes	•	2 servings

ERIC'S OPTIONS

Other fish, such as salmon or cod, can replace the halibut. Instead of frozen chopped spinach, use a small bunch of fresh spinach, washed, stemmed, steamed, cooled, squeezed of excess moisture and chopped. If you are not fond of the taste of capers, simply omit them from the sauce.

THE FISH

Squeeze all the moisture from the spinach and set aside. Heat the 1 Tbsp (15 mL) butter in a small skillet over medium heat. Add the shallot and garlic and cook until softened, about 2 minutes. Add the spinach and season with salt and pepper. Remove from the heat and set aside. Preheat the oven to 400°F (200°C).

Lay a sheet of phyllo on a work surface. Brush lightly with melted butter. Top with another sheet and brush again. Repeat until all the sheets are used. Cut the stacked sheets in half. Divide the spinach mixture and place near the bottom center of each sheet stack. (See photos.) Set the halibut on top of the spinach and season with salt and pepper. Fold the sides of the phyllo over to partially cover the halibut and then roll it up to form a package and seal the filling inside. Place on a parchment paper–lined baking tray. Brush the tops with butter. Bake in the middle of the oven for 20 to 25 minutes until puffed and golden.

THE SAUCE

Melt the butter in a pot set over medium heat. Add the shallot and cook until softened, about 2 minutes. Add the lemon juice and continue cooking until it has almost all evaporated. Pour in the cream and cook until it thickens slightly. Add the capers and chives. Season with salt and pepper.

To serve, pour a pool of the sauce on 2 dinner plates. Cut each phyllo parcel in half at a slight angle. Arrange the pieces over the sauce.

HANDLING AND STORING PHYLLO PASTRY

Phyllo (also called filo) pastry is sold frozen in most supermarkets. Thaw at room temperature for 3 to 4 hours before using. Phyllo pastry is delicate. Make sure you have a clear, large workspace to move and fold it without tearing it. Carefully unfold the sheets and remove and set aside the number you require, covering them with a very slightly dampened tea towel. Refold the remaining sheets and tightly seal the package. Refrigerate any unused sheets for 2 to 3 weeks. Phyllo pastry can also be refrozen. Divide it into packages that contain the number of sheets you will most likely use each time.

Use a soft, bristled brush to butter or oil the sheets. A firm brush can easily cause tears. When you start to butter or oil the sheets, brush the outer edges first, as they are more prone to drying and cracking. Evenly and lightly coat the remainder of the sheet; do not overdo it with the butter or oil it or the layered sheets will become greasy and heavy. When layering the sheets, do so as neatly and evenly as possible, but do not become overly concerned if they are not perfectly aligned. If too much time is taken fussing around the sheets could dry out or break.

Phyllo pastry is best baked on a parchment paper–lined baking tray in the middle of the oven. The parchment paper will prevent sticking even if some of the filling leaks out; being centrally located in the oven will promote even cooking.

GRILLED HALIBUT FILLETS with BEAN and TOMATO SALAD

The flavor of this simply seasoned halibut is accented by a colorful Mediterranean-style salad, flavored with garlic, fresh herbs and extra virgin olive oil. See Fish Grilling Tips (page 239).

preparation time • 25 minutes
cooking time • 6–8 minutes
makes • 4 servings

THE SALAD

4 ripe Roma, or plum, tomatoes, cut into wedges

½ lb (250 g) wax beans, trimmed and blanched (see How to Blanch Vegetables on page 253)

½ small red onion, thinly sliced

16–20 black olives

1 garlic clove, crushed

3 Tbsp (45 mL) extra virgin olive oil

3 Tbsp (45 mL) balsamic vinegar

2 Tbsp (30 mL) chopped fresh oregano or basil

salt and freshly ground black pepper to taste

THE FISH

four 5 oz (150 g) halibut fillets

2 Tbsp (30 mL) olive oil

salt and freshly ground black pepper to taste

lemon wedges and oregano or basil sprigs for garnish

ERIC'S OPTIONS
Use green beans instead of wax beans, or use a combination of the two. A mix of small, different-colored tomatoes makes the salad even more colorful.

THE SALAD

Combine all the ingredients in a bowl and toss gently to combine. Cover and refrigerate until the halibut is ready.

THE FISH

Preheat the grill to medium-high. Brush the halibut with olive oil and season with salt and pepper. Lightly oil the grill if it's not nonstick. Grill the fillets for 3 to 4 minutes per side, or until just cooked through. To serve, mound the salad in the center of individual plates. Top with the halibut. Garnish with lemon wedges and oregano or basil sprigs.

FISH in CRISPY BEER BATTER

Foamy beer adds lightness and tanginess to this batter. Double the recipe if you're feeding a crowd of fish lovers.

vegetable oil for deep-frying

¾ cup (185 mL) all-purpose flour

¼ cup (60 mL) cornstarch

1 tsp (5 mL) baking powder

½ tsp (2 mL) salt

pinches paprika and white pepper

¾ cup (185 mL) ice-cold lager beer

1½ lb (750 g) fish fillets, such as cod, halibut, snapper or haddock, cut into 8 equal pieces

preparation time	• 5 minutes
cooking time	• 5–6 minutes
makes	• four 2-piece servings

ERIC'S OPTIONS
For darker, richer tasting batter use dark ale instead of lager.

Heat the oil in your deep-fat fryer to 350°F–375°F (175°C–190°C). Place the flour, cornstarch, baking powder, salt, paprika and pepper in a bowl and whisk to combine. Set a second bowl in a bowl filled with ice. Pour the beer into that bowl. Add the flour mixture and whisk until a smooth batter forms.

Preheat your oven to 200°F (95°C). Set a baking rack on baking sheet. Dip the fish in the batter, coating them evenly. Deep-fry the fish, in batches, for 5 to 6 minutes, turning once, or until golden brown and cooked through. Drain well, set on the baking rack, and keep the cooked pieces warm in the oven until all are cooked. Serve the fish with Tartar Sauce (page 217).

HADDOCK and WINTER VEGETABLE CASSEROLE

Here's a complete meal that is inexpensive to make and can be baked in one pan. Try it for a winter Sunday dinner.

preparation time • 25 minutes
cooking time • 20 minutes
makes • 4 servings

3 Tbsp (45 mL) melted butter

4 medium red-skinned potatoes, cut into wedges

2 medium carrots, halved lengthwise and sliced diagonally

2 cups (500 mL) chopped green cabbage

four 5 oz (150 g) haddock fillets

salt and freshly ground black pepper to taste

½ cup (125 mL) white wine

½ cup (125 mL) fish, chicken or vegetable stock

2 garlic cloves, finely chopped

½ cup (125 mL) frozen peas

1 Tbsp (15 mL) chopped fresh parsley

ERIC'S OPTIONS
Use cod, snapper, salmon or halibut fillets if haddock is unavailable. If you wish, replace the wine with stock.

Preheat the oven to 425°F (220°C). Brush a 9- × 13-inch (3.5 L) baking dish with 1 Tbsp (15 mL) of the melted butter. Place the potatoes and carrots in a large pot and cover with 3 inches (8 cm) of cold water. Bring to a boil and cook until firm-tender. Add the cabbage and cook just until it brightens in color, about 2 minutes. Drain the vegetables well and place in the casserole. Set the haddock fillets on top; season with salt and pepper. Combine the remaining butter, wine, stock and garlic in a bowl. Spoon the mixture over the haddock and vegetables. Sprinkle in the frozen peas. Cover and bake for 20 minutes, or until the haddock is cooked through. Sprinkle with the parsley and serve.

POACHED SABLEFISH with CHAMPAGNE HOLLANDAISE

Sablefish is a sleek, black-skinned fish harvested from the cold, deep waters of the North Pacific. For years it was most often smoked and was known as black cod, and still is in some areas. Restaurant chefs and knowledgeable home cooks now prefer it unsmoked. With its pearly white flesh and sweet, rich flavor, it's easy to understand why.

THE HOLLANDAISE

3 large egg yolks

¼ cup (60 mL) champagne or sparkling wine

¼ lb (125 g) butter, melted

2 Tbsp (30 mL) finely chopped green onions or chives

salt and white pepper to taste

THE FISH

1 cup (250 mL) dry white wine

3 cups (750 mL) fish stock or water

2 bay leaves

1 medium onion, thinly sliced

2 garlic cloves, thinly sliced

3–4 lemon slices

½ tsp (2 mL) dried thyme

½ tsp (2 mL) whole black peppercorns

4 parsley sprigs

four 5 oz (150 g) sablefish fillets

preparation time • 40 minutes
cooking time • 20 minutes
makes • 4 servings

ERIC'S OPTIONS
To make the poaching liquid a little more upscale and give the fish a golden hue, add ½ tsp (2 mL) of crumbled saffron threads when you add the wine. The poaching liquid can be used to cook just about any kind of fish fillets or steaks, such as salmon, cod, halibut and skate.

THE HOLLANDAISE

Place the egg yolks in a heatproof bowl and whisk in the wine. Place the bowl over (but not touching) boiling water and whisk steadily until the mixture begins to lighten and thicken like lightly whipped cream. Remove from the heat and very, very slowly whisk in the melted butter. Mix in the onion or chives and season with salt and pepper. Cover the bowl with plastic wrap and keep the sauce someplace warm, such as near the stove, until the fish is cooked. (Don't put the sauce somewhere hot, or the eggs will cook.)

THE FISH

Place the wine, stock or water, bay leaves, onion, garlic and lemon in a medium-sized pot. Tie the thyme, peppercorns and parsley in a piece of cheesecloth. Drop into the wine mixture. Bring the mixture to a simmer over medium heat and simmer for 10 minutes. Add the fish fillets. Cover and simmer for 7 to 8 minutes, or until the fish is just cooked through.

Remove the fish to serving plates, using a large slotted spoon or lifter. Top each fillet with a spoonful of the hollandaise, and serve the rest alongside.

GRILLED TUNA STEAKS
with PAPAYA GINGER SALSA

Tuna is a firm, meaty fish that's perfect for grilling.
The bright-tasting, tropical salsa is a fine accent.

preparation time • 20 minutes
cooking time • 6–8 minutes
makes • 4 servings

½ fresh, ripe papaya, about ½ lb (250 g) peeled and
   cut into ¼ inch (6 mm) cubes

¼ cup (60 mL) finely chopped green bell pepper

1 small, ripe tomato, finely chopped

2 tsp (10 mL) grated fresh ginger

2 tsp (10 mL) brown sugar

1 lime, juice of

¼ tsp (1 mL) cayenne pepper, or to taste

four 5 oz (150 g) ahi, albacore or other tuna steaks

1 Tbsp (15 mL) vegetable oil

salt and freshly ground black pepper to taste

lime slices and cilantro sprigs to garnish

ERIC'S OPTIONS
If papaya is not available, make the
salsa with a medium-sized mango.
A wide range of other grilled fish
steaks go well with this salsa, such as
salmon or halibut.

Combine the papaya, bell pepper, tomato,
ginger, sugar, lime juice and cayenne pepper in
a bowl. Cover and let the flavors meld at room
temperature for 30 minutes. Preheat a nonstick or
lightly oiled grill to medium-high. Brush the tuna
with the oil; season with salt and pepper. Grill
2 minutes per side, or until still slightly rare in
the middle. (If you like your tuna entirely cooked
through, cook 1 to 2 minutes more per side). Top
each steak with a spoonful of the salsa and serve
the rest alongside. Garnish with lime slices and
cilantro sprigs.

Firm-fleshed fish steaks and fillets, such as swordfish, tuna, salmon or shark, are best for cooking directly on the grill. When buying them, choose firm-looking ones tightly holding their shape. If they have several soft spots or are falling apart in places, they won't grill well.

Before cooking, I like to let the fish warm at room temperature for 20 minutes or so. I've found that setting refrigerator-cold fish on a hot grill makes it more prone to sticking. Excess moisture can also cause the fish to stick. Before seasoning and cooking, pat the fish dry. If it's been marinated, remove as much of the wet marinade off the fish as you can.

Before cooking, properly preheat your grill. If the fish is set on just a slightly warm grill, it won't quickly form a protective crust and will likely fuse itself to the grill. Unless it's a high-quality nonstick grill, another way to help prevent sticking is to lightly oil the grill before setting on the fish.

SHRIMP-STUFFED SOLE FILLETS

This elegant fish dish for two can be put together quite quickly. Complement it with baby potatoes and tiny carrots with their tops, and green beans or asparagus.

preparation time • 20 minutes
cooking time • 15–20 minute
makes • 2 servings

THE FILLING

5 oz (150 g) small cooked salad shrimp,
    coarsely chopped

1 tsp (5 mL) chopped fresh dill

1 large egg white

1 garlic clove, crushed

¼ cup (60 mL) breadcrumbs

salt, white pepper and lemon juice to taste

ERIC'S OPTIONS
Use crabmeat in the filling instead of shrimp. Use other thin, boneless fish fillets suitable for rolling, such as flounder or plaice, instead of sole.

THE FISH

4 sole fillets, totaling ¾ lb (375 g)

salt and white pepper to taste

2 Tbsp (30 mL) olive oil

1 tsp (5 mL) chopped fresh dill

1 garlic clove, crushed

¼ cup (60 mL) white wine

dill sprigs and lemon wedges

Place the filling ingredients in a bowl and mix well. Preheat the oven to 375°F (190°C). Season the fillets with salt and pepper and lay flat on a work surface. Divide and mound the filling at the narrow end of each fillet. Roll up tight and place in a small baking dish. (The fish can be prepared to this point several hours before cooking and stored in the refrigerator.) Combine the oil, chopped dill, garlic and wine in a bowl. Pour over the fish. Cover with foil and bake for 15 to 20 minutes, or until the fish begins to flake and turn opaque. To serve, place 2 pieces of sole on each plate and spoon the pan juices overtop. Garnish with dill and lemon.

POULTRY

CORN-CRUSTED CHICKEN STRIPS with HONEY MUSTARD SAUCE

The taste of these crispy-coated chicken strips, which take only minutes to make oven-ready, is miles above the mass-produced chicken strips available in supermarkets.

3 Tbsp (45 mL) vegetable oil

¼ cup (60 mL) mayonnaise

3 Tbsp (45 mL) Dijon mustard

½ cup (125 mL) cornmeal

¾ cup (185 mL) breadcrumbs

pinch cayenne pepper

½ tsp (2 mL) ground sage

20 boneless, skinless chicken breast fillets (see Note)

½ cup (125 mL) honey

preparation time	•	15 minutes
cooking time	•	about 20 minutes
makes	•	20 strips

NOTE
Chicken breast fillets are tender strips that are sold separately. You'll find them in the meat section of most supermarkets; if you can't, cut 3 to 4 boneless, skinless chicken breasts into 20 long strips.

ERIC'S OPTIONS
For a sweeter corn crust, substitute the cornmeal and breadcrumbs with 1¼ cups (310 mL) cornflakes.

Preheat the oven to 375°F (190°C). Line a baking sheet with parchment paper. Brush the parchment paper with the vegetable oil. Place the mayonnaise and 1 Tbsp (15 mL) of the mustard in a bowl and whisk well to combine. Combine the cornmeal, breadcrumbs, cayenne and sage in a shallow dish. Add the chicken to the mayonnaise-mustard bowl and toss well to thoroughly coat. Set a few of the chicken breast fillets in the cornmeal-breadcrumb mixture, turning them to coat and gently pressing the crumbs on. Arrange the crusted chicken in a single layer on the baking sheet. Repeat with the remaining chicken breast fillets. Bake the chicken strips for 10 minutes, then turn over and bake for 8 to 10 minutes more, or until the chicken is cooked through. Meanwhile, in a small bowl, mix the honey with the remaining mustard. Arrange the chicken strips on a serving tray and serve with the honey mustard sauce alongside for dipping.

GARLIC-STUFFED CHICKEN LEGS
with PAN GRAVY

Serve this with a couple of favorite vegetables and
Buttermilk Yukon Gold Mashed Potatoes (page 349) and
you'll have a very comforting, budget-friendly supper.

preparation time • 20 minutes
cooking time • 50–60 minute
makes • 4 servings

4 large chicken legs

6 garlic cloves, thinly sliced

1 tsp (5 mL) dried herbs, such as sage, thyme
and rosemary

salt and freshly ground black pepper to taste

2½ cups (625 mL) chicken stock

3 Tbsp (45 mL) all-purpose flour

ERIC'S OPTIONS
Use bone-in chicken breasts instead
of legs. Cooking time may be a little
less, depending on the size of the
breasts.

Preheat the oven to 400°F (200°C). Carefully lift the skin from the thigh
end of a chicken leg. Stuff a quarter of the garlic slices underneath,
pushing them to different points around the leg. Repeat with the
remaining legs. Place the chicken in a stovetop and ovenproof pan.
Sprinkle the herbs over the chicken and season with salt and pepper.
Bake, basting with the pan juices occasionally, for 45 to 50 minutes, or
until cooked through.

When the chicken is ready, remove it from the pan and keep it warm.
Remove excess fat from the pan and set over medium heat. Pour in 2 cups
(500 mL) of the stock. Mix the flour with the remaining ½ cup (125 mL)
of stock until it is lump-free. Add it to the pan in a slow stream, whisking
constantly. Bring the gravy to a simmer and cook until it thickens and the
flour is cooked through. Season with salt and pepper. Serve the chicken
with the gravy alongside.

TERIYAKI CHICKEN and VEGETABLE STIR-FRY

This dish is easy, quick and colorful, and it's all made in one pan. All you need to complete the meal is a pot of steamed rice.

preparation time • 15 minutes
cooking time • 15 minutes
makes • 4 servings

2 Tbsp (30 mL) vegetable oil

four 6 oz (175 g) boneless skinless chicken breasts

salt and freshly ground black pepper to taste

¼ cup (60 mL) cornstarch

1 medium red bell pepper, halved, seeded and cubed

1 medium carrot, halved lengthwise and thinly sliced on the bias

1 cup (250 mL) pineapple chunks, tinned or fresh

3 green onions, cut into 1-inch (2.5 cm) pieces

½–¾ cup (125–185 mL) teriyaki sauce

ERIC'S OPTIONS

Try using thin-cut pork chops or small tender beef steaks, about 1 inch (2.5 cm) thick, instead of chicken. Cook as for the chicken, reducing the time a little if you like your beef rare.

Heat the oil in large skillet over medium-high heat. Season the chicken with salt and pepper and then lightly coat in cornstarch, shaking the excess off. Cook the chicken for 2 to 3 minutes on each side. Remove from the pan and set aside. Add the bell pepper and carrot to the pan and stir-fry for 2 to 3 minutes. Stir in the pineapple and green onions. Set the chicken on top of the mixture and pour the teriyaki sauce into the pan. Cover, reduce the heat to medium, and cook until the vegetables are tender and the chicken is cooked through, about 3 to 5 minutes.

SINGAPORE-STYLE CHICKEN SATAY with PEANUT SAUCE

I got the marinade recipe for these satay from a street vendor in Singapore. I'm pretty sure he didn't give me his exact list of ingredients: such recipes are usually closely guarded secrets. But what he did suggest ended up tasting mighty fine.

preparation time • 25 minutes
cooking time • about 10 minutes
makes • 24 satay

THE PEANUT SAUCE

⅓ cup (80 mL) creamy peanut butter

1 cup (250 mL) coconut milk

1 lime, juice and grated zest of

1 Tbsp (15 mL) packed brown sugar

2 Tbsp (30 mL) soy sauce

2 tsp (10 mL) grated fresh ginger

¼ tsp (1 mL) crushed chili flakes

THE SATAY

2 Tbsp (30 mL) vegetable oil

1 Tbsp (15 mL) packed brown sugar

1 tsp (5 mL) salt

1 lime, juice and grated zest of

2 tsp (10 mL) grated fresh ginger

2 tsp (10 mL) ground cumin

1 tsp (5 mL) ground turmeric

1½ lb (750 g) boneless, skinless chicken breast or thigh, cut into 24 thin strips

2 Tbsp (30 mL) chopped fresh cilantro

twenty-four 6-inch (15 cm) wooden skewers (soaked in cold water for at least an hour)

NOTE

Even after soaking the wooden skewers, they can still burn. To help prevent that, set a double-thick strip of aluminum foil, the same width as the top, non–meat-covered area of the skewers on the front portion of your grill. When grilling the skewers, set the meat portion over the open flame, and the wooden end on the foil, preventing the latter from burning.

ERIC'S OPTIONS

Use thin, tender slices of boneless pork, beef or lamb instead of chicken. Make the peanut sauce more or less spicy by simply increasing or decreasing the amount of crushed chili flakes.

THE PEANUT SAUCE

Place the peanut sauce ingredients in a small pot over medium heat and bring to a simmer. Continue simmering for 5 minutes, whisking until a smooth sauce forms. Remove from the heat and serve hot or at room temperature.

THE SATAY

Combine the oil, brown sugar, salt, lime zest and juice, ginger, cumin and turmeric in a medium bowl. Add the chicken and toss well to thoroughly coat. Allow the chicken to marinate in the refrigerator for 2 to 3 hours. When marinated, thread a chicken strip on end of each skewer (do not thread it all the way up the skewer or the chicken will be hard to pull off). Discard any leftover marinade. Preheat an indoor or outdoor grill to medium-high. Lightly oil the grill and cook the chicken skewers for 2 minutes per side or until cooked through (see Note). Arrange the chicken satay on a platter and sprinkle with the chopped cilantro. Serve with a bowl of the peanut sauce for dipping.

TANDOORI CHICKEN WINGS
with MINT CHUTNEY

Tandoori paste is a mildly spiced Indian ingredient used to marinate meats, giving them a deliciously subtle flavor and a striking, almost fuchsia-like color. It's available in the Asian foods aisle of most supermarkets.

1 cup (250 mL) packed fresh mint leaves

3 green onions, coarsely chopped

1 small jalapeño pepper, seeded and coarsely chopped

1 garlic clove, chopped

2 Tbsp (30 mL) vegetable oil

2 Tbsp (30 mL) water

¼ cup (60 mL) freshly squeezed lime juice

1 Tbsp (15 mL) sugar

1 tsp (5 mL) ground cumin

1 tsp (5 mL) salt

¾ cup (185 mL) plain yogurt

2 Tbsp (30 mL) tandoori paste

24 chicken wingettes or drumettes, or a mix of both (see Note)

preparation time	• 25 minutes
cooking time	• 25–35 minutes
makes	• 24 wings

NOTE
Most supermarkets sell chicken wingettes, the middle part of the wing, and drumettes, the meatier portion of the wing. If you can't find them, buy whole wings and cut them yourself.

ERIC'S OPTIONS
If you prefer the flavor of cilantro, use an equal amount of it instead of mint to make the chutney. If you like things really spicy, use a small, fiery-hot serrano chili in the chutney instead of the milder jalapeño.

Place all the ingredients in a food processor; pulse until finely chopped and well combined. Transfer to a bowl and keep in the refrigerator, covered, until wings are ready.

Combine the yogurt and tandoori paste in a large bowl. Add the wings and toss well to thoroughly coat. Marinate in the refrigerator for 2 hours. Preheat the oven to 425°F (220°C). Line a baking sheet with parchment paper. Set the wings on the baking sheet in a single layer. Bake for 25 to 35 minutes, turning once, or until cooked through. When done, if you prefer a crispier, darker skin, broil the wings a few minutes. Arrange on a platter and serve with mint chutney for dipping.

PICNIC CHICKEN

Cornmeal, sage, honey and mustard give this baked chicken its flavorful coating. Chilled well overnight in the refrigerator and kept in a cooler, it's perfect picnic food.

¾ cup (185 mL) dried breadcrumbs

¼ cup (60 mL) cornmeal

1 tsp (5 mL) ground sage

½ tsp (2 mL) salt

½ tsp (2 mL) freshly ground black pepper

⅓ cup (80 mL) mayonnaise

2 tsp (10 mL) Dijon mustard

2 tsp (10 mL) liquid honey

6 chicken drumsticks

6 chicken thighs

preparation time	•	20 minutes
cooking time	•	40–45 minutes
makes	•	six 2-piece servings

ERIC'S OPTIONS
For a sweeter, crisper crust, replace the breadcrumbs and cornmeal with 1 cup (250 mL) cornflake crumbs.

Preheat the oven to 375°F (190°C). Line a baking sheet with parchment paper. Combine the breadcrumbs, cornmeal, sage, salt and pepper in a wide, shallow bowl. Combine the mayonnaise, mustard and honey in another bowl. Add the chicken and toss to coat each piece well. Coat each piece of chicken in the breadcrumb mixture, gently pressing it on to help it adhere, and transfer to the baking sheet. Bake for 40 to 45 minutes, or until cooked through. Cool the chicken to room temperature. Chill in the refrigerator for at least 4 hours or overnight, before packing into an ice-cold cooler to enjoy at your picnic.

CRANBERRY MAPLE CHICKEN

This is a sumptuous dish created by braising chicken thighs and drumsticks with a fine mix and balance of flavors that include tangy cranberries, sweet maple syrup and rich, buttery pecans. It's pretty rich, so two pieces per person is an ample portion size. Serve the chicken with Mixed-Vegetable Rice Pilaf (page 160) and Broccoli Florets with Roasted Peppers (page 345).

8 chicken drumsticks

8 chicken thighs

salt and freshly ground black pepper to taste

½ cup (125 mL) cornstarch

5 Tbsp (75 mL) vegetable oil

2 medium onions, halved and thinly sliced

2 Tbsp (30 mL) chopped fresh ginger

1 cup (250 mL) maple syrup

1 cup (250 mL) chicken stock

½ cup (125 mL) white wine

½ cup (125 mL) balsamic vinegar

1 tsp (5 mL) herbes de Provence (see Note)

2 cups (500 mL) fresh or frozen cranberries

1 cup (250 mL) pecan halves

preparation time	•	25 minutes
cooking time	•	about 75 minutes
makes	•	eight 2-piece servings

NOTE
Herbes de Provence is a French-style blend made with herbs such as basil, marjoram, rosemary, fennel seed, lavender, summer savory, sage and thyme. The type and quantity of each herb used to make it can vary greatly depending on the maker. Herbes de Provence is available at most supermarkets, in bulk or in small bottles.

ERIC'S OPTIONS
If you're only serving 4, this recipe can easily be halved and cooked in 1 casserole dish, not 2. Instead of pecans, top the chicken with ½ cup (125 mL) lightly toasted sliced almonds.

Season the chicken pieces with salt and pepper. Place the cornstarch in a medium bowl. Add the chicken and toss to coat. Heat 3 Tbsp (45 mL) of the oil in a large skillet over medium-high heat. Shake the excess cornstarch off the chicken and add it to the skillet in batches. Brown on all sides. Divide the chicken between two 9- x 13-inch (3.5 L) casserole dishes. Preheat the oven to 375°F (190°C).

Heat the remaining 2 Tbsp (30 mL) of oil in a small pot over medium heat. Add the onion and cook 3 to 4 minutes. Add the ginger and cook 1 minute more. Add the maple syrup, stock, wine and vinegar, increase the heat to medium-high and bring to a boil. Divide and pour the mixture over the chicken. Sprinkle the chicken with the herbes de Provence. Nestle the cranberries and pecans around the chicken. Cover and bake for 60 minutes, or until the chicken is cooked and deliciously tender.

SLOW COOKER CHICKEN COCONUT CURRY

Serve this curry with steamed basmati rice, chutney, yogurt and pappadums, a crisp, cracker-like bread sold in the Asian foods aisle of most supermarkets.

2 Tbsp (30 mL) vegetable oil

1 lb (500 g) boneless, skinless chicken thighs, cubed

1 Tbsp (15 mL) cornstarch

3 medium red potatoes, cubed

1 medium onion, halved and sliced

one 28 oz (796 mL) can diced tomatoes

one 14 oz (398 mL) can coconut milk

1 cup (250 mL) chicken stock

1–2 Tbsp (15–30 mL) curry powder

salt to taste

24 snow or snap peas, blanched (see How to Blanch Vegetables on page 253)

Heat the oil in a large skillet over medium-high heat. Coat the chicken with the cornstarch, add to the skillet and brown on all sides. Place the browned chicken, potatoes, onion, tomatoes, coconut milk, stock and curry powder in the slow cooker and stir to combine. Cover and cook on the low setting for 8 hours. When ready to serve, season with salt and stir in the blanched peas; they'll heat through in 1 to 2 minutes.

preparation time	•	25 minutes
slow-cooker time	•	8 hours
finishing time	•	1–2 minutes
makes	•	4 servings

NOTE
This recipe is designed for a slow cooker with 4½ to 6½ quart (4.5 to 6.5 L) capacity.

ERIC'S OPTIONS
Substitute cubed turkey thighs or pork tenderloin for the chicken thighs. Reduce the calorie and fat content by using light coconut milk.

HOW TO BLANCH VEGETABLES

Blanch vegetables by plunging and cooking them in boiling water until they are firm-tender. The cooking time depends on the type of vegetable used and for how long (if at all, as in the case of salads) the vegetable will cook afterwards. In general, quick-cooking vegetables, such as asparagus, green beans, corn, snap peas and broccoli florets, will take one to two minutes; firmer vegetables, such as Brussels sprouts, five to six. Once you've blanched the vegetables, quickly chill them in ice-cold water to stop the cooking process and set their color, before draining them well and patting them dry.

SLOW COOKER CHICKEN in SOUR CREAM PAPRIKA SAUCE

In this dish, chicken is cooked in a paprika-rich sauce until it is deliciously tender. Serve the chicken with egg noodles and a green vegetable to add color to the plate.

6 chicken drumsticks

6 chicken thighs

salt and freshly ground black pepper to taste

2 small to medium onions, halved and sliced

2 small to medium celery stalks, halved lengthwise and sliced

2 small to medium carrots, halved lengthwise and sliced

2 garlic cloves, minced

2½ cups (625 mL) chicken stock

3 Tbsp (45 mL) all-purpose flour

2 Tbsp (30 mL) sweet paprika (see About Paprika on page 257)

1 tsp (5 mL) ground marjoram

½ cup (125 mL) regular or low-fat sour cream

½ cup (125 mL) frozen peas

chopped fresh parsley to taste

preparation time	•	20 minutes
slow-cooker time	•	6 hours
finishing time	•	15 minutes
makes	•	4–6 servings

NOTE
This recipe is designed for a slow cooker with 4½ to 6½ quart (4.5 to 6.5 L) capacity.

ERIC'S OPTIONS
For a smoky paprika taste, replace 2 tsp (10 mL) of the regular sweet paprika with smoked paprika.

Set an oven rack 6 inches (15 cm) below the broiler. Preheat the broiler to high.

Set the chicken on a nonstick baking sheet and season with salt and pepper. Broil the chicken until lightly browned, 4 to 5 minutes per side. Remove the chicken from the oven.

Place the onions, celery, carrots and garlic in your slow cooker and mix to combine. Nestle the chicken into the vegetables. Place the stock, flour, paprika and marjoram in a bowl and whisk to combine. Pour this mixture over the chicken. Cover and cook on the low setting for 6 hours, or until the chicken is very tender.

Preheat the oven to 200°F (95°C).

Carefully lift the chicken out of the slow cooker and set in a 13- x 19-inch (3.5 L) serving casserole. Keep the chicken warm in the oven. Ladle ½ cup (125 mL) of the sauce from the slow cooker into a small bowl and whisk in the sour cream. Add this mixture to the remaining sauce and vegetables in the slow cooker and mix well to combine. Stir in the peas, cover and cook for 10 minutes more to heat the sour cream and peas through. Season to taste with salt and pepper. Pour the mixture over the chicken, sprinkle with parsley and serve.

SLOW COOKER DURBAN-STYLE CHICKEN CURRY

The South African city of Durban is famous for its red-hued curries, introduced to the area by Indian immigrants. This very tasty version is flavored with hot curry powder, and sweet paprika and crushed tomatoes give it a reddish color. Serve this with steamed basmati rice, warm wedges of naan bread and Fresh Mint Chutney (page 358).

3 Tbsp (45 mL) vegetable oil

8 chicken thighs

½ tsp (2 mL) sweet paprika (see About Paprika on page 257)

salt and freshly ground black pepper to taste

1 medium onion, diced

1 garlic clove, minced

1 Tbsp (15 mL) peeled, chopped fresh ginger (see About Fresh Ginger on page 264)

1–2 Tbsp (15–30 mL) hot curry powder

one 14 oz (398 mL) can crushed tomatoes

one 14 oz (398 mL) can regular or light coconut milk

1 Tbsp (15 mL) golden brown sugar

2 Tbsp (30 mL) fresh lime juice

1 Tbsp (15 mL) cornstarch

2 Tbsp (30 mL) chopped fresh cilantro or sliced green onion

preparation time • 25 minutes
slow-cooker time • 6 hours
makes • 4 servings

NOTE
This recipe is designed for a slow cooker with 4½ to 6½ quart (4.5 to 6.5 L) capacity.

ERIC'S OPTIONS
For a milder curry, use mild or medium curry powder instead of the hot.

Place the oil in a large skillet set over medium-high heat. Sprinkle and rub the chicken with the paprika and salt and pepper. Brown the thighs on both sides and place in your slow cooker. Drain off most of the fat from the skillet, add the onion, garlic and ginger and cook for 2 to 3 minutes. Mix in the curry powder and cook for 1 minute more. Mix in the crushed tomatoes, coconut milk and brown sugar. Combine the lime juice and cornstarch in a small bowl to dissolve the cornstarch. Stir this into the coconut milk mixture, bring to a simmer and pour over the chicken. Cover and cook on the low setting for 6 hours, or until the chicken is very tender. Sprinkle servings of the chicken with cilantro or green onion.

ABOUT PAPRIKA

Paprika is a spice made from dried, ground, sweet red pepper pods. Although there are several types, the spice is divided into two main varieties, sweet paprika and hot paprika. Hot paprika is made from peppers that have some heat to them. Supermarkets usually sell the sweeter varieties of paprika in containers that are generically labeled "paprika," not "sweet paprika." Tins or jars of hot paprika will be labeled "hot." Smoking the peppers before they are dried and ground creates a spice called smoked paprika. You'll find smoked paprika at fine food stores and some supermarkets.

QUICK CHICKEN STEW
for TWO

Here's a simple, but tasty dish that, unlike stews made with tougher cuts of meat, takes minutes, not hours, to cook. If time allows, whip up a batch of Buttermilk Biscuits (page 366), to serve alongside. Any leftover biscuits will taste great with butter and jam for breakfast the next day.

1 Tbsp (15 mL) vegetable oil

½ lb (250 g) boneless, skinless chicken breast or thigh, cut into bite-sized cubes

⅓ cup (80 mL) chopped onion

⅓ cup (80 mL) chopped carrot

⅓ cup (80 mL) chopped celery

1½ Tbsp (22 mL) all-purpose flour

pinch dried sage leaves (see Note on page 128)

1½ cups (375 mL) chicken stock

¼ cup (60 mL) frozen peas or corn

salt and freshly ground black pepper to taste

preparation time •	20 minutes
cooking time •	about 20 minutes
makes •	2 servings

ERIC'S OPTIONS
Make turkey stew by replacing the chicken with boneless, skinless turkey breast or thigh.

Heat the oil in a large skillet over medium-high heat. Add the chicken, onion, carrot and celery and cook, stirring frequently, for 4 to 5 minutes, or until the chicken is light golden brown on all sides. Stir in the flour and sage and cook for 1 minute. Slowly add the stock, stirring constantly. Bring to a boil and reduce the heat until the stew is gently simmering. Cook until the vegetables are tender and the chicken is cooked through, about 10 minutes. (Add a little more stock if the stew becomes too thick.) Add the peas or corn and cook for 2 minutes, until heated through. Season with salt and pepper and serve immediately.

CORNISH HEN with RASPBERRY GINGER GLAZE

This rich red raspberry sauce spiked with fresh ginger tastily glazes the succulent hen.

one 1½ lb (750 g) Cornish game hen

salt and freshly ground black pepper to taste

⅓ cup (80 mL) raspberry jam

1 Tbsp (15 mL) soy sauce

1 Tbsp (15 mL) balsamic vinegar

1 Tbsp (15 mL) water

1 tsp (5 mL) chopped fresh ginger

¼ tsp (1 mL) dried tarragon

preparation time • 15 minutes
cooking time • 50 minutes
makes • 2 servings

ERIC'S OPTIONS
Make the glaze with another type of jam, such as blackberry or red currant. For added texture, sprinkle the hens with 2 tsp (10 mL) toasted sesame seeds after the second basting.

Preheat the oven to 375°F (190°C). With kitchen shears or a sharp knife, cut along both sides of the hen's backbone and remove the bone. Place the hen breast side up and press it flat. Cut it in half down the middle of the breastbone. Place the hen halves, skin side up, in a roasting pan; season with salt and pepper, and roast for 30 minutes.

While the hen roasts, place the jam, soy sauce, vinegar and water in a small saucepan. Bring to a simmer and stir until the jam is melted and well combined with the other ingredients. Strain the mixture through a fine sieve into a bowl. Mix in the ginger and tarragon. When the hen halves have roasted 30 minutes, baste with half the raspberry mixture. Roast 10 minutes longer, and then baste with the remaining glaze. Roast 10 minutes more, or until cooked through.

ROAST CORNISH HENS GLAZED with MAPLE and DIJON

The glaze for these succulent hens is easy to make and hard to resist. It's a sweet, spicy and herbaceous mix of maple syrup, Dijon mustard and sage. For Christmas dinner, this dish makes a fine alternative to roast turkey.

four 1½ lb (750 g) Cornish hens

salt and freshly ground black pepper to taste

⅓ cup (80 mL) maple syrup

⅓ cup (80 mL) Dijon mustard

3 Tbsp (45 mL) chopped fresh sage, or 2 tsp (10 mL) dried sage leaves (see Note on page 128)

Preheat the oven to 375°F (190°C). Place 1 hen on a secure work surface and use kitchen shears or a sharp knife to cut along either side of the backbone and remove it. Place the hen breast side up and press it flat. Cut it in half down the middle of the breastbone. Place the hen halves, skin side up, in a large roasting pan. Repeat with the remaining hens. Season with salt and pepper. (The hens can be cut and made oven-ready several hours in advance of serving. Keep refrigerated until ready to roast.) Roast for 30 minutes. Combine the maple syrup, mustard and sage in a bowl. Brush half the mixture over the hens and roast for 10 minutes. Brush with the remaining mixture and roast 10 to 15 minutes more, or until cooked through.

preparation time	•	25 minutes
cooking time	•	50–55 minute
makes	•	8 servings

ERIC'S OPTIONS
Instead of maple syrup, use honey in the glaze for the hens. Instead of sage, flavor the hens with chopped fresh rosemary.

ABOUT ROCK CORNISH GAME HENS

Rock Cornish game hen is not actually a game bird, although its small size and use in more refined preparations make it seem like it is. It is actually a hybrid of Cornish and White Rock chickens, hence its name.

This fowl, often simply called Cornish game hen, averages in weight from about 1 to 2 pounds (500 g to 1 kg). Because the meat-to-bone ratio is relatively small, if you were just serving the hen with a few side dishes, and were able to find sufficient amounts of birds in the 1- to 1¼-pound (500 to 600 g) range, you could serve a whole one per person.

However, I prefer to buy larger ones, somewhere in 1½-pound (750 g) range, split them in two before cooking, and serve half a hen per person. It always seems to be the perfect amount and halving the hens is fairly easy to do.

SPICE-ROASTED DUCK
with HOISIN GLAZE

The wonderful aromas of five-spice powder, ginger and hoisin sauce will fill your house as the duck roasts. Close your windows if you don't want your neighbours knocking on the door looking for an invitation to dinner!

preparation time • 30 minutes
cooking time • 1¾–2 hours
makes • 3–4 servings

one 4–5 lb (1.8–2.2 kg) duck, rinsed in cold
    water and patted dry

⅓ cup (80 mL) soy sauce

½ cup (125 mL) white wine or dry sherry

½ tsp (2 mL) salt

1 Tbsp (15 mL) five-spice powder

1 Tbsp (15 mL) vegetable oil

1 medium onion, halved and sliced

2 Tbsp (30 mL) coarsely chopped fresh ginger

3 garlic cloves, minced

2 Tbsp (30 mL) hoisin sauce, plus some to
    serve with the cooked duck

Using a fork, prick the skin of the duck all over. Combine 2 Tbsp (30 mL) of the soy sauce, white wine or sherry, salt and 2 tsp (10 mL) of the five-spice powder in a large bowl. Add the duck and brush it with the mixture inside and out. Cover and marinate in the refrigerator for 4 hours, turning and basting the duck from time to time.

Heat the oil in a pot over medium-high heat. Add the onion, ginger and garlic and cook for 2 to 3 minutes.

Continued . . .

NOTE
This style of duck is often served with thin pancakes that are used to wrap up delicious morsels of meat and a little hoisin sauce. However, for a quicker and lighter alternative, I like to use small whole lettuce leaves, such as butter, leaf or iceberg, to wrap the meat. Steamed rice and a mound of quickly stir-fried vegetables would also go great with the duck.

ERIC'S OPTIONS
The stuffing in this dish infuses incredible flavor into the meat but is not meant to be eaten. However, the duck carcass with stuffing makes a delicious soup stock. Simmer, just covered in water, for 1½ to 2 hours. For a quick soup, simmer any leftover duck meat and Chinese-style vegetables, such as bok choy and Chinese cabbage, in the stock for a few minutes, then pour it over some cooked Chinese-style noodles. Sprinkle with green onions and serve. Flavor the soup with a little soy sauce and hot sauce if desired.

SPICE-ROASTED DUCK
with HOISIN GLAZE (*continued*)

Add 2 Tbsp (30 mL) of the soy sauce and the remaining 1 tsp (5 mL) of five-spice powder. Cook for 2 minutes more. Remove from heat and cool. Stuff this mixture inside the duck and use skewers or string to enclose it. Tie the legs together with string and fold the wings under the body.

Preheat the oven to 425°F (220°C). Place the duck, breast side up, on a rack in a roasting pan. Fill the pan with hot water to a level just below the duck. Cover tightly so the water in the pan will steam the duck. Roast for 90 minutes.

Increase the heat to 475°F (240°C). Make the hoisin glaze by combining the hoisin sauce with the remaining 1 Tbsp (15 mL) of soy sauce in a small bowl. Uncover the duck and brush with the glaze. Roast, uncovered, until the skin is richly glazed and crispy, about 20 to 30 minutes.

Allow the duck to rest for 10 to 15 minutes before carving. Thinly slice the meat, arrange it on a platter, and serve it with extra hoisin sauce for dipping.

ABOUT FRESH GINGER

Ginger is the tan-colored, knobby rhizome of a perennial herb whose botanical name is *Zingiber officinale*. When purchasing ginger, look for firm pieces with fairly smooth skin. If it appears shriveled or has spongy spots, it's old or was improperly stored and should be avoided. It will be difficult to peel, cut or grate.

Unpeeled very fresh ginger, if placed in a tightly sealed plastic bag, can be kept in your refrigerator crisper for up to 3 weeks. For the freshest ginger taste, buy only what you can use within a reasonable length of time.

If you've purchased a pile of fresh ginger, place it in a tightly sealed plastic bag and freeze it for up to 2 months. Slice, chop or grate the ginger when still partially frozen, as it will be harder to do so when thawed. Another option is to peel and slice the ginger, place it in a jar, top it with sake, dry sherry or vodka, tightly screw on the lid and store it in the refrigerator for a month or more. These two processes will alter the original lively, fresh ginger taste.

BEAN and TURKEY ENCHILADAS

Here's a Mexican-style way to use those leftovers from a Thanksgiving, Christmas or Sunday roast turkey dinner. For a side dish, serve Grilled Corn with Lime and Cumin (page 342).

preparation time • 20 minutes
cooking time • 20–25 minutes
makes • 4 servings

ERIC'S OPTIONS
Substitute cooked and shredded chicken, pork or beef for the turkey.

one 14 oz (398 mL) can tomato sauce

1 tsp (5 mL) chili powder

½ tsp (2 mL) ground cumin

hot pepper sauce, such as Tabasco to taste

four 10-inch (25 cm) tortillas

one 14 oz (398 mL) can refried beans

2 cups (500 mL) shredded, cooked turkey

1½ cups (375 mL) grated Monterey Jack or cheddar cheese

1 large, fresh jalapeño pepper, thinly sliced (optional)

Preheat the oven to 375°F (190°C). Line a baking sheet with parchment paper. Combine the tomato sauce, chili powder, cumin and hot pepper sauce in a bowl. Place the tortillas on your work surface and spread an equal amount of the refried beans down the center of each.

Top the beans with the turkey. Drizzle 1½ Tbsp (22 mL) of the sauce over the turkey on each tortilla. Roll the tortillas into cylinders and place on the baking sheet, spacing them about 2 inches (5 cm) apart. Spoon the remaining sauce evenly over the tortillas and sprinkle with the cheese. Top each enchilada, if desired, with a few thin slices of jalapeño pepper. Bake for 20 to 25 minutes, or until heated through and the cheese is melted.

TURKEY SHEPHERD'S PIE with YUKON GOLD MASHED POTATOES

This twist on the classic casserole can be readied ahead, cooled and refrigerated, and then cooked later that day or the next. It also freezes very well unbaked.

preparation time • 30 minutes
cooking time • 30–40 minutes
makes • 6 servings

2½–3 lb (1.25–1.5 kg) Yukon Gold (yellow-fleshed) potatoes, peeled and quartered

2 Tbsp (30 mL) olive or vegetable oil

1½ lb (750 g) ground turkey

1 medium onion, finely chopped

1 small carrot, grated

2 garlic cloves, chopped

1 tsp (5 mL) dried thyme

2 Tbsp (30 mL) all-purpose flour

1 cup (250 mL) tomato sauce

1 cup (250 mL) chicken stock

1 cup (250 mL) frozen (thawed) peas

1 cup (250 mL) frozen (thawed) corn

salt, black pepper and Worcestershire sauce to taste

2 Tbsp (30 mL) butter

½–¾ cup (125–185 mL) milk

3–4 green onions, finely chopped

salt and freshly ground black pepper to taste

ERIC'S OPTIONS
Use other ground meats, such as beef or lamb, instead of turkey. For tangy potatoes, replace the milk with buttermilk.

Preheat the oven to 375°F (190°C). Boil the potatoes until very tender. While the potatoes are cooking, heat the oil in a large skillet over medium-high heat. Add the ground turkey, onion, carrot, garlic and thyme. Cook, stirring to break the turkey into small pieces, until the meat is cooked through. Stir in the flour, and then mix in the tomato sauce, stock, peas and corn. Season with salt, pepper and Worcestershire sauce. Bring just to a simmer, remove from the heat, and spoon into a 9- × 13-inch (23 × 33 cm) baking dish.

Mash the potatoes, and then whip in the butter, milk and green onions. Season the potatoes with salt and pepper. Spread or pipe the potatoes over the turkey mixture. (If you are making the shepherd's pie in advance, cool to room temperature, wrap and then refrigerate or freeze. If freezing, thaw in the refrigerator overnight before baking.) Bake the shepherd's pie for 30 to 40 minutes (a little longer if it has been refrigerated), until the potatoes are golden and the filling is bubbling.

SLOW COOKER SWEET-and-SOUR TURKEY MEATBALLS

Tender, Asian-style meatballs are simmered with bits of green bell pepper and chunks of golden pineapple. Serve the meatballs on steamed rice or Cashew Fried Rice (page 159).

1 lb (500 g) lean ground turkey

¼ cup (60 mL) dried breadcrumbs

1 large egg, beaten

2 tsp (10 mL) peeled, grated fresh ginger
(see About Fresh Ginger on page 264)

1 garlic clove, minced

½ tsp (2 mL) salt

freshly ground black pepper to taste

one 14 oz (398 mL) can tomato sauce

¼ cup (60 mL) ketchup

¼ cup (60 mL) rice vinegar

3 Tbsp (45 mL) honey

1 Tbsp (15 mL) soy sauce

2 tsp (10 mL) cornstarch

one 19 oz (540 mL) can unsweetened
pineapple chunks

1 medium green bell pepper, diced

2 green onions, thinly sliced

preparation time	•	35 minutes
slow-cooker time	•	6 hours
makes	•	4–6 servings

NOTE
This recipe is designed for a slow cooker with 4½ to 6½ quart (4.5 to 6.5 L) capacity.

ERIC'S OPTIONS
Make sweet, sour and spicy meatballs by adding hot Asian-style chili sauce, to taste, when mixing the tomato sauce and other liquid ingredients.

Preheat the oven to 375°F (190°C). Line a baking sheet with parchment paper.

Place the turkey, breadcrumbs, egg, ginger, garlic, salt and pepper in a bowl and mix to combine. Moisten your hands with cold water. Roll the meat mixture into 1½ inch (4 cm) balls and set on the prepared baking sheet. Roast for 20 minutes, or until cooked through.

Place the tomato sauce, ketchup, vinegar, honey, soy sauce and cornstarch in your slow cooker and whisk to combine. Add the meatballs, pineapple (fruit and juice) and bell pepper and gently swirl to combine. Cover and cook on the low setting for 6 hours, or until the meatballs are tender. Sprinkle servings of the meatballs with green onion.

ROAST TURKEY with HERBES de PROVENCE and BUTTER

Herbes de Provence is a French-style combination of herbs. Spread over the turkey before roasting, it gives the finished bird a wonderful flavor, aroma and appearance.

one 12–14 lb (5.5–6.3 kg) fresh or frozen (thawed) grade A or free-range turkey

3 Tbsp (45 mL) butter, softened

1 Tbsp (15 mL) herbes de Provence (see Note on page 250)

salt and freshly ground black pepper to taste

3½ cups (875 mL) chicken or turkey stock

⅓ cup (80 mL) all-purpose flour

preparation time • 20 minutes
cooking time • 2¾–3¼ hour
makes • 8 servings

ERIC'S OPTIONS
Before roasting, stuff the bird with Wh. Wheat Turkey Dressing with Apple and Bacon (page 329). For tips on stuffing bird, see A Guide to Preparing a Roast Turkey (page 272).

Preheat the oven to 325°F (160°C). Place the turkey in a roasting pan. Remove the neck and innards from the cavity. Place the neck in the roasting pan and discard the innards unless you want—and know how—to use them. Tie the legs together with string; fold and tuck the wings under the body. Combine the butter and herbes de Provence in a bowl. Brush over the surface of the turkey; season with salt and pepper. Roast the turkey uncovered for 1½ hours, and then give the roasting pan a 180-degree turn. Roast the turkey another 1 hour and 15 minutes.

Insert an instant-read meat thermometer deep into an inner thigh of the turkey, not touching the bone. If it reads 170°F (77°C), the turkey is ready. If not, baste the bird with the pan juices and roast 15 to 30 minutes more, or until the 170°F (77°C) temperature is achieved. Transfer the turkey and neck to a large platter, tent with foil and let it rest until you're ready to carve, at least 15 minutes.

To make the gravy, skim the fat from the pan drippings. Place the pan over medium-high heat. Add 3 cups (750 mL) of the stock and bring to a boil. Place the flour and the remaining ½ cup (125 mL) stock in a bowl and whisk until smooth. Whisk the mixture into the pan and simmer until the gravy thickens, about 5 minutes. Carve the turkey and serve the gravy in a sauceboat alongside.

A GUIDE TO PREPARING ROAST TURKEY

WHAT SIZE TO BUY

Many guides suggest allowing 1 lb (500 g) per person when buying turkey. If you're serving six people, however, it's unlikely you're going to find a 6 lb (2.7 kg) bird—tiny for a turkey. I recommend 1¼ to 1½ lb (625 to 750 g) per person, or even a little more if you want ample turkey leftovers from which to make sandwiches, soup and other dishes. Remember that the bigger the bird, the higher the meat-to-bone ratio tends to be, so it's safer to estimate less weight per person (1¼ lb/ 625 g) when buying a very large turkey, such as one that weighs over 20 lb (9 kg).

STORING AND THAWING

Buy fresh turkey a maximum of two to three days before you'll cook it and, if it's packed and sold at a supermarket, always check the best-before date. If buying a frozen bird, they tend to go on sale a few weeks before Thanksgiving and before Christmas, so buy it then and keep frozen until needed. Never thaw turkey on the kitchen counter at room temperature. The bird's exterior will thaw first and this may cause bacterial growth before the center of the turkey is thawed. The safest way is in the refrigerator. Allow 24 hours thawing time for every 5 lb (2.2 kg) of turkey, or even a bit more for very large birds. For example, a 12 to 14 lb (5.5 to 6.3 kg) turkey will take about three days to thaw.

TO STUFF OR NOT TO STUFF

You can make dressing for turkey and bake it separately from the bird as described in Whole Wheat Turkey Dressing with Apple and Bacon (page 329). It will taste delicious and can be made oven-ready ahead of time, and you won't have to worry about the process of safely stuffing it inside the turkey.

However, many prefer to stuff the bird, as it can enhance the flavor of mild-tasting turkey and also produce a richer-tasting dressing. Always stuff the bird just before you put it in the oven. Fill the main cavity, making sure it's loosely stuffed, not packed in. If you pack it in, it won't get hot enough to kill any bacteria present in the turkey. Also stuff the cavity behind the large flap of skin at the neck end of the bird. You can pack the dressing tighter here as it's closer to the heat. Any leftover stuffing can be baked in a casserole dish.

Remove the stuffing from the turkey as soon as the bird is cooked. Transfer to a heatproof serving dish and keep warm in the oven while the turkey rests before carving. If the stuffing does not feel hot, bake until it reaches a bacteria-killing 165°F (74°C) when tested with an instant-read thermometer.

TO BASTE OR NOT TO BASTE

Some folks put the turkey in the oven and don't open the door until it's done. Others occasionally baste it with the pan juices to keep the bird moist and give it a rich color. The more you open the oven door, however, the longer it will take for the turkey to cook.

I take an in-between approach. I let the turkey roast undisturbed until my first temperature check, which usually comes at a time when the bird is not quite cooked. Since I've opened the oven door to test the bird, it makes sense to baste it then as it will improve its color when it is fully cooked.

COOKING TIMES

The charts below are for cooking a whole turkey without basting at an oven temperature of 325°F to 350°F (160°C to 175°C), using a regular (not a convection) oven. If you look at the whole turkeys for sale at your supermarket, you'll notice that even if they are the same weight, they will not all be uniform in shape. Some birds will have thicker breasts, others longer, thinner legs, all of which can affect cooking time. That's why it is important to check for doneness about one hour before the end of the recommended roasting time. The turkey is done when an instant-read meat thermometer inserted deep into the inner thigh, not touching the bone, reads 170°F (77°C) for an unstuffed turkey or 175°F (80°C) for a stuffed one.

Continued . . .

A GUIDE TO PREPARING
ROAST TURKEY (*continued*)

Roasting times for an unstuffed turkey	
6–8 lb (2.7–3.5 kg)	2½–2¾ hours
8–10 lb (3.5–4.5 kg)	2¾–3 hours
10–12 lb (4.5–5.5 kg)	3–3¼ hours
12–16 lb (5.5–7.25 kg)	3¼–3½ hours
16–20 lb (7.25–9.0 kg)	3½–4½ hours
20–25 lb (9.0–11.25 kg)	4½–5 hours

Roasting times for a stuffed turkey	
6–8 lb (2.7–3.5 kg)	3–3½ hours
8–10 lb (3.5–4.5 kg)	3¼–3½ hours
10–12 lb (4.5–5.5 kg)	3½–3¾ hours
12–16 lb (5.5–7.25 kg)	3¾–4 hours
16–20 lb (7.25–9.0 kg)	4–5 hours
20–25 lb (9.0–11.25 kg)	5–6 hours

CARVING THE BIRD

After roasting, lift the turkey out of the pan and onto a large platter. Tent with foil and rest at least 15 minutes to set the juices (the turkey will stay hot a surprisingly long time). Use a sharp, thin-bladed carving knife to remove the leg and wing on one side of the turkey. Cut the leg into drumstick and thigh pieces; thinly slice meat from them. Carve the breast by making thin, slightly angled, vertical slices that run parallel to the breastbone. Repeat the process on the other side of the bird. Unless you're carving at the table, arrange the meat on a platter.

HANDLING LEFTOVERS

When the meal is done, remove any meat on the carcass as soon as you can. The cooked meat can be refrigerated for 2 to 3 days. You can also slice or dice the meat, put it in freezer bags or containers, and freeze for up to 2 months. To make turkey stock, break or cut the carcass into large chunks and place in a tall, large pot. Add a sliced onion, carrot, a celery stalk or two, a few whole black peppercorns, a pinch or two of dried thyme and 2 or 3 bay leaves. Add about 12 cups (3 L) of cold water, ensuring the bones are well covered. Gently simmer the stock (small bubbles should just break on the surface), uncovered, for 2 to 3 hours, or until a rich turkey taste is achieved. Add additional water during simmering, if necessary.

Strain the stock, cool and refrigerate. Remove any fat that has solidified on the surface. The stock is ready to use or be frozen for up to 2 months.

ROASTED TURKEY BREAST
with SAGE and PAN GRAVY

Serve the turkey with Buttermilk Yukon Gold Mashed Potatoes (page 349) and Cider-Glazed Brussels Sprouts (page 335). Any leftover turkey makes great sandwiches the next day.

preparation time • 15 minutes
cooking time • 75 minutes
makes • 6 servings

2½ lb (1.25 kg) boneless turkey breast roast

2 Tbsp (30 mL) melted butter

2 tsp (10 mL) dried crumbled sage

1 tsp (5 mL) coarsely ground black pepper

salt to taste

2½ cups (625 mL) chicken stock

3 Tbsp (45 mL) all-purpose flour

ERIC'S OPTIONS
To make mushroom gravy, melt 1 Tbsp (15 mL) of butter in a skillet over medium heat. Add ½ lb (250 g) of sliced white or brown mushrooms and cook until tender, about 5 minutes. Mix the mushrooms into the gravy just before serving.

Preheat the oven to 350°F (175°C). Place the turkey in a roasting pan. Brush with the melted butter and sprinkle with the sage, pepper and salt. Roast the turkey for 75 minutes, or until the center of the roast reaches 170°F (77°C) on an instant-read meat thermometer. Remove the turkey from the pan and set on a plate; loosely cover with foil and let it rest for 10 minutes before serving.

Meanwhile, drain the excess fat from the roasting pan and set the pan on the stovetop over medium-high heat. Whisk the stock and flour in a bowl until smooth. Add to the roasting pan and bring to a simmer, scraping the brown bits off the bottom of the pan to add taste and color to the gravy. Simmer until slightly thickened, about 4 to 5 minutes. Season with salt and pepper and transfer the gravy to a serving dish. Slice the turkey and serve the gravy alongside.

MEATS

BAKED HAM GLAZED with HONEY, MUSTARD and SPICE

It's hard to go wrong with a baked glazed ham. It's easy to cook because the ham sold in supermarkets, unless it's labeled as fresh raw ham, is fully cooked and simply needs to be heated through. This is where you can add your own tasty glazing. After the meal, there always seem to be some leftovers for making tasty sandwiches.

6–7 lb (2.7–3.15 kg) bone-in, shank portion ham (see Note)

⅓ cup (80 mL) liquid honey, warmed

3 Tbsp (45 mL) Dijon mustard

1 tsp (5 mL) pure vanilla extract

½ tsp (2 mL) ground cinnamon

¼ tsp (1 mL) ground nutmeg

¼ tsp (1 mL) ground cloves

preparation time	•	15 minutes
cooking time	•	1 hour
		55 minutes
makes	•	10–12 servings

NOTE
Ham comes from the back leg of the pig and often is cut into the shank portion (the lower part of the leg) and the hip portion (the upper part of the leg). I prefer the shank portion as it's meatier and easier to carve.

ERIC'S OPTIONS
Instead of honey, use an equal amount of maple syrup in the glazing mixture.

Preheat the oven to 325°F (160°C). Trim the ham of any tough outer skin and some of the excess fat, leaving a thin layer of the latter intact. Score the top of the ham in a diamond pattern, making shallow cuts 1 inch (2.5 cm) apart. Place the ham in a roasting pan and bake for 75 minutes. While the ham bakes, combine the honey, mustard, vanilla, cinnamon, nutmeg and cloves in a bowl.

When the ham has baked 75 minutes, brush it with half of the glaze and bake 20 minutes longer. Brush with the remaining glaze and bake a further 20 minutes. Remove from the oven, loosely cover with foil and let it rest for 10 to 15 minutes before carving it into thin slices.

ERIC'S
TOURTIÈRE

I serve my version of this classic French Canadian meat pie every Christmas Eve. Using a trio of ground meat gives it a more complex flavor. Make the filling the day before to allow the flavors to blend and develop. Serve the tourtière with pickled beets, mustard pickles, chutneys and relishes—homemade if you have them.

½ lb (250 g) ground veal

½ lb (250 g) ground pork

½ lb (250 g) ground beef

1 medium onion, diced

2 cloves garlic, chopped

1 tsp (5 mL) dried thyme

½ tsp (2 mL) ground cloves

1½ tsp (7 mL) ground cinnamon

2 Tbsp (30 mL) all-purpose flour

1¼ cups (310 mL) hot beef stock

1¼ cups (310 mL) water

1 cup (250 mL) small potato cubes, cooked firm-tender

1 Tbsp (15 mL) chopped fresh parsley

salt and black pepper to taste

one 9-inch (23 cm) deep-dish double crust pie shell
(see Flaky Pie Dough on page 375)

egg wash (1 large egg mixed with 2 Tbsp (30 mL) milk)

preparation time • 40 minutes
cooking time • 45–50 minutes
makes • 6–8 servings

ERIC'S OPTIONS
Use either a store-bought or homemade pie crust. You can make the tourtière and freeze it unbaked. Thaw in the refrigerator overnight before baking.

Place the meats, onion and garlic in a pot over medium heat. Cook until the meat is no longer pink, then drain away the fat. Add the thyme, cloves, cinnamon and flour and mix well. While stirring, slowly pour in the beef stock and water. Simmer until the liquid has almost evaporated, then mix in the potatoes and parsley. Season with salt and pepper. Remove from the heat, cool to room temperature and refrigerate overnight.

Preheat the oven to 425°F (220°C). Place the filling in the bottom pie crust. Brush the edges with egg wash. Place the top crust on, crimping the edges to seal. Decorate the top with extra pastry if desired. Brush the top of the pie with egg wash. Cut a small hole in the center of the top crust to allow steam to escape. Bake for 20 minutes. Reduce the heat to 350°F (175°C) and cook 25 to 30 minutes more. Allow the tourtière to sit for about 10 to 15 minutes before slicing.

OAK BAY
BAKED BEANS

For lack of a better name, I decided to call my version of baked beans after the area where I live. After placing my beans in the oven to bake one day, I went for my morning stroll. On the way back, at least a block from my house, I could smell their heavenly aroma wafting around the Oak Bay neighborhood. I made my beans with pork, but this is an excellent vegetarian dish without the meat.

preparation time	•	1¼–1½ hours (includes precooking the beans)
cooking time	•	3–4 hours
makes	•	8 servings as main course, 12 as a side dish

2 lb (1 kg) small white beans, presoaked
   if desired (see method and Note)

½ cup (125 mL) maple syrup

½ cup (125 mL) molasses

½ cup (125 mL) barbecue sauce

2 medium onions, chopped

2½ cups (625 mL) tomato sauce

2–3 tsp (10–15 mL) dry mustard

1 Tbsp (15 mL) Worcestershire sauce

2 bay leaves

1 small smoked pork hock or ½ lb (250 g)
   salt pork cut in 2 pieces (optional)

2 cups (500 mL) cold water

salt and freshly ground black pepper to taste

NOTE
The small white beans called for in this recipe are sometimes labeled white pea beans or navy beans. The older the beans, the longer they will take to cook. If they take forever to become tender, it's time to buy new ones. When purchasing beans, buy them from a location that sells a lot of them and therefore has a higher rate of turnover.

ERIC'S OPTIONS
The recipe can be halved. Try substituting lima beans or black-eyed peas for the small white beans. The time it takes to precook each legume will vary slightly.

Place the beans in a large pot and cover with 3–4 inches (8–10 cm) of cold water. Bring to a boil, then reduce the heat to a gentle simmer. Cover and cook until tender, but still slightly firm to the bite. If you've presoaked the beans overnight in cold water, this will take about 45 to 60 minutes. If you cook unsoaked beans, it will take about 60 to 75 minutes. Skim away any foam that rises to the top as the beans cook. Add more water during cooking if required.

Preheat the oven to 300°F (150°C). Drain the beans and transfer to a Dutch oven or casserole with a capacity of 16 to 20 cups (4 to 5 L). In a bowl, combine the maple syrup, molasses, barbecue sauce, onions, tomato sauce, mustard and Worcestershire sauce. Stir into the beans. Nestle in the bay leaves and the pork hock or salt pork, if desired. Pour the 2 cups (500 mL) cold water over the beans. Cover and bake for 3 to 4 hours, or until the beans are tender. Check the beans occasionally during cooking and add more water if they become too dry.

If you included the pork, remove it when the beans are finished cooking, cut the edible portions into pieces and mix them back in. Season the beans with salt and pepper.

GLAZED MEATLOAF
with ONION GRAVY

You can never have too many recipes for meatloaf. Here's my version; you can make it in a loaf pan or on a baking sheet.

THE GLAZE

½ cup (125 mL) sweet chili sauce or ketchup

2 Tbsp (30 mL) brown sugar

1 Tbsp (15 mL) red wine or cider vinegar

THE MEATLOAF

¾ lb (375 g) lean ground beef

¾ lb (375 g) ground pork

2 large eggs, beaten

4 green onions, finely chopped

2 garlic cloves, chopped

½ cup (125 mL) breadcrumbs

¼ cup (60 mL) milk

½ cup (125 mL) sweet chili sauce or ketchup

1 tsp (5 mL) dried thyme

1 tsp (5 mL) salt

1 tsp (5 mL) freshly ground black pepper

THE GRAVY

3 Tbsp (45 mL) butter or vegetable oil

1 medium onion, finely chopped

¼ cup (60 mL) flour

2½ cups (625 mL) hot beef stock

salt and freshly ground black pepper to taste

preparation time • 20 minutes
cooking time • 60–75 minut‹
makes • 4–6 servings

ERIC'S OPTIONS
Ground turkey could replace the beef and pork. Use barbecue sauce instead of sweet chili sauce or ketchup. Use ½ medium onion, finely chopped, instead of the green onions.

THE GLAZE
Combine all the ingredients in a small bowl.

THE MEATLOAF
Preheat the oven to 350°F (175°C). Place all the meatloaf ingredients in a bowl and gently mix to combine. Place the mixture in a nonstick or lightly oiled 9- × 5-inch (23 × 12.5 cm) loaf pan. (You could also shape it into a free-form loaf of similar size on a nonstick or parchment paper–lined baking sheet.) Spread the glaze ingredients over the meatloaf. Bake for 60 to 75 minutes, or until cooked through. A meat thermometer inserted in the center of the meatloaf should read 160°F (71°C).

THE GRAVY
When the meatloaf is almost done, you can make the gravy. Heat the butter or oil in a pot over medium to medium-high heat. Add the onion and cook until tender. Mix in the flour and cook until the mixture turns a very light brown. Slowly whisk in the beef stock. Simmer until thickened. Season with salt and pepper. Keep warm over low heat.

When the meatloaf is done, remove from the oven, cover and let it rest for 10 minutes. Drain any fat from the pan before unmolding the meatloaf. Slice and serve with the gravy alongside.

CHINESE-STYLE BARBECUE PORK

Fattier cuts of pork, such as those taken from the shoulder, are often used to make this dish. However, I like to use pork tenderloin because it's very tender, lean and easy to slice when cooked. Make the pork part of a three-dish Chinese-style meal by serving it with Green Bean Stir-Fry (page 182) and Cashew Fried Rice (page 159).

2 Tbsp (30 mL) soy sauce

2 Tbsp (30 mL) hoisin sauce

2 Tbsp (30 mL) ketchup

2 Tbsp (30 mL) honey

2 Tbsp (30 mL) Chinese rice wine, sherry or brandy

½ tsp (2 mL) five-spice powder

2 tsp (10 mL) sesame oil

2 garlic cloves, finely chopped

1 Tbsp (15 mL) chopped fresh ginger

2 whole pork tenderloin, trimmed of any fat and sinew

chopped green onions (optional) for garnish

preparation time •	10 minutes + marinating tir
cooking time •	40 minutes
makes •	8 servings

ERIC'S OPTIONS
This pork can also be sliced or diced and added to all sorts of Chinese dishes, such as fried rice, chow mein or wonton soup. This is something you may wish to do if you have any pork left over after serving it as an appetizer. Any leftover pork will freeze well.

Combine the soy and hoisin sauce, ketchup, honey, rice wine, sherry or brandy, five-spice powder, sesame oil, garlic and ginger in a sided dish just large enough to hold the pork. Add the pork and turn to coat. Cover and marinate in the refrigerator for 4 hours or overnight. When the pork is marinated, preheat the oven to 375°F (190°C). Place the pork on a rack set over an aluminum foil–lined baking sheet. Brush with half the remaining marinade in the bowl and roast for 20 minutes. Brush with the remaining marinade and roast for 20 minutes more, or until the pork is just cooked through. Place the pork on a plate and tent with aluminum foil; rest for 10 minutes to allow the pork's juices to set. Thinly slice the pork and arrange on a platter; sprinkle, if desired, with chopped greens onions and serve.

ROAST PORK with MCINTOSH APPLE SAUCE

A large leg roast might take over two hours to cook, but this lean, boneless pork loin roast cooks in an hour or a little more. You can come home from work, quickly get the roast in the oven and by the time you relax a bit and whip up a few vegetables to serve alongside, the meat is done. Any leftovers make delicious sandwiches for lunch the next day.

2½ lb (1.25 kg) boneless pork loin roast

2 Tbsp (30 mL) olive oil

1 tsp (5 mL) dried sage leaves (see Note on page 128)

½ tsp (2 mL) sweet paprika (see About Paprika on page 257)

salt and freshly ground black pepper to taste

McIntosh Apple Sauce to taste (see recipe on page 355)

preparation time • 25 minutes
cooking time • 60–70 minutes
makes • 6 servings

ERIC'S OPTIONS
Instead of sage, try another herb in this recipe, such as thyme or rosemary.

Preheat the oven to 450°F (230°C). Place the roast in a shallow roasting pan. Combine the oil, sage and paprika in a small bowl and brush over the pork. Sprinkle with salt and pepper. Roast for 20 minutes, and then reduce the heat to 325°F (160°C). Roast for 40 to 50 minutes more, or until the internal temperature reaches 160°F (71°C) on an instant-read meat thermometer inserted into the center of the roast. Remove from the oven, cover loosely with foil and allow to rest for 10 minutes. Cut into thin slices and serve the applesauce alongside.

HAWAIIAN-STYLE RIBS

Chinese immigrants introduced their style of cooking ribs to Hawaiians, and it quickly became very popular around the island chain. In this version, the ribs are cut into single-bone pieces perfect for snacking on.

preparation time • 15 minutes
cooking time • 1½ hours
makes • 6 servings

½ cup (125 mL) soy sauce

½ cup (125 mL) ketchup

¼ cup (60 mL) honey

1 tsp (5 mL) five-spice powder

1 tsp (5 mL) coarsely cracked black peppercorns

1-inch (2.5 cm) piece fresh ginger, peeled and chopped (see About Fresh Ginger on page 264)

¼ cup (60 mL) dry sherry

2 garlic cloves, crushed

3 lb (1.5 kg) pork side or back ribs, trimmed well and cut into 4- to 6-bone racks (see About Pork Ribs on page 291)

ERIC'S OPTIONS
To give these ribs a more complex Chinese-style flavor, replace ½ the ketchup with hoisin sauce. For a spicy kick, mix in Asian-style hot chili sauce to taste when combining the other marinade ingredients.

Combine the soy sauce, ketchup, honey, five-spice powder, peppercorns, ginger, sherry and garlic in a large bowl. Add the ribs and turn to coat. Cover, marinate and refrigerate for 4 hours or overnight, turning occasionally.

Preheat the oven to 325°F (160°C). Place the ribs in a single layer, meaty side up, in a shallow baking pan. Pour in 1 cup (250 mL) of water. Brush half the marinade left in the bowl over the ribs; store the remaining marinade in the refrigerator. Cover and bake the ribs for 1 hour. Uncover and brush the ribs with the remaining marinade. Bake, uncovered, for 30 minutes more, or until the ribs are tender and nicely glazed. Turn the oven to broil; broil the ribs for a few minutes to glaze and deepen their color. Remove from the oven and cool the ribs for a few minutes before cutting each rack into single-bone pieces. Arrange on a platter, spoon some of the pan juices overtop and serve.

PORK RIBS with CHIPOTLE BARBECUE SAUCE

After the initial oven cooking to tenderize, these flavorful ribs are grilled, sauced and finished off on the barbecue. Try them with corn on the cob and Southern-style Brown Rice Salad, page 98.

preparation time • 20 minutes
cooking time • about 2 hour
makes • 4 servings

2 large whole racks pork side ribs
    (see About Pork Ribs on page 291)

salt and freshly ground black pepper to taste

1¾ cups (435 mL) beer

2 Tbsp (30 mL) olive oil

1 medium onion, finely chopped

2 garlic cloves, finely chopped

2 chipotle peppers, finely chopped, (see Note)

1½ cups (375 mL) ketchup

2 tsp (10 mL) chili powder

2 tsp (10 mL) dry mustard

3 Tbsp (45 mL) packed brown sugar

2 Tbsp (30 mL) red wine vinegar

2 tsp (10 mL) Worcestershire sauce

salt to taste

ERIC'S OPTIONS
For added color and flavor, sprinkle the ribs once on the plate with sliced green onion or chopped fresh cilantro.

NOTE
Chipotle peppers are smoked jalapeño peppers. They are sold in tins in the Mexican foods aisle of most supermarkets. Refrigerate any leftover peppers in a tightly sealed jar; they keep for a few weeks. Use them in chilis, sauces and Tex-Mex dishes.

Preheat the oven to 325°F (160°C). Cut the racks in half. Lay them in a single layer in a baking dish. Season generously with salt and pepper and pour in 1 cup (250 mL) of the beer. Cover and bake for 115 minutes, or until the ribs are quite tender, but still holding their shape.

While the ribs are cooking, heat the oil in a pot over medium heat. And the onion and garlic and cook until tender, about 4 minutes. Stir in the remaining ingredients, including the three-quarter cup (185 mL) of remaining beer. Bring the sauce to a gentle simmer, adjusting the heat downward to maintain that simmer. Partially cover and simmer 30 minutes, stirring occasionally, until rich and tasty, then remove from the heat. Thin the sauce with a little water if it thickens overly.

Preheat your barbecue to medium-high. Grill the ribs on both sides for a few minutes to accent their color. Set the ribs meaty side up and thickly brush with some of the chipotle barbecue sauce. Cook for 5 to 10 minutes more, or until nicely glazed. Serve any remaining sauce in a bowl and let diners spoon it on to their ribs tableside.

ABOUT PORK RIBS

The two main types of pork ribs available for sale are back ribs and side ribs, also called spare ribs. Back ribs are cut from the pork loin, the same portion of the pig that pork chops come from. These ribs are fairly lean and have a generous amount of meat between the bones, which explains why they're more costly.

Side ribs are taken from the side (belly) of the animal. They contain more bone than meat and are fairly fatty and should be trimmed well before cooking. However, cooks are attracted to side ribs because they know that the bones and fat enhance the flavor of the meat as it cooks. St. Louis–style ribs are pork side ribs with the brisket bone removed. This creates a long, even rack of ribs popular for slow cooking on the barbecue.

SLOW COOKER BARBECUE PORK BACK RIBS with BOURBON

To quickly get the ribs cooking in the morning, trim and grill them the night before, cool to room temperature and refrigerate overnight. Serve the ribs with baked potatoes, pickles and Sweet and Tangy Six-Vegetable Coleslaw (page 76).

2 Tbsp (30 mL) chili powder

1 Tbsp (15 mL) ground cumin

½ tsp (2 mL) cayenne pepper

½ tsp (2 mL) salt

3 medium-sized racks pork back ribs, trimmed of excess fat and cut into 2- to 3-rib portions

1¾ cups (435 mL) barbecue sauce

¾ cup (185 mL) bourbon

¾ cup (185 mL) apple juice

3 Tbsp (45 mL) apple cider vinegar

2 Tbsp (30 mL) honey

preparation time • 20 minutes
slow-cooker time • 8 hours
makes • 4–6 servings

NOTE
This recipe is designed for a slow cooker with 4½ to 6½ quart (4.5 to 6.5 L) capacity.

ERIC'S OPTIONS
Replace the pork back ribs with 2½ lb (1.25 kg) of pork side ribs, well trimmed and cut into 2- to 3-rib portions.

Preheat an indoor or outdoor grill to medium-high. Combine the chili powder, cumin, cayenne and salt in a small bowl; rub the mixture on the ribs. Lightly oil the bars of your grill and cook the ribs for 3 to 4 minutes per side, or until nicely seared but not cooked through.

Place the ribs in the slow cooker. Combine the remaining ingredients in a bowl and pour over the ribs. Cover and cook on the low setting for 8 hours.

CRISPY OVEN-BAKED PORK CUTLETS

Mayonnaise, which in this recipe replaces the more common flour and egg coating that is used to ensure the crumb coating adheres, gives these cutlets a tangy flavor and helps them stay moist. Serve the cutlets with store-bought or McIntosh Apple Sauce (page 355).

2 Tbsp (30 mL) vegetable oil

¾ cup (185 mL) cornflake crumbs

½ tsp (2 mL) ground sage

¼ tsp (1 mL) paprika

pinch cayenne pepper (optional)

salt and freshly ground black pepper to taste

¼ cup (60 mL) mayonnaise

four 5 or 6 oz (150 or 175 g) pork cutlets

preparation time • 15 minutes
cooking time • 10–12 minutes
makes • 4 servings

ERIC'S OPTIONS
Instead of pork, use turkey or veal cutlets. Plain breadcrumbs can replace the cornflake crumbs.

Preheat the oven to 450°F (230°C). Line a baking sheet with parchment paper and brush with the oil. Combine the cornflake crumbs, sage, paprika, cayenne (if using), salt and pepper in a shallow dish and mix well. Evenly coat each pork cutlet with a thin layer of mayonnaise and place on the crumb mixture. Coat on all sides, gently pressing on the crumbs to help them adhere. Place on the prepared baking sheet. Bake for 5 minutes, then flip the cutlets over and bake for another 5 to 7 minutes, or until just cooked through, with just a hint of pale pink in the middle.

SLOW COOKER PULLED PORK SANDWICHES

I'm not going to say this pork is as good as if it had been cooked over a wood-fired barbecue pit, but it is slow-cooked, very succulent and dripping with barbecue sauce. Serve the sandwiches with pickles, Sweet and Tangy Six-Vegetable Coleslaw (page 76) and Crispy Oven Fries (page 351).

1½ cups (375 mL) barbecue sauce

1¼ cups (310 mL) lager beer or chicken stock

¼ cup (60 mL) packed golden brown sugar

¼ cup (60 mL) apple cider vinegar

2 tsp (10 mL) sweet paprika (see About Paprika on page 257)

2 tsp (10 mL) chili powder

2 tsp (10 mL) ground cumin

1 tsp (5 mL) salt

3 lb (1.5 kg) boneless pork shoulder roast

2 Tbsp (30 mL) olive oil

8 hamburger buns or large crusty rolls, split and warmed

Place the barbecue sauce, beer, brown sugar and vinegar in your slow cooker and whisk to combine. On a wide plate, mix together the paprika, chili powder, cumin and salt. Set the pork on the plate and roll it to coat evenly with the spice mix.

preparation time	•	15 minutes
slow-cooker time	•	8 hours
finishing time	•	20 minutes
makes	•	8 sandwiche

NOTE
This recipe is designed for a slow cooker with 4½ to 6½ quart (4.5 to 6.5 L) capacity.

ERIC'S OPTIONS
Instead of sandwiches, make pulled pork burritos by rolling the meat in tortillas with diced onion, shredded lettuce and grated Monterey Jack cheese.

Place the oil in a large skillet set over medium-high heat. Add the pork and sear on all sides. Set the pork in the slow cooker, turning it to coat with the sauce. Cover and cook on the low setting for 8 hours, or until very tender. Remove the pork from the sauce and set it in a bowl. Skim off any fat from the surface of the sauce, then cover and keep the sauce warm in the slow cooker.

When the pork is cool enough to handle, shred it with 2 forks. Add the meat to the sauce, cover and heat through for 10 minutes. Pile the pork into the buns and serve.

HOW TO SEAR MEAT PROPERLY

If you've ever wondered why those pork chops or cubes of stewing beef you were hoping to turn a rich brown seem to steam rather than sear in the skillet, you've likely made a few simple missteps during the process. Prepackaged meats, including pork, beef, veal and chicken, may have small pools of liquid in the package. If you want the meat to sear properly, you need to get rid of any moisture on the meat before cooking. To do so, simply pat the meat dry with a paper towel.

Once that's done, you can still end up with meat that does not properly sear if you add it to the skillet before the latter is properly heated. If you add the meat when the skillet and oil are only slightly warm, there's not much chance of it quickly searing and browning nicely.

Lastly, even if you add the meat to a nice hot skillet, if you add too much at once, it still won't brown properly as the skillet will cool down. Also, any moisture in the meat will not have a chance to evaporate, which will cause the meat to steam, rather than sear.

SLOW COOKER OSSO BUCCO
with GREMOLATA

This succulent, slow-cooked veal shank is sprinkled with gremolata, a palate-awakening parsley, citrus zest and garlic mixture. I like to serve this with something that will blend tastily with the sauce, such as creamy polenta or Saffron Risotto (page 162).

four 7–8 oz (200–250 g) veal shanks

salt and freshly ground black pepper to taste

¼ cup (60 mL) all-purpose flour

3 Tbsp (45 mL) olive oil

1 small onion, finely diced

1 large celery stalk, finely diced

1 small carrot, finely diced

2–3 garlic cloves, minced

2 tsp (10 mL) dried sage leaves (see Note on page 128)

28 oz (796 mL) can diced tomatoes

½ cup (125 mL) dry white wine

2 Tbsp (30 mL) tomato paste

1 bay leaf

6 sprigs Italian parsley

1 garlic clove, thickly sliced

1 tsp (5 mL) grated lemon zest

1 tsp (5 mL) grated orange zest

preparation time • 30 minutes
slow-cooker time • 7–8 hours
finishing time • 1–2 minutes
makes • 4 servings

NOTE
This recipe is designed for a slow cooker with 4½ to 6½ quart (4.5 to 6.5 L) capacity.

ERIC'S OPTIONS
Make lamb osso bucco by replacing the veal shanks with lamb shanks.

Season the veal with salt and pepper, then coat in the flour, shaking off any excess. Place the oil in a large skillet and set over medium-high heat. When hot, add the veal and brown deeply on both sides. Set the veal in your slow cooker.

Add the onion, celery and carrot to the skillet and cook for 2 to 3 minutes. Add the garlic and sage and cook for 1 minute more. Add the diced tomatoes, wine, tomato paste and bay leaf, bring to a simmer and pour over the veal. Cover and cook the veal on the low setting for 7 to 8 hours, or until very tender.

For the gremolata, finely chop the parsley, sliced garlic clove, lemon zest and orange zest together.

To serve, carefully lift the veal shanks out of the slow cooker and set 1 on each of 4 plates. Skim off any fat from the sauce, then taste and add salt and pepper, if needed. Top the veal with some of the sauce and sprinkle with gremolata to serve.

LAMB CHOPS with BLACKCURRANT SAUCE

Sweet, sour and spicy flavors accent the lamb in this vibrant dish. To complete a spring feast, serve these chops with small, new potatoes, baby carrots and asparagus.

4–6 lamb chops

salt to taste

1 Tbsp (15 mL) olive oil

1 Tbsp (15 mL) finely chopped shallot or onion

1 Tbsp (15 mL) balsamic vinegar

1 tsp (5 mL) freshly ground black pepper

¼ cup (60 mL) blackcurrant jelly or jam

¼ cup (60 mL) red wine

1 Tbsp (15 mL) chopped fresh mint

preparation time	•	5 minutes
cooking time	•	10 minutes
makes	•	2 servings

ERIC'S OPTIONS
Use ½ tsp (2 mL) dried mint instead of the fresh herb. Add it when you add the other sauce ingredients to the pan.

Season the lamb with salt. Heat the oil in a small skillet over medium-high heat. Cook the lamb for 2 to 3 minutes per side, until it is nicely browned and partially cooked. Remove from the skillet and set aside.

Place the shallot or onion in the skillet and cook for 1 minute. Add the vinegar, pepper, jelly or jam and wine, and simmer until the sauce thickens slightly. Sprinkle in the mint and return the lamb to the pan. Cook 3 to 4 minutes more, turning the chops. Divide the lamb between two plates. Top with the sauce and serve.

LEMONY LAMB CHOPS with ARTICHOKES, OLIVES and MINT

Serve this one-pan lamb dish with boiled new potatoes and boiled orzo, a small, rice-shaped pasta.

12 lamb chops, trimmed of excess fat

salt and freshly ground black pepper to taste

2–3 Tbsp (30–45 mL) olive oil

one 14 oz (398 mL) can quartered artichoke hearts

⅓ cup (80 mL) whole black olives

⅓ cup (80 mL) whole green olives

1 grated zest and juice of lemon

1 cup (250 mL) white wine or chicken stock

2 Tbsp (30 mL) chopped fresh mint

lemon slices for garnish

preparation time • 20 minutes
cooking time • 22 minutes
makes • 4–6 servings

ERIC'S OPTIONS

For another hit of flavor, add ¼ cup (60 mL) of coarsely chopped sun-dried tomatoes to the casserole along with the artichokes and olives.

Preheat the oven to 450°F (230°C). Season the lamb with salt and pepper. Heat the oil in a large skillet over medium-high heat and quickly brown the lamb on both sides. Transfer the chops to a casserole large enough to hold them in a single layer. Arrange the artichokes and olives around the lamb. Top with the lemon zest and juice. Pour in the wine or stock. Cover and bake for 20 minutes, or until the lamb reaches the desired degree of doneness. Uncover and sprinkle with the chopped mint. Garnish with lemon slices and serve.

ROAST RACK of LAMB for TWO

This tender lamb has an irresistible mustard and herb crust and a delicious red wine sauce that's perfect for a special dinner. Use a good wine to make it and enjoy the remainder with the meal! Serve with boiled small potatoes tossed with chopped fresh mint and Roasted Asparagus with Peppers and Pine Nuts (page 341).

preparation time • 20 minutes
cooking time • 27–35 minute
makes • 2 servings

2 Tbsp (30 mL) dried breadcrumbs

1 tsp (5 mL) herbes de Provence (see Note on page 250)

¼ tsp (1 mL) salt

¼ tsp (1 mL) freshly ground black pepper

one 8-rib frenched lamb rack (see Note)

1 Tbsp (15 mL) Dijon mustard

¼ cup (60 mL) red wine

¾ cup (185 mL) beef stock

1 Tbsp (15 mL) all-purpose flour

NOTE
Frenched lamb racks, with the rib bones exposed and the outer fat cap removed, are sold at most supermarkets and butcher shops.

ERIC'S OPTIONS
Give the sauce a sweeter taste by using port instead of red wine. If you prefer a coarser texture, coat the lamb with wholegrain Dijon mustard instead of smooth Dijon. Use 1 tsp (5 mL) chopped fresh rosemary to flavor the lamb instead of herbes de Provence.

Preheat the oven to 400°F (200°C). Combine the breadcrumbs, herbes de Provence, salt and pepper on a plate. Cut the lamb into two 4-rib racks. Brush the top and sides of the lamb with the mustard.

Dip the mustard-coated portions of the lamb in the breadcrumb mixture, pressing the crumbs on to help them adhere. Set the lamb in a small roasting pan. Roast for 22 to 25 minutes for rare; 25 to 28 minutes for medium-rare; and 30 minutes for medium. Transfer the lamb to a plate, cover loosely with foil and let rest for 5 minutes.

Meanwhile, place the roasting pan on the stovetop over medium-high heat. Add the wine and cook until reduced by half. Whisk the stock and flour together until smooth in a small bowl; add to the pan. Simmer until it forms a thickened sauce, about 2 minutes. To serve, pour a pool of sauce on each dinner plate and set the lamb racks on top.

SLOW COOKER LAMB CURRY with POTATOES and PEAS

Serve this coconut milk–based, tomatoey lamb curry with steamed basmati rice, Fresh Mint Chutney (page 358) and pappadums. Pappadums, which are great for dunking into the curry, are a wafer-thin, Indian-style flatbread sold at Indian food stores and most supermarkets. Simple cooking instructions are on the box.

3 Tbsp (45 mL) vegetable oil

1½ lb (750 g) cubed stewing lamb

salt and freshly ground black pepper to taste

1 medium onion, diced

2 Tbsp (30 mL) all-purpose flour

1 Tbsp (15 mL) mild, medium or hot curry powder

½ tsp (2 mL) sweet paprika (see About Paprika on page 257)

one 14 oz (398 mL) can regular or light coconut milk

one 28 oz (796 mL) can diced tomatoes

2 medium white-skinned potatoes (unpeeled), cubed

2 Tbsp (30 mL) golden brown sugar

1 cup (250 mL) frozen peas

2 Tbsp (30 mL) chopped fresh cilantro or mint

preparation time	•	20 minutes
slow-cooker time	•	6–8 hours
finishing time	•	5 minutes
makes	•	6 servings

NOTE
This recipe is designed for a slow cooker with 4½ to 6½ quart (4.5 to 6.5 L) capacity.

ERIC'S OPTIONS
Make chicken curry with potatoes and peas by replacing the lamb with an equal weight of boneless, skinless chicken thigh, cubed. The chicken won't take as long to cook, so reduce the cooking time to 5 to 6 hours.

Place the oil in a large skillet set over medium-high heat. Season the lamb with salt and pepper. Brown the lamb in batches, setting the cooked pieces in your slow cooker as you go. Add the onion to the skillet and cook for 2 to 3 minutes. Mix in the flour, curry powder and paprika and cook for 1 minute more. Slowly, while stirring, mix in the coconut milk. Add the diced tomatoes, potatoes and brown sugar, bring to a simmer and pour over the lamb. Cover and cook on the low setting for 6 to 8 hours, or until the lamb is tender. Mix in the peas and cilantro or mint. Cover and cook for 5 minutes more, or until the peas are heated through.

BRAISED LAMB SHANKS with HOT MUSTARD and WHISKY

Rich-tasting lamb made even more rich-tasting by slowly braising it in a full-flavored mix of ingredients, including spicy mustard and smoky-tasting whisky. Try serving the lamb over Mashed Rutabagas with Buttermilk and Parsley (page 340).

preparation time	•	20 minutes
cooking time	•	about 2¾ hours
makes	•	6 servings

3 Tbsp (45 mL) vegetable oil

6 lamb shanks, each about 10 oz (300 g)

salt and freshly ground black pepper to taste

1 medium onion, halved and thinly sliced

2–3 garlic cloves, chopped

one 28 oz (796 mL) can diced tomatoes

1 cup (250 mL) beef stock mixed with 2 Tbsp (30 mL) flour

½ cup (125 mL) Scotch whisky

3 Tbsp (45 mL) tomato paste

3 Tbsp (45 mL) brown sugar

3 Tbsp (45 mL) hot English-style mustard

1 Tbsp (15 mL) chopped fresh rosemary

ERIC'S OPTIONS
Instead of lamb shanks, use 6 meaty veal shanks in this recipe. The method and cooking time remain the same.

Preheat the oven to 325°F (160°C). Heat the oil in a large skillet over medium-high heat. Season the lamb with salt and pepper. Deeply brown the lamb on all sides and place in a single layer in a large casserole dish. Combine the remaining ingredients in a bowl. Pour over the lamb. Cover and braise the lamb in the oven for 2½ hours, or until the meat is very tender. Skim any fat from the surface of the lamb. Serve the lamb with the sauce on individual plates.

ROAST LEG of LAMB
with MINT PESTO CRUST

There's no mint jelly in this updated version of roast lamb. Instead, the juicy meat is lusciously crusted and flavored with mint pesto—a rich, forest-green paste made by puréeing fresh mint with olive oil, garlic, Parmesan cheese and pine nuts.

preparation time	•	25 minutes
cooking time	•	depends on desired doneness
makes	•	8 servings

1½ cups (375 mL) loosely packed fresh mint leaves

½ cup (125 mL) pine nuts

⅓ cup (80 mL) freshly grated Parmesan cheese

½ cup (125 mL) extra virgin olive oil

4 medium garlic cloves, sliced

one 5–7 lb (2.2–3.15 kg) leg of lamb

coarse sea salt and freshly ground black pepper to taste

¼ cup (60 mL) dried breadcrumbs

3 cups (750 mL) beef stock

ERIC'S OPTIONS
For a quicker and easier-to-make pesto, mix 1 cup (250 mL) of store-bought basil pesto in a bowl with ¼ cup (60 mL) chopped fresh mint. Thin the pesto with a little extra virgin olive oil if too thick.

Preheat the oven to 450°F (230°C). Place the mint, pine nuts, cheese, oil and garlic in a food processor and pulse until well combined. Place the lamb, fatty side up, in a large, shallow roasting pan. Spread the pesto on the top and sides of the lamb. Sprinkle with the salt, pepper and breadcrumbs. Roast the lamb for 20 minutes, and then reduce the heat to 325°F (160°C) and cook to the desired doneness (see Lamb Roasting Guide, page 307). Set the lamb on a platter, tent with foil and let it rest for 15 minutes.

While the lamb rests, make jus to serve with it. Remove excess fat from the roasting pan, place the pan on the stovetop and pour in the beef stock. Bring to a simmer, scraping the bottom of the pan to get the brown bits off the bottom; simmer 5 minutes.

Carve the lamb and arrange the meat on a warmed platter. Serve the jus in a sauceboat for drizzling on top of the meat.

LAMB ROASTING GUIDE

The roasting times below factor in the 15 minutes the lamb rests to set the juices after it's removed from the oven, during which time the lamb continues to cook. Because lamb legs can vary in thickness, an instant-read meat thermometer, sold at most stores selling kitchenware, is the best tool to use to gauge doneness. Insert it into the center of the thickest part of the leg to gauge how the lamb is progressing.

RARE Allow 20 minutes per pound (500 g). Internal temperature of the lamb should be 125°F to 130°F (50°C to 55°C) before you remove it from the oven.

MEDIUM RARE Allow 20 to 25 minutes per pound (500 g). Internal temperature should be 130°F to 135°F (55°C to 57°C) before you remove it from the oven.

MEDIUM Allow 25 minutes per pound (500 g). Internal temperature should be 140°F (60°C) before you remove it from the oven.

WELL DONE Allow 30 minutes per pound (500 g). Internal temperature should be 150°F (65°C) before you remove it from the oven.

HOW TO CARVE A WHOLE LEG OF LAMB

If the meat has been tied with string, remove it after the lamb has rested. Make sure the leg is sitting on your cutting board fat side up. Insert a meat fork into the narrow, shank end of the leg and lift the lamb up at a 45-degree angle away from you. Using a sharp, thin carving knife, cut the meat into thin slices starting at the thicker, hip end of the leg. If your butcher has not removed the hip, or hitch bone, from the leg, you will have to make the slices more parallel to the leg bone. Continue slicing until you reach the joint where the lower and upper leg bones meet. Carefully move up the leg and cut thin slices from the shank end of the leg, where the meat is quite succulent. Turn the leg over and slice the meat from that side of the leg.

SLOW COOKER VEAL MEATBALLS
in TOMATO SAUCE with BASIL

The milk helps to give these meatballs a more delicate texture, and the basil adds a lively, fresh flavor and wonderful green color. Serve the meatballs on cooked pasta, such as spaghetti or rigatoni.

preparation time • 30 minutes
slow-cooker time • 6–8 hours
makes • 4–6 servings

1¼ lb (625 g) ground veal

⅓ cup (80 mL) dried breadcrumbs

2 Tbsp (30 mL) milk

1 large egg, beaten

1–2 garlic cloves, minced

1 tsp (5 mL) salt, plus some to taste

½ tsp (2 mL) freshly ground black pepper, plus some to taste

one 28 oz (796 mL) can diced tomatoes

one 14 oz (398 mL) can crushed tomatoes

½ cup (125 mL) red wine or beef stock

½ tsp (2 mL) sugar

pinch crushed chili flakes

¼ cup (60 mL) chopped fresh basil

NOTE
This recipe is designed for a slow cooker with 4½ to 6½ quart (4.5 to 6.5 L) capacity.

ERIC'S OPTIONS
Make open-faced meatball sandwiches by piling these meatballs onto thick slices of Italian bread. For deluxe meatball sandwiches, scoop these meatballs onto Roasted Garlic Bread (page 374). Make beef meatballs by replacing the veal with ground beef.

Preheat the oven to 375°F (190°C). Line a baking sheet with parchment paper. Place the veal, breadcrumbs, milk, egg, garlic, salt and pepper in a bowl and mix to combine. Moisten your hands with cold water. Roll the meat mixture into 1½ inch (4 cm) balls and set on the prepared baking sheet. Roast for 20 minutes, or until cooked through.

Place the diced tomatoes, crushed tomatoes, wine or stock, sugar and chili flakes in your slow cooker and stir to combine. Drain off any fat from the meatballs and add them to the sauce. Cover and cook on the low setting for 6 to 8 hours, or until the meatballs are tender. Gently stir the fresh basil into the meatballs and serve.

CHERYL'S BEEF and POTATO MOUSSAKA

This is my wife's delicious rendition of the classic Greek dish. She serves it with Greek salad and warm pita bread.

1½ lb (750 g) lean ground beef

1 large onion, finely chopped

2 garlic cloves, crushed

one 5½ oz (156 mL) can tomato paste

¾ cup (185 mL) water

¼ cup (60 mL) chopped fresh parsley

1 tsp (5 mL) dried mint

1 tsp (5 mL) ground cinnamon

salt and freshly ground black pepper to taste

8 medium white potatoes

¼ cup (60 mL) butter

¼ cup (60 mL) all-purpose flour

2 cups (500 mL) milk

4 large eggs

½ cup (125 mL) freshly grated Parmesan cheese

salt and freshly ground black pepper to taste

preparation time • 40 minutes
cooking time • 60–70 minutes
makes • 6–8 servings

ERIC'S OPTIONS
You can make this with ground lamb instead of beef or use thin slices of eggplant instead of potatoes.

Preheat the oven to 375°F (190°C). Place the meat, onion and garlic in a pot and cook over medium heat, stirring frequently, until the meat is no longer pink. Drain off the fat. Add the tomato paste, water, parsley, mint, cinnamon, salt and pepper. Simmer until thickened, about 10 minutes. Remove from the heat and set aside. Peel the potatoes and slice them thinly. Place the slices in cold water as you work.

For the moussaka sauce, melt the butter in a pot over medium heat. Add the flour and stir and cook until it's absorbed by the butter. Slowly whisk in the milk. Simmer, stirring, just until the sauce thickens. Remove from the heat. Beat the eggs to a slight froth in a bowl. Mix ½ cup (125 mL) of the white sauce into the eggs, whisking constantly until well combined. Whisk this mixture back into the white sauce in the pot. Mix 6 Tbsp (90 mL) of the Parmesan cheese into the mixture. Season to taste with salt and pepper.

To assemble the moussaka, lightly butter a 9- x 13-inch (23 x 33 cm) baking dish. Drain the potatoes well and arrange half the slices in the bottom of the dish. Pour half the moussaka sauce over the potatoes. Top with the meat mixture. Place the remaining potatoes over the meat and top with the remaining moussaka sauce. Sprinkle with the remaining 2 Tbsp (30 mL) Parmesan cheese. Bake for 60 to 70 minutes, or until the potatoes are tender and the top is browned. Test for doneness by inserting the point of a small knife in the center of the moussaka to see if the potatoes are cooked. Let the moussaka rest for 10 minutes to allow it to set before cutting into serving portions.

POT ROAST BRAISED
with PORT and ROSEMARY

Pot roast is not the most exciting dish around. But this one, thanks to flavor-enhancing ingredients such as port, Dijon mustard and shallots, is robust and rewarding. It is also relatively inexpensive to make and cooks in one pan.

2 Tbsp (30 mL) vegetable oil

2½–3 lb (1.25–1.5 kg) chuck, blade or baron of
    beef roast, trimmed of excess fat

salt and freshly ground black pepper to taste

2 cups (500 mL) beef stock

1 cup (250 mL) port

1 Tbsp (15 mL) chopped fresh rosemary

2 Tbsp (30 mL) Dijon mustard

1 Tbsp (15 mL) Worcestershire sauce

1 bay leaf

3 cloves garlic, peeled and sliced

¼ cup (60 mL) all-purpose flour

½ cup (125 mL) water

1 lb (500 g) baby carrots

12 small shallots, peeled

4 medium white potatoes, cut in quarters

chopped green onion or fresh parsley to taste (optional)

preparation time • 30–40 minutes
cooking time • 2¼–2½ hours
makes • 4–6 servings

ERIC'S OPTIONS
For a touch of spiciness, add 2–3 Tbsp (30–45 mL) of green peppercorns to the pot when you add the port. You could replace the shallots with 2 medium onions, halved and sliced. If you don't have fresh rosemary, use 1 tsp (5 mL) dried.

Preheat the oven to 325°F (160°C). Heat the oil in a large Dutch oven or deep-sided roasting pan over medium-high heat. Season the roast with salt and pepper and brown it on all sides. Remove it from the pan and set aside. Drain the excess fat from the pan.

Add the stock, port, rosemary, mustard, Worcestershire sauce, bay leaf and garlic to the pan and bring to a simmer. In a small bowl, blend the flour and water and slowly whisk it into the simmering mixture. Cook until the sauce thickens. Return the roast to the pot. Cover and cook in the oven for 1¾ hours, turning once. Add the carrots, shallots and potatoes. If the sauce is too thick, add a little water. Cover and cook 30 to 45 minutes more, or until the vegetables and beef are tender.

Remove the meat from the pot, cover and let rest for 10 minutes. With a slotted spoon, scoop out the vegetables and arrange them on one side of a platter. Slice the beef and place it on the other side. Sprinkle with chopped green onions or fresh parsley, if using. Ladle the sauce into a gravy boat and serve it alongside.

BRAISING AND STEWING MEAT

Braising and stewing are cooking methods designed to cook tougher cuts of meat to a succulent tenderness.

To braise meat, first sear it, then add a small amount of flavored liquid, cover tightly and cook at a low temperature for a long period of time. The meat should be surrounded by the liquid, not immersed in it. Steam released from the liquid flavors and tenderizes the meat. It's important to have a tight lid, but additional liquid is sometimes required during the long cooking process. Braised meats are most often roasts or individual portions, such as lamb shanks.

For stewing, sear the meat and then entirely cover it in the stewing liquid. The meat is most often cut into bite-sized pieces and requires less cooking time. Both braising and stewing can be done on the stovetop or in the oven. For both methods, most often, I do the initial browning on the stovetop and finish the cooking in the oven. It cooks more evenly, won't stick or burn on the bottom, and allows me to do other things while the meat cooks.

SOUTHERN-STYLE SHORT RIBS

Roasting short ribs in a hot oven before braising helps render away the excess fat. Serve with Buttermilk Biscuits (page 366) to soak up the delectable sauce.

preparation time • 30 minutes
cooking time • 2–2½ hours
makes • 4 servings

2 tsp (10 mL) ground cumin

2 tsp (10 mL) chili powder

1 tsp (5 mL) ground coriander

1 tsp (5 mL) dried thyme

1 tsp (5 mL) dried oregano

1 tsp (5 mL) salt

1 tsp (5 mL) freshly ground black pepper

¼ tsp (1 mL) cayenne pepper

eight to twelve 2-inch-thick (5 cm) beef short ribs

1 medium onion, coarsely chopped

2 garlic cloves, halved and sliced

1½ cups (375 mL) tomato sauce

1 cup (250 mL) beef stock

1 Tbsp (15 mL) brown sugar

2 Tbsp (30 mL) chopped cilantro or fresh parsley

ERIC'S OPTIONS
Use 8 beef back ribs (prime rib or standing rib bones) in place of the short ribs. For a smoky chili taste, add 2 to 3 finely chopped chipotle peppers to the tomato mixture before spooning it over the short ribs.

Preheat the oven to 450°F (230°C). In a bowl combine the cumin, chili powder, coriander, thyme, oregano, salt, pepper and cayenne. Rub the spice mix on the ribs. Place the ribs in a roasting pan just large enough to hold them and roast for 30 minutes. Remove from the oven and drain away the excess fat. Reduce the oven temperature to 325°F (160°C). Combine the onion, garlic, tomato sauce, stock and brown sugar in a bowl. Pour over the ribs. Cover and bake for 1½ to 2 hours, or until the meat is very tender and falling off the bone. Transfer the ribs to a platter. Skim the fat from the sauce and adjust the seasoning. Spoon the sauce over the ribs, sprinkle with cilantro or parsley and serve.

OVEN-BRAISED STEAK
with ROSEMARY and GARLIC

While the steak tenderizes in the oven, prepare side dishes to serve with it, such as frozen peas heated in a little melted butter and Buttermilk Yukon Gold Mashed Potatoes (page 349).

1½ lb (750 g) round steak, cut into 8 pieces

salt and freshly ground black pepper to taste

1½ cups (375 mL) beef stock

2 Tbsp (30 mL) all-purpose flour

2 Tbsp (30 mL) olive oil

2 garlic cloves, chopped

1 Tbsp (15 mL) chopped fresh rosemary

1 Tbsp (15 mL) Worcestershire sauce

preparation time • 15 minutes
cooking time • 70–75 minutes
makes • 4 servings

ERIC'S OPTIONS
If you don't have fresh rosemary, use 1 tsp (5 mL) dried. Make oven-braised veal or pork by replacing the round steak with four 5–6 oz (150–175 g) pork or veal cutlets. Cooking method remains the same.

Preheat the oven to 350°F (175°C). Season the steaks with salt and pepper. Whisk the stock and flour in a bowl until smooth. Heat the oil in a skillet over medium-high heat. Add the steak and brown on both sides; transfer to a 9- × 13-inch (3.5 L) casserole.

Drain the oil from the skillet. Add the stock mixture, garlic, rosemary and Worcestershire sauce and bring to a boil. Pour the mixture over the steaks. Cover and bake until quite tender, about 65 to 75 minutes.

SLOW COOKER SAUERKRAUT-STUFFED BEEF ROULADEN

Rouladen is a German-style dish in which very thinly sliced pieces of beef, often cut from the round, are rolled around a filling, in this recipe sauerkraut. You can buy the meat for rouladen cut and ready to use at most supermarkets, or ask the butcher at your local butcher shop to cut it for you. I like to serve this version of rouladen with Mixed-Vegetable Rice Pilaf (page 160) or Potato Pancakes (page 350).

8 very thin pieces beef rouladen (each about
  8 inches/20 cm long and 4 inches/10 cm wide)

8 tsp (40 mL) Dijon mustard

eight 3–4 inch (8–10 cm) carrot sticks

eight 3–4 inch (8–10 cm) celery sticks

2 cups (500 mL) sauerkraut, rinsed and drained well

salt and freshly ground black pepper to taste

3 Tbsp (45 mL) vegetable oil

2½ cups (625 mL) beef stock

¼ cup (60 mL) all-purpose flour

preparation time • 35 minutes
slow-cooker time • 7–8 hours
makes • 4 servings

NOTE
This recipe is designed for a slow cooker with 4½ to 6½ quart (4.5 to 6.5 L) capacity.

ERIC'S OPTIONS
Instead of rolling a carrot and celery stick inside each rouladen, roll a long, thin slice of dill pickle. Instead of regular Dijon mustard, try using wholegrain Dijon, which has a coarser texture.

Set a piece of rouladen flat on a work surface. Brush the top of it with 1 tsp (5 mL) of the mustard. Set a carrot and celery stick at one end of the meat and top with ¼ cup (60 mL) of sauerkraut. Roll the meat into a cylinder and secure with string or a toothpick. Repeat with the remaining rouladen and fillings. Season rouladen with salt and pepper.

Continued . . .

SLOW COOKER SAUERKRAUT-
STUFFED BEEF ROULADEN (*continued*)

Place the oil in a large skillet set over medium-high heat. When hot, add the stuffed rouladen, in batches if necessary, and brown on all sides. Set the rouladen in your slow cooker.

Drain the excess oil from the skillet. Place the stock and flour in a bowl and whisk to combine. Pour this mixture into the skillet. Bring to a boil and cook until slightly thickened, about 2 minutes. Pour this mixture over the rouladen. Cover and cook on the low setting for 7 to 8 hours, or until the beef is very tender.

To serve, remove the string or toothpicks from the rouladen. Set 2 pieces of rouladen on each of 4 plates. Top with some of the sauce in the slow cooker and serve.

BEEF TENDERLOIN STEAKS with CRAB-STUFFED MUSHROOMS

Here's a tasty version of "surf and turf"—an ultratender steak paired with crab-stuffed mushroom caps. Add a baked potato and some buttery green beans or zucchini to each plate, and dinner is ready. For tips on cooking the meat, see Grilling the Perfect Steak (page 325).

preparation time	•	20 minutes
cooking time	•	about 20 minutes
makes	•	6 servings

¾ cup (185 mL) canned or fresh crabmeat

⅓ cup (80 mL) spreadable cream cheese

1 garlic clove, crushed

1 green onion, thinly sliced

½ tsp (2 mL) hot pepper sauce

salt, freshly ground black pepper and lemon juice to taste

18 medium white or brown mushrooms, stems removed

¼ cup (60 mL) freshly grated Parmesan cheese

six 5 oz (150 g) beef tenderloin steaks

ERIC'S OPTIONS

Instead of tenderloin, use any tender steak, such as rib eye or top sirloin medallions. Instead of crab in the mushroom stuffing, use an equal amount of finely chopped cooked salad shrimp.

Line a 9- × 13-inch (3.5 L) baking dish with parchment paper.

Place the crabmeat, cream cheese, garlic, green onion, hot pepper sauce, salt, pepper and lemon juice in a bowl and mix well to combine. Stuff the crab mixture inside the mushroom caps. (The mushrooms can be stuffed in the morning, covered and refrigerated. Add a few minutes cooking time if you cook the mushrooms from a chilled state.) Set the mushroom caps in the baking dish; sprinkle with the Parmesan cheese.

Preheat the oven to 350°F (175°C). Preheat your grill to medium-high. Bake the mushrooms 15 to 20 minutes, or until tender and the stuffing is golden brown. While the mushrooms bake, season the steaks with salt and pepper. Lightly oil the bars of the grill. Grill the steaks, 2 to 3 minutes per side for rare, and 3 to 4 minutes for medium-rare to medium. Serve the steaks and mushrooms together.

SLOW COOKER
BEEF DAUBE

The beef in this dark, rich, French-style dish is given a wonderful flavor even before it makes it into the slow cooker. After slices of garlic are cooked until golden in a skillet and removed, the beef is seared in the remaining oil and infused with a divine, garlicky taste. For an ultradecadent meal, serve this with Roquefort and Chive Mashed Potatoes (page 347).

¼ cup (60 mL) olive oil

4 large garlic cloves, halved and thinly sliced

2 lb (1 kg) boneless chuck or blade steak, cut into 1½ inch (4 cm) cubes

salt and freshly ground black pepper to taste

3 medium carrots, halved lengthwise and sliced

1 large onion, diced

3 Tbsp (45 mL) all-purpose flour

1 cup (250 mL) beef stock

1 cup (250 mL) red wine

one 14 oz (398 mL) can diced tomatoes

2 Tbsp (30 mL) tomato paste

2 bay leaves

½ tsp (2 mL) dried thyme

pinch ground cloves

chopped fresh parsley to taste

preparation time	•	30 minutes
slow-cooker time	•	6–8 hours
makes	•	4–6 servings

NOTE
This recipe is designed for a slow cooker with 4½ to 6½ quart (4.5 to 6.5 L) capacity.

ERIC'S OPTIONS
Make lamb daube by replacing the beef with a 2 lb (1 kg) piece of boneless lamb leg, cubed.

Place the olive oil in a large skillet set over medium-low to medium heat. Add the garlic and cook until lightly golden and aromatic, 4 to 5 minutes. Remove the skillet from the heat. Lift the garlic out of the skillet with a slotted spoon and set it in your slow cooker.

Return the skillet to the stovetop and increase heat to medium-high. Season the beef with salt and pepper, then sear in batches, setting the browned pieces in your slow cooker as you go. (see How to Sear Meat Properly on page 297.)

Add the carrot and onion to the skillet and cook for 3 to 4 minutes. Stir in the flour and cook for 2 minutes more. Slowly, while stirring, mix in the stock. Mix in the wine, diced tomatoes, tomato paste, bay leaves, thyme and cloves and bring to a simmer. Pour this mixture over the beef and stir to combine. Cover and cook on the low setting for 6 to 8 hours, or until the beef is very tender. Sprinkle servings with chopped parsley.

ROAST BEEF TENDERLOIN
for TWO

The most tender cut of beef served with an easy-to-make red wine sauce. Because of the small size of this roast tenderloin, you will likely need to get a butcher to custom cut it for you.

preparation time • 10 minutes
cooking time • 25–30 minutes
makes • 2 servings

1½ Tbsp (22 mL) olive oil

1 lb (500 g) beef tenderloin roast

coarse sea salt and freshly ground black
    pepper to taste

1 cup (250 mL) beef stock

1 Tbsp (15 mL) all-purpose flour

⅓ cup (80 mL) richly flavored red wine,
    such as Cabernet Sauvignon

ERIC'S OPTIONS
To make green peppercorn sauce, add 1 tsp (5 mL) green peppercorns to the skillet when reducing the wine. Green peppercorns are sold in small tins or jars at most supermarkets and fine food stores.

Preheat the oven to 400°F (200°C). Heat the oil in an ovenproof skillet over medium-high heat. Season the beef with salt and pepper, place in the skillet and sear on all sides. Place the skillet in the oven and roast 20 minutes for rare to medium-rare beef, 25 minutes for medium-rare to medium. (See introduction to Roast Strip Loin with Dijon and Herbes de Provence on page 323.)

Transfer the beef to a plate, tent with foil and let rest while you make the sauce.

Place the stock and flour in a bowl and whisk to combine. Drain the excess fat from the skillet and set on the stovetop over medium-high heat. Add the wine to the skillet and cook until it's reduced by half. Pour in the stock/flour mixture, bring to a simmer and simmer until lightly thickened. Season the sauce with salt and pepper and set aside on low heat. Thinly slice the beef, arrange it on a small serving platter and drizzle with some of the sauce. Serve the remaining sauce in a small sauceboat alongside.

ROAST STRIP LOIN with DIJON and HERBES de PROVENCE

Strip loin roasts can vary in thickness depending on what end of the loin they were cut from, and that can affect cooking time. I've given approximate cooking times below, but it's best to use an instant-read meat thermometer, inserted into the center of the thickest part of the roast, to gauge doneness. Cook the meat to 125°F (50°C) for rare, 125°F to 135°F (50°C to 57°C) for medium-rare, 140°F (60°C) for medium. Remember that the meat will continue to cook when you let it rest before slicing.

3 lb (1.5 kg) strip loin roast

2 Tbsp (30 mL) Dijon mustard

1 Tbsp (15 mL) herbes de Provence (see Note on page 250)

coarse sea salt and coarsely ground black pepper to taste

½ cup (125 mL) red wine

2½ cups (625 mL) beef stock

preparation time • 10 minutes
cooking time • depends on desired doneness
makes • 6 servings

ERIC'S OPTIONS

If you prefer its coarser texture, use wholegrain Dijon mustard instead of the smooth type of Dijon. If you don't use alcohol, use another ½ cup (125 mL) of beef stock to make the jus.

Preheat the oven to 450°F (230°C). Place the beef, fat side up, in a medium-sized roasting pan. Combine the mustard and herbes de Provence in a small bowl. Brush the beef with the mustard mixture; season with salt and pepper. Roast the beef for 20 minutes. Lower the oven temperature to 325°F (160°C) and cook the roast to the desired doneness, approximately 30 to 40 minutes for rare and 40 to 50 minutes for medium-rare to medium.

Set the roast on a plate, cover with foil and let it rest for 10 minutes before carving it into thin slices.

To make jus, set the roasting pan on the stovetop over medium-high heat. Add the wine and bring to a simmer, scraping the bottom of the pan to lift off the tasty brown bits. Add the stock and simmer a few minutes more. Pour the jus into a sauceboat and serve alongside the beef.

GRILLED RIB STEAK
with SUMMER SALAD

Celebrate a summer holiday evening in your backyard with this dinner that sees a prime, juicy beef rib steak deliciously paired with an easy-to-make summer salad.

1 lb (500 g) small white or Yukon Gold potatoes, cut into small wedges

2 cobs of corn, kernels removed

3 Tbsp (45 mL) olive oil

1 tsp (5 mL) ground cumin

1 tsp (5 mL) chili powder

½ lb (250 g) green beans, trimmed, halved and blanched (see How to Blanch Vegetables on page 253)

2–3 Tbsp (30–45 mL) fresh lime juice

pinch sugar

salt and freshly ground black pepper to taste

four 8 oz (250 g) beef rib steaks

preparation time	•	20 minutes
cooking time	•	about 25 minutes
makes	•	4 servings

ERIC'S OPTIONS
Grill any tender steak, such as T-bone or strip loin. For added flavor, brush the steaks with your favorite barbecue sauce when almost done.

Boil the potatoes in lightly salted water until just tender. Drain well and place in a wide bowl to cool. Preheat your barbecue to medium-high. Line a baking pan with parchment paper. Place the corn kernels, oil, cumin and chili powder in a bowl and toss to coat. Spoon into the baking pan. Set the pan on the upper rack of the barbecue and roast 10 minutes, stirring occasionally, until the corn is tender and nicely caramelized. Spoon the roasted corn and its cooking oil over the potatoes. Add the green beans and sprinkle the lime juice, sugar, salt and pepper over the salad. Toss to combine the ingredients.

Season the steaks with salt and pepper. Lightly oil the grate of your grill. Grill the steaks to the desired degree of doneness, allowing 2 to 3 minutes per side for rare, and 3 to 4 minutes per side for medium-rare to medium. Serve the steaks on individual plates with a generous spoonful of salad.

GRILLING THE PERFECT STEAK: IT'S ALL A MATTER OF TOUCH

If you like rare or medium-rare steaks, choose those that are at least 1 inch (2.5 cm) thick. At high heat, they can be nicely seared on the outside while the inside remains rare. If you like steaks well done, choose thinner cuts, as thicker ones take a long time to cook through and become dried out.

When it's time to grill the steak, let it warm at room temperature for 20 minutes or so, depending on how hot a day it is. Never put an ice-cold steak on the grill; it won't cook evenly, as the outside will char and shrivel before the middle even gets warm. Be sure your grill is properly preheated before setting on the meat. If it's not, the meat can stick and you won't get nice grill marks.

Steaks become firmer the longer they cook. To see how it is progressing, lightly press the steak in the center (without squeezing out the juice) using the tips of your tongs or, carefully, with your finger. A rare steak will feel soft to the touch in the very center. Medium-rare ones will be somewhat soft, but offer a little resistance.

A medium steak will start to feel firm but still have a little give in the middle. Well-done steaks will feel firm all over.

Determining doneness by touch takes practice. To judge how your skill is progressing, make a small incision into the thickest part of a steak to check its doneness. After you've practiced and perfected your steak cooking skills, you won't have to do this.

BURGER
BUFFET

Celebrate summer by having a backyard barbecue with your family and friends. Place the grilled burgers on a platter, provide a basketful of buns and arrange the condiments and toppings in bowls and on plates. Then relax and allow your guests to build their own perfect burgers.

2½ lb (1.25 kg) lean ground beef

⅓ cup (80 mL) breadcrumbs

4 green onions, thinly sliced

1 large egg, beaten

1 Tbsp (15 mL) Worcestershire sauce

1 tsp (5 mL) Tabasco sauce

1 Tbsp (15 mL) chopped fresh rosemary

1 tsp (5 mL) salt

1 tsp (5 mL) freshly ground black pepper

8 crusty burger buns, warmed

assorted burger toppings, such as shredded lettuce, sliced tomatoes, onion, hot peppers, pickles, crispy bacon, grated cheddar and mozzarella cheese, relish, mustard, ketchup, barbecue sauce, salsa and guacamole

preparation time •	30 minutes
cooking time •	about 8 minutes
makes •	8 burgers

ERIC'S OPTIONS
For a more complex taste, use a mix of ground beef, pork and veal to make the burgers. Or, make lamb burgers by using ground lamb instead of beef.

Place the beef, breadcrumbs, green onions, egg, Worcestershire, Tabasco, rosemary, salt and pepper in a large bowl and mix until just combined. Moisten your hands with cold water and shape the meat into 8 patties, each about ¾ inch (2 cm) thick, placing them in a single layer on a large platter. (These can be prepared several hours in advance; cover and refrigerate.) Preheat your barbecue to medium-high. Grill the burgers for about 4 minutes per side, or until entirely cooked through and the center of each burger reaches 160°F (71°C) on an instant-read meat thermometer. Place the burgers on a clean platter with the buns nearby, set out the toppings and serve.

CONDIMENTS AND SIDE DISHES

WHOLE WHEAT TURKEY DRESSING
with APPLE and BACON

This fiber-rich dressing is flavored with a pleasing mix of ingredients, such as sweet apples, smoky bacon and earthy sage. Serve it with Roast Turkey with Herbes de Provence and Butter (page 270).

preparation time	•	25 minutes
cooking time	•	about 45 minutes
makes	•	8 servings

10–12 slices whole wheat bread, cut into ½-inch (1 cm) cubes

4 strips bacon, diced

1 medium onion, finely chopped

2 celery ribs, finely chopped

1 large red apple, cored and cut into small cubes

1½ cups (375 mL) chicken or turkey stock

2 tsp (10 mL) dried sage leaves

salt and freshly ground black pepper to taste

2 Tbsp (30 mL) butter, softened

ERIC'S OPTIONS
The dressing can be made oven-ready several hours in advance. After spooning into the baking dish, cool to room temperature, then refrigerate. Pop the stuffing in the oven the moment the turkey is done.

Place the bread cubes in a large bowl. Fry the bacon until crispy in a large skillet over medium to medium-high heat. Add the onion, celery and apple and cook 5 minutes more, or until tender. Spoon the mixture over the bread cubes. Add the stock, sage, salt and pepper and toss to combine.

Coat a 9- × 13-inch (3.5 L) baking dish with the butter. Spoon the dressing into the baking dish and cover with foil.

Preheat the oven to 375°F (190°C). Bake the dressing for 20 minutes. Uncover and bake 15 minutes more, or until the dressing is hot and crisp and golden on top.

MINI-CARROTS with HONEY, GINGER and LEMON

Peeled and ready to use, mini-carrots, also called baby carrots, take just minutes to cook. In this recipe, the flavor goes up several notches thanks to the addition of sweet honey, spicy fresh ginger and tart lemon juice. I like to dress up simply cooked main dishes, such as grilled or sautéed boneless, skinless chicken breasts or baked ham, with this tasty dish.

1 lb (500 g) mini-carrots

2 Tbsp (30 mL) butter

1 tsp (5 mL) freshly grated ginger, or to taste

1 Tbsp (15 mL) honey

1 Tbsp (15 mL) freshly squeezed lemon juice

salt and freshly ground black pepper to taste

1 Tbsp (15 mL) chopped fresh parsley (optional)

preparation time • 5 minutes
cooking time • 7–8 minutes
makes • 4 servings

ERIC'S OPTIONS
For a different sweet taste, use maple syrup instead of honey. Instead of mini-carrots, peel an equal weight of regular carrots and slice into coins.

Place the carrots in a pot, cover with cold water and set over medium-high heat.

Bring to a boil and cook until just tender. Drain and return the pot to the stove over low heat. Add the butter, ginger, honey, lemon juice, salt and pepper to the carrots and cook, stirring, until the butter melts and the carrots are nicely coated, about 2 minutes. Sprinkle in the parsley, if using, and serve.

Mini-Carrots with Honey, Ginger and Lemon, top (page 330),
Roasted Asparagus with Peppers and Pine Nuts, bottom (page 341)

BRUSSELS SPROUTS
with GREMOLATA

Gremolata is an Italian-style garnish made from a mix of chopped parsley, citrus zest and garlic. It's most often used to add a last-minute, fresh taste to osso bucco (braised veal shanks). I discovered one day, having some gremolata leftover from making osso bucco, that it can also be a flavor-enhancing topping for a green vegetable, such as these Brussels sprouts. The gremolata ingredients can be chopped (together) a few hours in advance and refrigerated.

preparation time • 20 minutes
cooking time • 4–5 minutes
makes • 6–8 servings

ERIC'S OPTIONS
Try the gremolata on other steamed or boiled green vegetables, such as asparagus, green beans or broccoli.

1 tsp (5 mL) coarsely grated lemon zest

1 tsp (5 mL) coarsely grated orange zest

8 parsley sprigs

1 garlic clove, thickly sliced

1½ lb (750 g) Brussels sprouts

2 Tbsp (30 mL) melted butter

salt and freshly ground black pepper to taste

Bring a large pot of water to a boil. Place the lemon and orange zest, parsley and garlic together on a cutting board. Finely chop all the ingredients and place in a small bowl.

Boil the Brussels sprouts until just tender, about 4 to 5 minutes depending on size. (The Brussels sprouts used for this recipe were approximately 1 inch/2.5 cm in diameter. If yours are much larger, you'll need to boil them 1 to 2 minutes longer.) Drain well and place in a wide serving dish.

Drizzle with the melted butter, season with salt and pepper, sprinkle with the gremolata and serve.

When purchasing Brussels sprouts, choose vibrant green, firm sprouts that feel heavy for their size. Avoid yellowish sprouts with a lot of loose leaves—a sign they've been sitting around too long. To ensure even cooking, pick Brussels sprouts of roughly the same size. If you like a milder, somewhat sweeter taste, choose smaller ones, approximately 1 inch (2.5 cm) in diameter.

To prepare them for cooking, rinse the sprouts well in cold water, trim the stems and remove any loose outer leaves. Use a paring knife to cut a shallow cross into the bottom of the stem end of each Brussels sprout. This will allow the cooking liquid or steam to reach the center of the sprout and promote even cooking.

To cook, bring a large pot of water to a boil, then add the Brussels sprouts. Return to a boil, reduce the heat to a gentle boil and cook until the stem ends are just tender when pierced with a paring knife. This can take 4 to 8 minutes, depending on the size of the sprouts. If you prefer, steam the Brussels sprouts for a similar amount of time.

A good make-ahead technique, used in Cider-Glazed Brussels Sprouts (page 335) is to blanch the sprouts in advance and reheat them with the flavorings when ready to serve.

Brussels sprouts have a bad reputation among some people that probably stems from improper cooking and past-their-due-date vegetables. If overcooked, this bold-tasting vegetable can intensify in flavor and aroma and turn an unpalatable grayish/green color. Properly cooked and seasoned, sprouts can be a staple of the winter table!

CIDER-GLAZED BRUSSELS SPROUTS

Sweet apple cider helps tame the intense flavor of Brussels sprouts. This side dish goes particularly well with poultry and pork, such as Roasted Turkey Breast with Sage and Pan Gravy (page 276) or Crispy Oven-Baked Pork Cutlets (page 295).

preparation time • 5 minutes
cooking time • 6–8 minutes
makes • 4 servings

1 lb (500 g) small to medium Brussels sprouts, trimmed (see Cooking Brussels Sprouts on page 334)

½ cup (125 mL) apple cider (non-alcoholic)

1 Tbsp (15 mL) butter

salt and freshly ground black pepper to taste

ERIC'S OPTIONS
You could blanch the sprouts several hours before needed and keep them refrigerated until ready to simmer in the cider and serve. For a richer taste, toss in ⅓ cup (80 mL) of lightly toasted walnut or pecan pieces just before serving.

Bring a large pot of water to a boil. Add the Brussels sprouts, return to a boil and boil for 3 to 4 minutes, or until crisp-tender. Drain well, cool in ice-cold water, and drain well again. Place the apple cider and butter in a large skillet and bring to a boil over high heat. Add the Brussels sprouts, lower the heat to medium and simmer until the Brussels sprouts are tender and the cider mixture is a little syrupy, about 3 to 4 minutes. Season with salt and pepper and serve immediately.

GLAZED YAMS with CRANBERRIES and PECANS

Here's a rich-tasting side dish that can be readied hours in advance and baked later. This makes it a good item for a holiday dinner; it will be ready to go when your guests arrive, allowing you to spend more time with them, rather than in the kitchen.

6 medium yams (see About Sweet Potatoes and Yams on page 337)

⅓ cup (80 mL) fresh or frozen cranberries (thawed), coarsely chopped

⅓ cup (80 mL) pecan pieces

3–4 Tbsp (45–60 mL) butter, at room temperature

salt and freshly ground black pepper to taste

¼ cup (60 mL) brown sugar

½ tsp (2 mL) ground cinnamon

pinch ground nutmeg

preparation time • 20 minutes
cooking time • 75–90 minutes (includes pre-cooking the yams)
makes • 8 servings

ERIC'S OPTIONS
Use 2 to 3 Tbsp (30 to 45 mL) of slightly warmed maple syrup or liquid honey instead of brown sugar. This will give the yams a shinier look and a slightly sweeter taste.

Preheat the oven to 350°F (175°C). Prick the yams several times with a fork. Place on a baking sheet and bake until tender but still slightly firm, about 60 minutes, depending on the size. Remove and set aside until cool enough to handle.

When still warm, carefully remove the skin with a small knife. Slice the yams into ¾-inch (2 cm) thick rounds and place in slightly overlapping rows in a lightly buttered 9- × 13-inch (23 × 33 cm) baking dish. Scatter the cranberries and pecans overtop. Melt the remaining butter and drizzle over the top. Season with salt and pepper. Combine the sugar, cinnamon and nutmeg in a small bowl. Sprinkle the mixture over the yams. (The dish could be made to this point several hours in advance and stored in the refrigerator until needed.) Bake for 20 to 30 minutes, or until the yams are heated through and nicely glazed.

ABOUT SWEET POTATOES AND YAMS

You'll find sweet potatoes and yams for sale in most supermarkets. However, most often those yams are actually the orange-fleshed variety of sweet potato. True yams, a staple ingredient in many Asian countries, are much larger than sweet potatoes and can grow up to 3 feet (90 cm) long. While sweet potatoes can be cooked in their skin and the skin eaten, the skin of a true yam must be deeply peeled before cooking and is never eaten because it contains irritating crystals of calcium oxalate.

Why, you may wonder, is the orange-fleshed variety of sweet potato called a yam in North America? It was a marketing ploy designed to help consumers distinguish it from the other sweet potato, which has a pale yellow flesh and pale brown skin. The skin of the orange-fleshed vegetable is most often a copper color and its flesh is moist, dense and quite sweet. The yellow-fleshed variety is drier in texture, less sweet and has an almost nutty flavor. The two varieties are suited to different preparations. If you are looking for a sweet potato to use in a salad or casserole, one that will hold its shape when cooked, the orange-fleshed variety is best. The yellow-fleshed variety, which has a starchy character like that of a baking potato, is best eaten as you would a potato—baked whole; cut into wedges, tossed with oil and spices and roasted; or peeled, boiled, mashed and mixed with buttermilk, butter, and salt and pepper.

In this book, in line with common practice, the orange-fleshed sweet potato is referred to as a yam.

SPICED YAM ROUNDS

This is an ultrasimple recipe, and I always get compliments when I serve it with such things as roast turkey and baked ham. You simply bake yams with the skin on, then cool, slice and set on a baking sheet. Baste them with this sweet, sour and spice-filled butter mixture, then bake. It's not rocket science!

3 small to medium yams (each about 3 inches/
    8 cm in diameter)

3 Tbsp (45 mL) honey

3 Tbsp (45 mL) melted butter

2 Tbsp (30 mL) fresh lemon juice

¼ tsp (1 mL) ground cinnamon

pinch ground nutmeg, ginger and cloves

salt and freshly ground black pepper to taste

1 Tbsp (15 mL) chopped fresh parsley

preparation time	•	10 minutes
cooking time	•	about 75 minutes
makes	•	8 servings

ERIC'S OPTIONS
Instead of yams, bake, slice and use sweet potatoes in this dish.

Preheat the oven to 325°F (160°C). Line a baking pan with parchment paper. Prick each yam several times with a fork and place in the pan. Bake until just tender, about 60 minutes. Cool the yams to room temperature. (The yams can be prepared to this point up to a day in advance. Cover and refrigerate until ready to slice and bake.)

Preheat the oven to 325°F (160°C). Line a baking sheet with parchment paper. Slice the yams into ½-inch-thick (1 cm) rounds and place on the baking sheet. Combine the honey, butter, lemon juice, cinnamon, nutmeg, ginger and cloves in a small bowl. Brush the mixture over the tops of the yams. Season with salt and pepper. Bake the yams, uncovered, for 20 minutes, or until heated through. Arrange on a platter, sprinkle with parsley and serve.

COLORFUL VEGETABLE MEDLEY

Red, green, orange and white vegetables make a colorful side dish to serve with roasts, fish, steaks and other entrées. The vegetables can be readied up to a day in advance and heated when needed.

1 lb (500 g) baby carrots

32 cauliflower florets, each about 1 inch (2.5 cm) across

½ lb (250 g) snap peas, tops trimmed

1 large red bell pepper, cut into small cubes

2 Tbsp (30 mL) butter

1 cup (250 mL) chicken or vegetable stock

1 garlic clove, minced

salt and freshly ground black pepper to taste

1 Tbsp (15 mL) chopped fresh parsley

preparation time • 15 minutes
cooking time • 12 minutes
makes • 8 servings

ERIC'S OPTIONS
Give this dish Italian-style flair by omitting the parsley and tossing in 2 to 3 Tbsp (30 to 45 mL) of pesto when heating the vegetables through. Sprinkle with freshly grated Parmesan cheese just before serving.

Place the carrots in a pot and cover with a generous amount of cold water. Boil until just tender but still a little firm. Add the cauliflower, snap peas and bell pepper, return to a boil, and cook 2 to 3 minutes more. Drain well, cool the vegetables in ice-cold water, and drain well again. (They can be prepared to this point a day in advance. Cover and refrigerate until needed.)

Place the butter, stock and garlic in a very large skillet and bring to a simmer; add the vegetables and heat through. Season with salt and pepper. Sprinkle the parsley overtop and serve.

MASHED RUTABAGAS with BUTTERMILK and PARSLEY

Mashed rutabagas, called "bashed neeps" in Scotland, are a traditional Scottish side dish with haggis. They also make a nice bed for something meaty and saucy, such as Braised Lamb Shanks with Hot Mustard and Whisky (page 304).

2½ lb (1.25 kg) rutabaga, peeled and cubed

3 Tbsp (45 mL) butter

½ cup (125 mL) buttermilk

2 Tbsp (30 mL) chopped fresh parsley

salt and freshly ground black pepper to taste

preparation time • 10 minutes
cooking time • 15 minutes
makes • 6 servings

ERIC'S OPTIONS
Try mixing 2 to 3 thinly sliced green onions into the mashed rutabagas.

Place the rutabaga in a pot, cover with a generous amount of water and boil until very tender, about 15 minutes. Drain well, and then thoroughly mash. Mix in the butter, buttermilk, parsley, salt and pepper.

ABOUT RUTABAGAS AND TURNIPS

Rutabagas are often mistaken for turnips, but the two vegetables, both members of the Brassica family, which includes cabbage and broccoli, are quite different. The skin of the turnip is smoother, thinner and white, and its top is tinged with purple. Turnips are usually smaller than rutabagas and the white flesh is crisper and blander, a result of being harvested when young. Older turnips can become woody and develop a very strong taste.

Rutabagas have long been popular in northern climates. They are hardy and some cold weather before picking can help sweeten the flesh. The flesh of rutabagas is golden and denser than turnip, which makes them good for mashing. The thick skin is golden on the bottom and tinged reddish-brown at the top.

ROASTED ASPARAGUS with PEPPERS and PINE NUTS

Red peppers and pine nuts add richness and color to this simple but divine asparagus dish.

1 lb (500 g) asparagus, stems trimmed

3 Tbsp (45 mL) olive oil

1 Tbsp (15 mL) balsamic vinegar

¼ cup (60 mL) finely chopped red bell pepper

2 Tbsp (30 mL) pine nuts

salt and freshly ground black pepper to taste

preparation time	•	10 minutes
cooking time	•	24 minutes
makes	•	4 servings

ERIC'S OPTIONS
This dish also tastes fine at room temperature, so don't worry if it cools down before you serve it. Recipe could be halved if you're only serving two.

Preheat the oven to 400°F (200°C). Bring a pot of water to a boil, add the asparagus and cook for 1 minute. Drain well, immerse in ice-cold water and drain well again. Place the asparagus in a single layer in a baking dish. Drizzle with the olive oil and balsamic vinegar; sprinkle with the red pepper, pine nuts, salt and pepper. Roast for 20 minutes and serve. *Pictured on page 331.*

GRILLED CORN
with LIME and CUMIN

Serve this corn with just about anything cooked on the barbecue, such as steaks, chicken, salmon, ribs and burgers. Cooking the shucked corn directly over the heat slightly chars and caramelizes the kernels—very tasty!

2 Tbsp (30 mL) butter

1 tsp (5 mL) ground cumin

2 Tbsp (30 mL) freshly squeezed lime juice

4 cobs of corn, shucked

salt and freshly ground black pepper to taste

4 lime wedges

preparation time • 10 minutes
cooking time • 4–5 minutes
makes • 4 servings

ERIC'S OPTIONS
For spicy grilled corn, add ¼ tsp (1 mL) of cayenne pepper to the butter mixture.

Preheat your barbecue or indoor grill to medium. Place the butter, cumin and lime juice in a small skillet over medium heat and cook just until the butter melts. Stir to combine and then remove from the heat. Place the corn on the grill. Cook, turning from time to time, until the corn is lightly charred and just tender, about 4 to 5 minutes. Set the corn on a platter. Brush with the butter mixture, sprinkle with salt and pepper and serve immediately, garnished with lime wedges.

GREEN BEANS with PECANS, LIME and HONEY

The beans in this quick-cooking side dish are sweetened with honey, made tangy with lime juice and enriched with the buttery taste of pecans.

preparation time • 6 minutes
cooking time • 5 minutes
makes • 4 servings

3 Tbsp (45 mL) honey

2 Tbsp (30 mL) fresh lime juice

1 lb (500 g) green beans, trimmed

⅓ cup (80 mL) pecan halves, coarsely chopped

salt and freshly ground black pepper to taste

ERIC'S OPTIONS
For a green and yellow color and two-bean taste, replace ½ lb (250 g) of the green beans with wax (yellow) beans.

Bring a large pot of water to a boil to cook the beans. Meanwhile, warm the honey and lime juice in a large skillet set over low heat.

When the water is boiling, add the beans and cook until they are a vibrant green and just tender, 2 to 3 minutes. Drain the beans well, then add them with the pecans and salt and pepper to the skillet, toss to combine and serve.

BROCCOLI FLORETS
with ROASTED PEPPERS

The green and red combination gives this side dish a Christmassy look, which is why it's nice to serve on that special day.

preparation time • 20 minutes
cooking time • 15–20 minutes
makes • 8 servings

24 medium-sized broccoli florets

1 large roasted red pepper, finely chopped (see Note)

1 cup (250 mL) chicken or vegetable stock

½ tsp (2 mL) dried oregano

1 garlic clove, finely chopped

salt and freshly ground black pepper to taste

NOTE
Roasted red peppers are available in jars at most supermarkets. If you wish to roast your own, see Eric's Options on page 253.

ERIC'S OPTIONS
The broccoli can be made oven-ready several hours in advance. Cover and refrigerate until you're ready to bake it.

Bring a large pot of water to a boil. Add the broccoli and cook until just tender, about 2 to 3 minutes. Drain well, cool in ice-cold water, and drain well again. Arrange the broccoli in a 9- × 13-inch (3.5 L) baking dish. Combine the roasted red pepper, stock, oregano and garlic in a bowl. Spoon the mixture over the broccoli, ensuring that each floret has some roasted red pepper on top. Season with salt and pepper. Bake the broccoli, covered with foil, in a 325°F oven (160°C) for 15 to 20 minutes, or until heated through.

MAKE-AHEAD YUKON GOLD MASHED POTATO BAKE

These mashed potatoes can be prepared up to a day in advance and baked when needed, eliminating that last-minute rush to mash potatoes when you're making a big meal—something every cook can appreciate!

4 lb (2 kg) Yukon Gold (yellow-fleshed) potatoes, peeled and quartered

1 cup (250 mL) warm milk

¼ cup (60 mL) butter, melted, plus some for casserole dish

salt and white pepper to taste

1½ cups (375 mL) grated white cheddar cheese

3 green onions, thinly sliced

preparation time • 15 minutes
cooking time • 40–45 minutes
makes • 8 servings

ERIC'S OPTIONS
Instead of the cheddar, use another flavorful cheese, such as Asiago or Swiss. For a tangy taste, use buttermilk instead of milk.

Place the potatoes in a pot and cover with at least 2 inches (5 cm) of cold water. Bring to a boil over medium-high heat. Reduce the heat until the potatoes simmer gently. Simmer until very tender, 18 to 20 minutes. Drain the potatoes well and mash thoroughly. Whip in the milk and melted butter. Season the potatoes with salt and pepper; mix in half of the cheese and two-thirds of the green onions.

Lightly butter the bottom and sides of a shallow 8-cup (2 L) casserole dish. Spread the potatoes in the casserole dish. Cool to room temperature, cover and refrigerate the potatoes and the remaining cheese and onion until needed. Preheat the oven to 375°F (190°C). Sprinkle the potatoes with the remaining cheese and bake, uncovered, for 25 to 30 minutes, or until heated through and golden. Sprinkle with the remaining green onions and serve.

ROQUEFORT and CHIVE MASHED POTATOES

Blue cheese lovers will adore these ultrarich mashed potatoes strewn with small nuggets of roquefort. Roquefort is one of France's most famous cheeses and French law says that only cheese aged in natural caves near Roquefort-sur-Soulzon, the birthplace of this cheese, can use that name.

2½ lb (1.25 kg) russet or baking potatoes, peeled and quartered

¾ cup (185 mL) milk

2 Tbsp (30 mL) butter, melted

salt and white pepper to taste

3½ oz (105 g) roquefort cheese, pulled into tiny nuggets

2 Tbsp (30 mL) snipped fresh chives

preparation time • 10 minutes
cooking time • 18–20 minutes
makes • 6 servings

ERIC'S OPTIONS
Instead of roquefort, try any other creamy blue cheese in this recipe. For golden-hued potatoes, use Yukon Gold potatoes instead of russets or baking potatoes. If you can't find chives, mix 2 thinly sliced green onions into the mashed potatoes.

Place the potatoes in a pot, cover with cold water by at least 2 inches (5 cm) and bring to a boil over medium-high heat. Reduce the heat until the potatoes simmer gently. Simmer until very tender, 18 to 20 minutes. Drain the potatoes well, then mash thoroughly. Mix in the milk and butter until well combined and season with salt and pepper. Mix in the cheese and chives and serve.

TIPS FOR MAKING MASHED POTATOES

If you want to make smooth, light, lump-free mashed potatoes, use a floury potato, such as a russet or baking potato. These types of potatoes have a high starch level that allows you to mash them vigorously until lump-free without worrying about them turning gummy and sticky.

Yukon Gold or yellow-fleshed potatoes have a medium starch level that yields a denser, slightly moister, yet still delicious, mashed potato. Waxy, low-starch potatoes, such as smooth-skinned red or white potatoes, turn unappealingly gummy if overly mashed. You can still mash them, but it's best to get them only just smooth or still a little coarse in texture. I often boil and mash these types of potatoes with the skin on.

When preparing the potatoes for cooking, cut them into evenly sized quarters, or even halves, depending on their size. If you cut the potatoes too small, they can become waterlogged and, when cooked, will taste more like water than potato. If you cut the potatoes unevenly, the smaller pieces will overcook and fall apart while you wait for the larger pieces to cook.

Cook the potatoes in a generous amount of cold water. I usually cover them with at least 2 inches (5 cm) of cold water. If you don't use a generous amount of water, starch leaching from the potatoes as they cook can concentrate and give the potatoes a gluey texture. Simmer the potatoes gently. If you boil them rapidly they'll cook too quickly and start to fall apart on the outside before the center is done.

When the potatoes are very tender, drain them well. If the potatoes seem overly moist, set the pot back on the heat to dry for a minute or so. To avoid lumps, be sure to mash them when they are piping hot. If they cool for too long, they won't mash as well. Add any ingredients such as butter and milk after the potatoes have been mashed. If you add them before, particularly if the ingredients are not warm, they can cool the potatoes down and cause them to lump, no matter how vigorously you mash them afterward.

BUTTERMILK YUKON GOLD MASHED POTATOES

The eye-appealing color and texture of Yukon Gold potatoes make them a favorite for mashing. Buttermilk gives them an added tanginess. These mashed potatoes go well with a range of dishes, from baked salmon to meatloaf to roast chicken.

preparation time • 5 minutes
cooking time • 20 minutes
makes • 4–6 servings

2½ lb (1.25 kg) Yukon Gold (yellow-fleshed) potatoes, peeled and halved

¾ cup (185 mL) warm buttermilk

2 Tbsp (30 mL) melted butter

salt and white pepper to taste

ERIC'S OPTIONS
Give the potatoes a hint of green by mixing in some chopped parsley or snipped chives after mashing. For saffron mashed potatoes, add ½ tsp (2 mL) saffron threads to the potatoes before you start boiling them.

Place the potatoes in a pot, cover with cold water by at least 2 inches (5 cm) and bring to a boil over medium-high heat. Reduce the heat until the potatoes simmer gently. Simmer until very tender, 18 to 20 minutes. Drain the potatoes well, then mash thoroughly. Mix in the remaining ingredients until well combined.

POTATO
PANCAKES

This savory, crispy, German-style potato dish is hard to resist. I like to serve it with Slow Cooker Sauerkraut-Stuffed Beef Rouladen (page 316), and alongside slices of Roast Pork with McIntosh Apple Sauce (page 287). These pancakes could also be served for breakfast; they make a nice base for a poached egg.

4 medium baking potatoes, peeled

2 large eggs, beaten

½ cup (125 mL) finely grated onion

2 Tbsp (30 mL) flour

½ tsp (2 mL) salt

¼ tsp (1 mL) ground white pepper

pinch ground nutmeg

2 Tbsp (30 mL) vegetable oil

preparation time • 25 minutes
cooking time • 6–8 minutes
makes • 8 pancakes

ERIC'S OPTIONS
The pancakes can be cooked in advance. Place on a large baking sheet lined with parchment paper, cool to room temperature, cover and refrigerate for up to a day. Reheat in a 300°F (150°C) oven for 10 to 15 minutes, or until heated through.

Preheat the oven to 200°F (95°C). Grate the potatoes, rinse well with cold water and drain in a colander. Thoroughly pat the potatoes dry with paper towels and place in a bowl. Mix in the egg, onion, flour, salt, white pepper and nutmeg. Coat the bottom of a large skillet or griddle with a thin layer of vegetable oil and warm over medium to medium-high heat. Working in batches (do not crowd the pan) and adding additional oil as needed, place dollops of the potato mixture in the pan using a ½ cup (125 mL) measure and spread them out to make 4- to 5-inch (10 to 12 cm) circles. Cook 3 to 4 minutes on each side, or until golden and crispy. Set the cooked pancakes on a heatproof platter and keep warm in the oven until all are cooked.

CRISPY OVEN FRIES

These potatoes don't last long around my house. They're crispy on the outside and fluffy in the middle, and they taste sublime sprinkled with malt vinegar or dunked into ketchup.

preparation time • 10 minutes
cooking time • 25 minutes
makes • 4–6 servings

3 Tbsp (45 mL) vegetable oil

1 tsp (5 mL) coarse sea salt, or to taste

1 tsp (5 mL) coarsely ground black pepper, or to taste

½ tsp (2 mL) sweet paprika (see About Paprika on page 257)

3 large baking potatoes

ERIC'S OPTIONS
Instead of using salt, pepper and paprika, season the potatoes to taste with your favorite brand of seasoning salt.

Place an oven rack in the middle position. Preheat the oven to 450°F (230°C).

Combine the oil, salt, pepper and paprika in a large bowl. Cut each potato in half lengthwise, then cut each half into 6 lengthwise wedges. Place the potatoes in the bowl and toss to coat. Arrange the potatoes in a single layer on a large nonstick baking sheet. Bake for 20 minutes, or until the potatoes are tender in the center and crisp on the bottom. Turn the oven to broil and cook the potatoes until golden and crispy on top, about 5 minutes. (Broiling eliminates the time-consuming step of trying to flip each potato individually and roasting them until brown on the other side.) Keep an eye on them as they broil so that they don't overbrown.

ROASTED POTATOES with HONEY, DIJON and PEPPER

Honey and mustard always go well together, whether in a dipping sauce for chicken or, in this case, a glaze for roasted potatoes. When roasted, these potatoes are sticky, sweet, peppery, crisply coated and yummy!

3 Tbsp (45 mL) olive oil

2 Tbsp (30 mL) honey

2 Tbsp (30 mL) wholegrain Dijon mustard

2 Tbsp (30 mL) fresh lemon juice

1 tsp (5 mL) coarsely ground black pepper

½ tsp (2 mL) salt

6 medium red- or white-skinned potatoes,
    cut into 1-inch (2.5 cm) cubes

2 green onions, thinly sliced

preparation time	•	10 minutes
cooking time	•	40–45 minute
makes	•	4–6 servings

ERIC'S OPTIONS
For a smoother texture, use regular Dijon mustard instead of wholegrain. Instead of cubing medium red or white new potatoes, cut 20 to 24 miniature red- or white-skinned new potatoes in half and toss and roast them in the honey and Dijon mixture.

Preheat the oven to 375°F (190°C). Line a baking sheet with parchment paper.

Place the oil, honey, mustard, lemon juice, pepper and salt in a large bowl and whisk to combine. Add the potatoes and toss to coat. Spread the potatoes in a single layer on the prepared baking sheet. Roast for 40 to 45 minutes, turning occasionally, until they are golden brown and tender. Spoon the potatoes into a serving dish, sprinkle with green onion and serve.

ROASTED RED PEPPER AIOLI

Aioli is a garlic-rich mayonnaise that originated in Provence, France. The roasted red pepper blended into this version gives it a greater depth of flavor and a pinkish-red color. I like to use this as a spread for sandwiches or a dip for raw vegetables, and for dolloping onto seafood soups, such as Bouillabaisse (page 64).

1 large roasted red pepper, thickly sliced (see Eric's Options)

¾ cup (185 mL) mayonnaise

1–2 garlic cloves, minced

2 Tbsp (30 mL) coarsely chopped fresh parsley

1 Tbsp (15 mL) fresh lemon juice

½ tsp (2 mL) finely grated lemon zest

salt and freshly ground black pepper to taste

Place all the ingredients in a food processor and pulse until smooth. (You could also use an immersion blender if it has a vessel designed for blending things in.) Transfer the aioli to a bowl, cover and refrigerate until needed.

preparation time • 5 minutes
cooking time • none
makes • 1¼ cups (310 mL)

ERIC'S OPTIONS
Roasted red peppers are sold at most supermarkets. If you want to roast your own red pepper, place a large red bell pepper in a small baking pan lined with parchment paper. Roast at 375°F (190°C) for 30 minutes, turning once or twice, or until the skin is blistered. Remove the pan from the oven and cover with foil. Let the pepper sit for 20 minutes. Uncover the pepper and slip off the skin. Cut the pepper in half and remove the seeds, and it's ready to use.

MANGO
CHUTNEY

This colorful and lively sweet-and-sour chutney makes a nice, fresh condiment to serve alongside a curry such as Slow Cooker Chicken Coconut Curry (page 252).

1 cup (250 mL) finely cubed ripe mango

1 small ripe tomato, finely chopped

2 Tbsp (30 mL) finely chopped onion

2 Tbsp (30 mL) chopped fresh cilantro

1 Tbsp (15 mL) fresh lime juice, or to taste

1 tsp (5 mL) sugar

salt to taste

preparation time	•	10 minutes
cooking time	•	none
makes	•	1½ cups (375 mL)

ERIC'S OPTIONS
Make fresh papaya chutney by replacing the mango with cubes of papaya. For spicy chutney, add crushed chili flakes to taste.

Place all the ingredients in a medium bowl and toss to combine. Cover and refrigerate until needed. This can be made several hours before serving, but it is at its best when served soon after making, when all the ingredients will be at their freshest.

ABOUT FRESH MANGOES

When purchasing mangoes, choose those with smooth, taut skin. A ripe mango has a heavenly tropical fruit aroma and the flesh under the skin yields slightly to gentle pressure. If a mango is unripe, simply leave it out at room temperature for a few days to ripen, as you would a banana. If you want to speed up the ripening process, place the mango in a paper bag. Ripe mangoes can be stored in the refrigerator for up to a week. Mangoes contain vitamins A, C and D and are a source of fiber and potassium, among other things.

MCINTOSH APPLE SAUCE

I like to use McIntosh apples to make applesauce for three reasons. They are sweet enough that you don't have to add much or any sugar; have just enough acidity to balance that sweetness; and they have a wonderful aroma that makes this sauce not just taste good, but also smell good.

8 medium McIntosh apples, peeled, cored and sliced

½ cup (125 mL) water

1 Tbsp (15 mL) lemon juice

sugar (optional) to taste

pinch salt and cinnamon (optional)

Place all ingredients in a pot and set over medium heat. Bring to a gentle simmer and cook, stirring occasionally, until the apple slices cook, break apart and dissolve into a sauce, about 15 to 20 minutes. Add additional water during cooking if required. Once your sauce has achieved the desired consistency, remove the heat. Cool the sauce too room temperature, transfer it to a tight-sealing container and store in the refrigerator until ready to serve. It will keep about 2 weeks. This sauce could also be frozen for up to 2 months.

preparation time	•	15 minutes
cooking time	•	about 20 minutes
makes	•	about 4 cups

ERIC'S OPTIONS

If you want a completely smooth sauce, pulse the cooked apples in a food processor a few seconds, until smooth. I prefer McIntosh, but you could make the sauce with another type of apple, such as Spartan, Fuji or Jonagold, or use a mix of apples to make the sauce.

PICKLED BEETS with BALSAMIC and SPICE

Sweet-and-sour-tasting beets are made inviting by canning them with balsamic vinegar. Make these in summer or fall and you'll have plenty of pickled beets to enjoy during the winter. These beets go great with tourtière (recipes page 186 and page 280).

5 lb (2.2 kg) beets without tops

2¼ cups (560 mL) sugar

2¾ cups (685 mL) water for pickling mixture

1¾ cups (435 mL) white vinegar

¾ cup (185 mL) balsamic vinegar

2 Tbsp (30 mL) pickling spice

preparation time • 40 minutes
cooking time • 50–60 minutes
makes • six 2-cup (500 mL) jars

ERIC'S OPTIONS
To make raspberry-flavored beets, replace the balsamic vinegar with an equal amount of raspberry vinegar.

Place the beets, unpeeled, in a pot and cover completely with cold water. Gently boil them until tender, 30 to 40 minutes, depending on their size. Drain, cool in ice-cold water and drain again. Sterilize six 2-cup (500 mL) canning jars in boiling water for 10 minutes. Peel the beets. The skins should just slip off in your fingers. Trim off the rough top part from each beet. Cut each beet into wedges or ¼- to ½-inch (6 mm to 1 cm) thick slices.

Pack the beets into the sterilized jars. Sterilize 6 snap-top canning jar lids in boiling water for 5 minutes. While the lids boil, place the sugar, water, vinegars and pickling spice in a pot. Bring to a boil. Boil, stirring to dissolve the sugar, for about 3 minutes. Carefully pour this mixture over the beets, leaving a ½-inch (1 cm) headspace at the top of each jar. Wipe the rims clean, then top each jar with a lid. Set on the jars' screwbands and turn just until fingertip-tight.

Heat-process the jars of beets in boiling water for 15 minutes. Set on a rack to cool at room temperature for 24 hours. Check the seal. A properly sealed lid will be concave (curve downward). Label, date and then store the beets in a cool, dark place.

TECHNICOLOR SUMMER SALSA

I named this Technicolor Summer Salsa because of the many colors—red, purple, yellow, orange and green—of the vegetables in it. Serve it as an appetizer with tortilla chips for dipping, or as a fresh and lively condiment for wraps, burgers and Mexican-style dishes, such as tacos and burritos.

3 ripe medium tomatoes, finely chopped

1 cup (250 mL) finely diced green zucchini

½ cup (125 mL) finely diced red onion

½ cup (125 mL) finely diced yellow bell pepper

½ cup (125 mL) finely diced orange bell pepper

1 garlic clove, crushed

1 small to medium fresh jalapeño pepper, halved, seeds removed, flesh finely chopped

¼ cup (60 mL) chopped fresh cilantro

¼ cup (60 mL) fresh lime juice

1 tsp (5 mL) ground cumin

1 tsp (5 mL) sugar

salt to taste

preparation time • 30 minutes
cooking time • none
makes • 4 cups (1 L)

ERIC'S OPTIONS
If you don't care for the taste of cilantro, mix 2 to 3 thinly sliced green onions into the salsa instead.

Place all the ingredients in a bowl and gently toss to combine. Can be made a few hours in advance; cover and refrigerate until needed. Gently toss the salsa again just before serving.

FRESH MINT CHUTNEY

This rich green, intensely flavored chutney can be used to accent savory dishes that might benefit from having a spicy hit of mint alongside, such as Slow Cooker Lamb Curry with Potatoes and Peas (page 303).

preparation time • 25 minutes
cooking time • none
makes • 1 cup
(250 mL)

1 cup (250 mL) fresh mint leaves, packed

3 green onions, thinly sliced

1 small, fresh green serrano chili, coarsely chopped including seeds

1 garlic clove, minced

¼ cup (60 mL) fresh lime juice

2 Tbsp (30 mL) vegetable oil

2 Tbsp (30 mL) water

1 Tbsp (15 mL) sugar

½ tsp (2 mL) ground cumin

½ tsp (2 mL) salt

ERIC'S OPTIONS
Make cilantro chutney by replacing the mint with cilantro leaves.

Place all the ingredients in a food processor and pulse until well combined and finely chopped. Transfer to a serving bowl. Cover and let the flavors meld for 20 minutes or so before mixing again and serving. Store any leftover chutney in a tight-sealing jar in the refrigerator. It will keep for 2 to 3 days and can be used to flavor any leftover curry or other dishes, such as grilled meat or fish.

PESTO

A vibrant green pesto to toss into pasta, spread on a pizza or sandwich, mix into a salad dressing or dip, or use in any of the recipes in this book calling for pesto.

4 cups (1 L) fresh basil leaves, loosely packed

3 medium garlic cloves, sliced

⅓ cup (80 mL) pine nuts, slivered almonds or walnut pieces

½ cup (125 mL) freshly grated Parmesan cheese (not the dried powdered stuff)

2 Tbsp (30 mL) freshly grated Romano pecorino cheese (see Eric's Options)

1 cup (250 mL) olive oil

preparation time • 10 minutes
cooking time • none
makes • about 1¼ cups (310 mL)

ERIC'S OPTIONS
If you prefer to use just Parmesan cheese, simply replace the quite tangy pecorino with 2 Tbsp (30 mL) more of it. The pesto could also be frozen in an ice cube tray. When frozen, unmold, transfer to a freezer bag or container, and keep frozen until needed.

Place all ingredients, except oil, in a food processor and pulse until chopped. Add the oil and process until well blended. Add a bit more oil if you find the pesto too thick. Refrigerate the pesto in a tightly sealed jar with a skim of olive oil on top. It will keep about 10 days.

TZATZIKI SAUCE

Serve this tangy, Greek-style sauce as a dip, spread or condiment for some of the entrées in this book, such as Lemony Lamb Chops with Artichokes, Olives and Mint (page 301).

½ medium English cucumber

1¼ cups (310 mL) thick, Greek-style yogurt

2 Tbsp (30 mL) chopped fresh mint

1 medium garlic clove, minced

½ tsp (2 mL) finely grated lemon zest

1 Tbsp (15 mL) lemon juice

salt and white pepper to taste

preparation time • 10 minutes
cooking time • none
makes • about
1½ cups
(375 mL)

ERIC'S OPTIONS
If you prefer its taste, instead of mint, use chopped fresh dill, to taste, in the sauce.

Set a large sieve over a bowl. Coarsely grate the cucumber into the sieve. Press on the cucumber and squeeze out as much liquid as you can. Discard the liquid.

Place the squeezed cucumber in a second bowl. Mix in the remaining ingredients. Cover and refrigerate until needed. Can be made several hours before needed.

BAKED GOODS AND DESSERTS

SODA BREAD with AGED CHEDDAR, OATS and GREEN ONIONS

This delicious loaf is flecked with fiber-rich oats, tangy cheese and fresh-tasting green onion. Use it for sandwiches or serve it alongside any of the soups or saucy entrées in this book.

preparation time • 15 minutes
cooking time • 30 minutes
makes • 1 loaf

1¼ cups (310 mL) all-purpose flour

1¼ cups (310 mL) whole wheat flour

½ cup (125 mL) large-flake oats

1½ tsp (7 mL) baking soda

½ tsp (2 mL) salt

¼ cup (60 mL) cold butter, cut into small cubes

1½ cups (375 mL) grated aged cheddar cheese

2 green onions, thinly sliced

1⅓ cups (325 mL) buttermilk (see About Buttermilk on page 367)

ERIC'S OPTIONS
Instead of cheddar, use another type of tangy cheese in this recipe, such as Gouda or Jarlsberg. Instead of green onion, give the loaf an herbaceous taste by mixing in 2 to 3 tsp (10 to 15 mL) of chopped fresh rosemary.

Preheat the oven to 425°F (220°C). Line a baking sheet with parchment paper.

Place the flours, oats, baking soda and salt in a bowl and whisk well to combine. With your fingers, 2 forks or a pastry cutter, work the butter into the flour mixture until thoroughly distributed. Mix in the cheese and green onions. Gently mix in the buttermilk until a loose dough forms, then turn it onto a floured surface. With floured hands, shape the dough into a round loaf about 6 inches (15 cm) in diameter. Place the loaf on the prepared baking sheet. With a floured knife, cut a shallow *x* into the center of the loaf. Bake the soda bread for 30 minutes, or until the loaf springs back when touched lightly in the very center.

ABOUT BAKING POWDER and BAKING SODA

Baking soda and baking powder are used to leaven baked goods, both savory and sweet, such as muffins, biscuits and cookies.

Baking soda is pure sodium bicarbonate and requires an acidic ingredient, such as buttermilk, lemon juice or yogurt, to activate a chemical reaction that produces bubbles and causes baked goods to rise. The reaction begins as soon as the baking soda is moistened, so act quickly and get your baking into the oven as soon as possible. If you don't do this, the rising action will occur in the mixing bowl, not in the oven, which may cause your baked good to deflate and be sunken after cooking.

Baking powder was invented to enable bakers to leaven dough that did not contain an acidic ingredient. It contains baking soda, a drying agent—usually cornstarch—and, most importantly, an acid, such as cream of tartar. With a built-in acidic ingredient it can be used in any baking recipe that needs a lift.

You may wonder why some recipes call for baking powder and baking soda, or why some recipes ask for what some home bakers deem too much baking powder. Baking powder's baking soda content is diluted with other ingredients, so it does not have the same leavening strength as baking soda. That's why in some recipes, particularly those for dense and moist baked goods, a generous amount of baking powder is used or, in some cases, some baking soda is added along with the baking powder.

When using baking powder and baking soda, it's important to whisk them thoroughly into the flour before they are moistened. This will help distribute them equally in the dough and ensure the baked good rises evenly.

If your baking soda or baking powder has been in your cupboard for some time, test it to see if it still works before you use it. To test baking soda, mix ¼ tsp (1 mL) with 2 tsp (10 mL) vinegar. Baking soda that is still good should bubble immediately. To test baking powder, mix 1 tsp (5 mL) with ½ cup (125 mL) hot water. If the baking powder is still good, this mixture should bubble immediately.

CORNBREAD with PEPPER JACK CHEESE

This moist and marvellous cornbread is spiced up with chili pepper–flavored cheese. It makes a nice side dish for such things as scrambled eggs, soups, chili and ribs.

soft butter or vegetable oil spray for greasing

1 cup (250 mL) cornmeal

1 cup (250 mL) all-purpose flour

¼ cup (60 mL) sugar

1 Tbsp (15 mL) baking powder

½ tsp (2 mL) salt

½ cup (125 mL) grated chili pepper–flavored
    Monterey Jack cheese (see Note)

1 large egg

1¼ cups (310 mL) buttermilk

¼ cup (60 mL) melted butter

Preheat the oven to 350°F (175°C). Lightly grease an 8½- × 4½-inch (1.5 L) loaf pan.

Place the cornmeal, flour, sugar, baking powder and salt in a medium bowl and whisk until thoroughly combined. Stir in the cheese.

Break the egg into a clean medium bowl and beat until the yolk and white are well blended. Mix in the buttermilk and melted butter. Add the wet ingredients to the dry and mix until just combined. Spoon the batter into the prepared pan. Bake for 50 minutes, or until the loaf springs back when touched gently in the very center. Cool the loaf on a baking rack for 15 minutes, then turn it out onto a cutting board. Slice and serve.

preparation time • 20 minutes
cooking time • 50 minutes
makes • 1 loaf

NOTE
Monterey Jack cheese flavored with spicy chilies, such as habañero or jalapeño peppers, is available in the dairy case of many supermarkets.

ERIC'S OPTIONS
If you don't like spicy cheese, use regular Monterey Jack cheese. To help prevent the loaf from sticking to the bottom of the loaf pan, cut a piece of parchment paper the size of the bottom of the pan. Set the paper in the pan after you've greased it, then spoon in the batter.

To make 12 cornbread muffins, divide and spoon the batter into a well-greased 12-cup muffin tin. Bake at 350°F (175°C) for 18 to 20 minutes, or until a muffin springs back when touched very gently in the center.

BUTTERMILK BISCUITS

I like to make these tasty biscuits fairly small by using a 2-inch (5 cm) cutter. When they're smaller, I don't feel guilty about having two or three of them! When the dough is ready to transfer to the work surface it will be fairly moist. Don't panic and add more flour—on the floured surface and shaped with your floured hands, the dough will attain the perfect consistency. Serve with the soup, stew and baked bean recipes in this book.

2 cups (500 mL) all-purpose flour

2 tsp (10 mL) baking powder

½ tsp (2 mL) baking soda

¼ tsp (1 mL) salt

¼ cup (60 mL) cold butter, cut into small cubes

1 cup (250 mL) buttermilk (see About Buttermilk on page 367)

1 large egg, beaten

Preheat the oven to 425°F (220°C). Line a baking sheet with parchment paper. Place the flour, baking powder, baking soda and salt in a bowl and whisk to combine. With your fingers, 2 forks or a pastry cutter, work the butter into the flour mixture until thoroughly distributed. Gently mix in the buttermilk until a loose dough forms, then turn it onto a floured surface. With floured hands, shape the dough into a ball, then flatten it into a 1-inch (2.5 cm) thick disk. Cut the dough into 2-inch (5 cm) rounds and place them on the baking sheet. (Gather up the scraps of dough, and press and cut into biscuits as well.) Brush the top of each biscuit lightly with beaten egg. Bake in the middle of the oven for 12 to 14 minutes, or until puffed and golden.

preparation time • 20 minutes
cooking time • 12–14 minute
makes • 20–24 biscuit

ERIC'S OPTIONS
For cheese biscuits, mix 3 oz (90 g) of grated cheddar cheese into the flour mixture before adding the buttermilk. Serve any leftover biscuits with jam and butter for breakfast the next day.

ABOUT BUTTERMILK

In the days when butter was still churned at home, buttermilk was the liquid left behind after the butter was made. It looked kind of like a lighter version of today's skim milk and had a slightly sour taste from the ripe cream used to make the butter.

Today, the buttermilk you see for sale in supermarkets is, of course, made at a commercial dairy. A special bacteria is added to low- or no-fat milk, giving it a slightly thickened texture and tangy flavor.

The acidity in buttermilk makes it an excellent ingredient for quick breads, such as biscuits and scones, as the baking soda often used in these items requires an acidic ingredient to activate it. It can also be used in marinades, such as those for chicken or calamari dishes that get coated in seasoned flour and then fried. Tangy buttermilk is also great mixed into mashed potatoes, such as Buttermilk Mashed Yukon Gold Mashed Potatoes (page 349).

ROSEMARY FLATBREAD

Why take the time to make your own flatbread when it is so easy to buy one ready-made? Well, try it once and you'll be surprised not only at how quickly and inexpensively the dough can be made, but at how wonderful the house smells and the bread tastes.

¾ cup (185 mL) lukewarm (not hot) water

1 tsp (5 mL) instant yeast

½ tsp (2 mL) sugar

1½ cups (375 mL) all-purpose flour, plus some for the table and kneading

2 tsp (10 mL) chopped fresh rosemary

¼ tsp (1 mL) salt

1 Tbsp (15 mL) olive oil, plus some for the bowl and baking sheet

coarse sea salt and coarsely ground black pepper to taste

preparation time	•	20 minutes (plus 60 minutes rising time)
cooking time	•	18–20 minutes
makes	•	1 loaf

ERIC'S OPTIONS
Instead of fresh rosemary, you could use ½ tsp (2 mL) of dried rosemary. Or flavor the dough Indian-style, with ½ tsp (2 mL) whole cumin seeds instead of rosemary. Add the cumin when you're asked to add the chopped rosemary. Instead of oil, brush the top of the loaf with 1 Tbsp (15 mL) of melted butter. Sprinkle with salt and pepper as described in the recipe, then bake.

Place the water, yeast and sugar in a medium bowl and stir to combine. Combine the flour, rosemary and salt in a second medium bowl. Add the wet ingredients to the dry and mix until the dough clumps together loosely. Transfer the dough to a lightly floured surface. Coat your hands with flour and knead until a smooth dough forms, 3 to 4 minutes.

Place the dough in a lightly oiled bowl. Cover and set in a warm, draft-free place. Let the dough rise and double in size, about 1 hour. When the dough has doubled in size, preheat the oven to 450°F (230°C). Lightly oil a nonstick baking sheet. Set the dough on the prepared baking sheet. Press and stretch the dough into a thin oblong about 10 inches (25 cm) long and 9 inches (23 cm) wide. Brush the top of the dough with the olive oil. Sprinkle with sea salt and pepper. Bake the bread for 18 to 20 minutes, or until puffed and golden.

ELISABETH'S CRANBERRY BREAD

This fine recipe is from my late friend and fellow chef Elisabeth Lawrence. It yields a moist and delicious loaf with tangy, citrus flavors. You can make it any time of year, but I like it best in autumn when fresh cranberries are available.

2 cups (500 mL) all-purpose flour

1 cup (250 mL) sugar

1½ tsp (7 mL) baking powder

½ tsp (2 mL) baking soda

1 tsp (5 mL) salt

¼ cup (60 mL) butter, softened

1 large egg, beaten

1 tsp (5 mL) grated orange zest

¾ cup (185 mL) orange juice

1½ cups (375 mL) fresh or frozen cranberries,
   coarsely chopped (see Note)

1½ cups (375 mL) golden raisins

preparation time	•	20 minutes
cooking time	•	70–75 minut
makes	•	1 large loaf

NOTE
The cranberries can be coarsely chopped with a sharp knife on a large cutting board, or pulsed in a food processor in batches.

ERIC'S OPTIONS
This recipe freezes well; double it and freeze one loaf for another time.

Preheat the oven to 350°F (175°C). Grease a 9- × 5-inch loaf (2 L) pan with vegetable oil spray. Line the bottom of the pan with parchment paper. Sift the flour, sugar, baking powder, baking soda and salt into a large bowl. Cut in the butter until the mixture is crumbly. Add the egg, orange zest and orange juice all at once; stir just until the mixture is evenly moist. Fold in the cranberries and raisins. Spoon the batter into the prepared pan.

Bake for 70 to 75 minutes, or until the loaf springs back when gently touched in the very center with the tip of your finger. Cool in the pan for 5 minutes, then remove the loaf and cool on a baking rack. Cut the loaf into slices about ½ inch (1 cm) thick, and arrange on a decorative plate to serve.

FRESH
PUMPKIN PIE

Pie pumpkins are smaller than the type of pumpkin you would carve for Halloween. They're about the size of a volleyball, but if you were to close your eyes and pick one up you would guess it was much larger because of its weight. The dense, sweet flesh is great for cooking, puréeing and making superb pie. Pie pumpkins are sold at roadside farm stands, farmers' markets and some supermarkets.

one 5½ lb (2.5 kg) pie pumpkin

dough for 2 single pie crusts (see Flaky Pie Dough on page 375)

4 large eggs

3½ cups (875 mL) fresh pumpkin purée

1½ cups (375 mL) evaporated milk

1½ cups (375 mL) packed golden brown sugar

1 tsp (5 mL) ground cinnamon

¼ tsp (1 mL) ground nutmeg

pinch ground cloves

½ tsp (2 mL) salt

1 cup (250 mL) whipping cream, whipped

mint sprigs and pecan halves for garnish (optional)

preparation time	•	60 minutes
cooking time	•	about 3 hours
makes	•	2 pies, 16 servings

ERIC'S OPTIONS
Make the pie crusts and the filling a day before you bake the pies. Cover and refrigerate separately. Give the filling a stir again before pouring into the shells and baking the pies. If time is short, these pies can also be made with an equal amount of canned pumpkin.

To make the purée, preheat the oven to 325°F (160°C). On a secured cutting board, trim off the stem of the pumpkin, and then cut the pumpkin into quarters. Use a paring knife to cut away most of the seeds and stringy bits and remove the rest with a large spoon.

Place the pumpkin in a large roasting pan, skin side down. Pour in cold water to a depth of 1 inch (2.5 cm). Tightly cover and bake the pumpkin 1¾ to 2 hours, or until the flesh is very tender. Uncover and cool to room temperature.

Remove the peel and purée the pumpkin flesh in a food processor. Spoon into a mixing bowl, cover and refrigerate until ready to make the filling.

To make the crusts, unwrap one of the disks of dough and place on a lightly floured work surface. Flour a rolling pin and roll the dough from the center out into a round large enough to fit a 10-inch (25 cm) wide pie plate with a 4-cup (1 L) capacity. Don't push too firmly; let the roller do the work. Turn the dough an eighth of a turn after each roll; this will help create a round shape and at the same time you can make sure the dough is not sticking. Sprinkle additional flour on the rolling pin and under the dough as necessary. When the round of dough is ready, carefully fold it in half and lay it across the center of the pie plate. Carefully unfold it and gently nestle it into the bottom of the plate. Crimp the top edges of the pie to create a finished look and trim off any excess dough from the side of the plate. Repeat with the other disk of dough. Refrigerate until the filling is ready.

When you are ready to prepare the filling, preheat the oven to 425°F (220°C). Beat the eggs in a large bowl until the yolks and whites are well blended. Whisk in the pumpkin, evaporated milk, brown sugar, cinnamon, nutmeg, cloves and salt. Pour the pumpkin mixture into the pie crusts. Bake for 15 minutes. Reduce the oven temperature to 350°F (175°C) and bake for 40 minutes more, or until the pie filling still jiggles slightly in the very center. Cool the pies on a baking rack to room temperature. Serve slices of the pie with a dollop of whipped cream and garnish with a mint sprig and pecan half.

ROASTED GARLIC BREAD

Roasting garlic mellows and sweetens its taste and infuses the olive oil it's cooked in with a heavenly flavor. Once the slices of garlic are roasted, they are mashed in the roasting oil and then both are mixed into softened butter, creating a very tasty spread for bread that's then topped with Parmesan cheese and baked. Double the recipe and serve it with Spaghetti and Meatballs for Eight (page 150).

4 garlic cloves, thickly sliced

1½ Tbsp (22 mL) extra virgin olive oil

½ cup (125 mL) butter, at room temperature

2 Tbsp (30 mL) chopped fresh parsley

eight 1-inch (2.5 cm) slices of Italian bread

freshly grated Parmesan cheese to taste

preparation time	•	10 minutes
cooking time	•	30–32 minute
makes	•	8 pieces

ERIC'S OPTIONS
For an even more dynamic-tasting roasted garlic bread, replace the Italian bread with slices of olive bread.

Preheat the oven to 325°F (160°C).

Place the garlic and olive oil in a small baking dish. Cover and roast for 20 minutes, or until the garlic is tender. Transfer the garlic and oil to a bowl. Mash the garlic into small pieces with the back of a small spoon and let it cool to room temperature. Add the butter and parsley to the garlic and oil and mix until well combined.

Increase the oven temperature to 375°F (190°C). Line a baking sheet with parchment paper.

Spread one side of each bread slice with the roasted garlic butter. Set the bread, buttered side up, on the prepared baking sheet. Sprinkle the top of the bread with Parmesan cheese to taste. Bake the roasted garlic bread for 10 to 12 minutes, or until lightly toasted.

FLAKY
PIE DOUGH

The generous amount of shortening, and a touch of butter, makes an ultraflaky crust.

3 cups (750 mL) all-purpose flour

½ tsp (2 mL) salt

1¼ cups (310 mL) cold vegetable shortening, cut into ½-inch (1 cm) cubes

¼ cup (60 mL) cold butter, cut into ½-inch (1 cm) cubes

1 large egg, beaten with ⅓ cup (80 mL) ice-cold water

preparation time	•	10 minutes
cooking time	•	none
makes	•	dough for 1 double-crust pie or 2 single-crust pies

Combine the flour and salt in a bowl. With a pastry cutter or 2 forks (or with the paddle attachment of your stand mixer), cut the shortening and butter into the flour until well blended. Pour the egg/water mixture into the bowl; gently work it until it forms a loose, moist dough that just holds together. Transfer the dough to a lightly floured work surface. With lightly floured hands, shape the dough into a ball. Cut the ball in half. Press each half into a ½-inch-thick (1 cm) disk. Wrap and refrigerate each disk for 20 minutes before rolling out. If you've refrigerated the dough for more than 20 minutes and the fat in it becomes very firm, let the dough warm at room temperature for a few minutes before rolling it out.

ERIC'S OPTIONS
The dough, if tightly wrapped and kept refrigerated, could be prepared up to 2 days in advance. This dough also freezes well, so if you make a lot of pies, consider making a double batch and freezing the unused dough for another time. If tightly wrapped, the dough will keep up to 2 months in the freezer.

BLACKBERRY and APPLE PIE

Use your favorite homemade or store-bought crust to make this pie.

6 medium apples, peeled, cored and sliced

1 Tbsp (15 mL) lemon juice

2 cups (500 mL) fresh or frozen (partially thawed) blackberries

¼ cup (60 mL) sugar

1 tsp (5 mL) ground cinnamon

¼ tsp (1 mL) ground nutmeg

2 Tbsp (30 mL) all-purpose flour

pinch salt

1 Tbsp (15 mL) butter

one 9-inch (23 cm) deep-dish double pie crust, store-bought or homemade (see Flaky Pie Dough on page 375)

egg wash (1 large egg beaten with 2 Tbsp/30 mL milk or cream)

preparation time • 30 minutes
cooking time • 50 minutes
makes • 8 servings

ERIC'S OPTIONS
For a sweet and crunchy crust, sprinkle the top of the pie with a little sugar before baking. Slightly underripe pears could replace the apples. Raspberries could replace the blackberries.

Combine the apples, lemon juice, blackberries, sugar, cinnamon, nutmeg, flour and salt in a large bowl and gently toss to combine. Do not overmix or you'll crush the blackberries. Spoon the filling into the bottom pie crust, gently packing it in. Dot the top with butter. Brush the edge of the bottom crust with egg wash. Place the top crust on, crimping the edges to seal. Brush the top of the pie with egg wash. Cut a small hole in the center of the pie to allow steam to escape. Refrigerate the pie 20 minutes to firm up the crust before baking.

Preheat the oven to 425°F (220°C). Bake the pie for 20 minutes. Reduce the heat to 325°F (160°C) and cook for 30 minutes more, or until the apples are tender when poked with a thin knife and the filling is bubbling in the center.

FAMILY-SIZED RHUBARB CRISP

This traditional family dessert is given a lift with the addition of orange juice and ginger. A scoop of vanilla ice cream or a dollop of whipped cream makes it even better.

preparation time • 20 minutes
cooking time • 45 minutes
makes • 8–10 servings

THE FILLING

10 cups (2.5 L) sliced fresh or frozen rhubarb

1 cup (250 mL) sugar

1 cup (250 mL) orange juice

1 cup (250 mL) water

2 Tbsp (30 mL) fresh lemon juice

2 tsp (10 mL) cornstarch

1 tsp (5 mL) pure vanilla extract

½ tsp (2 mL) ground ginger

THE TOPPING

2½ cups (625 mL) rolled oats

½ cup (125 mL) packed golden brown sugar

½ cup (125 mL) butter, softened

3 Tbsp (45 mL) all-purpose flour

1 tsp (5 mL) ground cinnamon

¼ tsp (1 mL) ground nutmeg

NOTE
If using fresh rhubarb, you'll need about 10 medium-sized stalks to get the 10 cups (2.5 L) required for this recipe. Cut it into slices about ¾ inch (2 cm) thick.

ERIC'S OPTIONS
Instead of ground ginger, flavor the rhubarb filling with ¼ to ⅓ cup (60 to 80 mL) finely chopped candied ginger, which is sold at most supermarkets. It will add a sweet and spicy taste to the rhubarb filling.

Mix the filling ingredients in a large bowl until well combined. Spoon into a 9- × 13-inch (3.5 L) baking dish. Set an oven rack in the middle position. Preheat the oven to 350°F (175°C). Place the topping ingredients in a medium bowl. Mix well with your fingertips to combine the butter with the other ingredients. Sprinkle the topping evenly over the filling. Bake for 45 minutes, until golden brown and bubbling.

BAKE and FREEZE
CARROT CAKE SQUARES

This recipe is for two cakes, yielding a total of 18 squares that freeze very well. For a quick midweek dessert, pull the required number of squares out of the freezer and thaw at room temperature for about 30 minutes. This moist and delicious cake substitutes applesauce for the usual oil, making it a little bit lighter.

preparation time • 40 minutes
cooking time • 35–40 minute
makes • 18 servings

ERIC'S OPTIONS
Instead of walnut or pecan halves, top each cake square with a bit of lightly toasted, unsweetened shredded coconut. I like a thick layer of cream cheese icing on my carrot. If you don't, cut the ingredients required for the icing in half and spread a thinner layer of icing on each cake.

THE CAKE

1½ cups (375 mL) sugar

1 cup (250 mL) unsweetened applesauce

4 large eggs

1 tsp (5 mL) pure vanilla extract

2 cups (500 mL) all-purpose flour

2 tsp (10 mL) baking soda

2 tsp (10 mL) baking powder

½ tsp (2 mL) salt

2 tsp (10 mL) ground cinnamon

¼ tsp (1 mL) ground nutmeg

3 cups (750 mL) grated carrot

1 cup (250 mL) chopped walnuts or pecans

⅔ cup (150 mL) raisins

THE ICING

one ½ lb (250 g) brick cream cheese,
    at room temperature

½ cup (125 mL) butter, at room temperature

3 cups (750 mL) icing sugar

18 walnut or pecan halves

Continued . . .

BAKE and FREEZE
CARROT CAKE SQUARES (*continued*)

THE CAKE

Place an oven rack in the middle position. Preheat the oven to 350°F (175°C). Cut two 8- × 12-inch (20 × 30 cm) pieces of parchment paper and fit them into the bottom and up 2 sides of two 8-inch-square (2 L) baking pans. (The parchment paper extending up the sides will help lift the cake out of the pan once it's baked.)

Combine the sugar, applesauce, eggs and vanilla in a large bowl and beat well. Whisk the flour, baking soda, baking powder, salt, cinnamon and nutmeg together in a separate bowl. Add the flour mixture to the applesauce mixture and stir until just combined. Stir in the carrot, chopped nuts and raisins. Spoon the batter into the prepared pans, dividing it evenly. Bake for 35 to 40 minutes, or until a cake tester inserted into the middle of the cake comes out clean. Cool the cake on a rack to room temperature.

THE ICING

Place the cream cheese and butter in a bowl and beat until thoroughly combined and lightened. Beat in the icing sugar until fully incorporated. Lift the cakes out of their pans. Spread the icing on the tops of both cakes. Chill the cake in the refrigerator until the icing is set before cutting into squares.

Cut each cake into 9 squares and top each square with half a walnut or pecan. Wrap each piece individually in wax paper or plastic wrap, place in an airtight container and freeze until needed.

TEN BAKING TIPS

1. Read the recipe carefully before starting.

2. Get organized by assembling the bowls, pans and utensils you will need.

3. Measure ingredients carefully; baking recipes are formulas and if you don't follow them exactly things can go terribly wrong. Use standard measuring cups and spoons (not the spoon you use to stir your coffee). Use level measurements, not heaped or almost-full tsp, cups, etc.

4. If your recipe says the ingredient, such as butter, must be at room temperature or should be cold, be sure that it is. If not, the recipe may not turn out as planned.

5. Don't make substitutions unless the recipe says you can. If it calls for a large egg use a large egg, not a small one. Unlike non-baked dishes, such as chili or soup, improvising and substituting the ingredients called for could ruin your recipe.

6. Focus on the job at hand. Distractions, such as answering the phone during a critical point in the recipe, can lead to mistakes.

7. Use the type of pan specified in the recipe. If you use one that's too small or too large, the cooking time will be thrown off and the baked good may be underdone or overbaked.

8. When shaping cookies, make sure all are uniform in thickness and size. If not, some will be done before the others are cooked through.

9. To promote even baking, place baking pans as near to the center of the oven as possible.

10. Don't place baking pans directly over one another. This can shield the top or bottom of the pan from the heat source and can cause uneven baking.

MOIST and DELICIOUS ONE-PAN CHOCOLATE CAKE

How easy can it get? This is a family-style cake that you mix right in the baking pan!

preparation time • 10 minutes
cooking time • 35–40 minutes
makes • 9 servings

1¼ cups (310 mL) all-purpose flour

1 cup (250 mL) sugar

¼ cup (60 mL) cornstarch

¼ cup (60 mL) unsweetened cocoa powder

1 tsp (5 mL) baking soda

½ tsp (2 mL) ground cinnamon

½ tsp (2 mL) salt

1 cup (250 mL) milk

⅓ cup (80 mL) vegetable oil

1 Tbsp (15 mL) lemon juice

1 tsp (5 mL) pure vanilla extract

whipped cream or ice cream (optional)

ERIC'S OPTIONS

For an elegant touch, once plated, decorate the cake with a mix of whole and sliced berries, such as strawberries, raspberries and blueberries.

Place an oven rack in the middle position. Preheat the oven to 350°F (175°C). Place the flour, sugar, cornstarch, cocoa, baking soda, cinnamon and salt in a nonstick 8-inch-square (2 L) baking pan. Mix with a fork or small whisk until well combined. Add the milk, oil, lemon juice and vanilla and mix until well combined. Bake for 35 to 40 minutes, or until a cake tester inserted in the center comes out clean. Cool on a rack for at least 15 minutes before cutting. (It can be served warm or at room temperature.) Serve plain or, if desired, top with a dollop of whipped cream or a scoop of vanilla ice cream.

PUMPKIN CHEESECAKE with MARZIPAN JACK-o'-LANTERNS

A moist, spice-filled cheesecake seasonally decorated with easy-to-make marzipan pumpkins. Marzipan is a paste made with ground almonds and sugar. It can be bought at some bakeries and supermarkets. Making the pumpkins takes some time and effort, but it's fun and can be a family activity.

THE PUMPKINS

½ lb (250 g) marzipan

orange and black food coloring (see Note)

THE CRUST

1¼ cups (310 mL) finely crushed gingersnaps or graham cracker crumbs

⅓ cup (80 mL) melted butter

¼ cup (60 mL) sugar

THE FILLING

1½ lb (750 g) brick cream cheese, softened

1 cup (250 mL) sugar

4 large eggs

one 14 oz (398 mL) can pumpkin

½ tsp (2 mL) pure vanilla extract

1 tsp (5 mL) ground cinnamon

¼ tsp (1 mL) ground cloves

¼ tsp (1 mL) ground nutmeg

Continued . . .

preparation time	•	30 minutes
cooking time	•	about 85 minutes
makes	•	12 servings

NOTE

Orange and black food coloring is available at stores that specialize in baking and decorating supplies. If you can't find them, use a mix of yellow and red food coloring, sold at most supermarkets, to create orange colored marzipan. Instead of black, simply use a color you do have, such as green.

ERIC'S OPTIONS

Cheesecake can be made up to 2 days in advance of serving. If you find that making the marzipan pumpkins is too time-consuming, omit the pumpkins and serve the cheesecake portions with dollops of lightly sweetened whipped cream instead, garnished, if desired, with pecan halves.

PUMPKIN CHEESECAKE with
MARZIPAN JACK-o'-LANTERNS (*continued*)

THE PUMPKINS

Set aside 3 Tbsp (45 mL) of the marzipan for decorating the pumpkins. Color the remaining marzipan orange by kneading drops of orange food coloring into it. Divide into 12 pieces and roll each into a ball. Gently press down on the balls to give them a squat, pumpkin shape. Use a wooden skewer or toothpick to mark in the ribs of the pumpkin.

Color the small piece of marzipan with black food coloring. Flatten it and cut or shape into handles, eyes, mouths and noses to decorate your marzipan pumpkins with. Set the pumpkins on a plate and cover and store at room temperature until needed. These can be made up to 2 days in advance.

THE CRUST

Combine the crust ingredients in a bowl and mix well. Press into the bottom and partially up the sides of a 10-inch (3 L) springform cake pan.

THE FILLING

Preheat the oven to 300°F (150°C). Place 1 rack in the lower third of the oven and another in the middle position. Beat the cream cheese in a bowl until smooth. Gradually beat in the sugar. Beat in the eggs one at a time, scraping the sides of the bowl after each addition. Mix in the pumpkin, vanilla, cinnamon, cloves and nutmeg. Pour the batter into the pan.

Place a shallow pan of water on the bottom rack of the oven; the steam rising from it will help prevent the cheesecake from cracking as it bakes. Set the cake on the rack above the water and bake 85 minutes, or until the center of the cake barely jiggles when the pan is tapped. Cool the cake on a baking rack for 15 minutes, and then run a sharp, thin and wet paring knife around the edges of the cake to a depth of 1 inch (2.5 cm). This will also prevent the cake from cracking as it cools and contracts. Cool the cake to room temperature. Cover and refrigerate in the pan for at least 3 hours.

When you're ready to serve the cake, run a wet paring knife completely around the outer edges of the pan to loosen the cake from the sides. Remove the cake pan's outer ring. Set the cheesecake on a cake plate. Arrange the pumpkins around the top edge of the cake. Slice and serve.

CREAMY COFFEE CHEESECAKE

This rich and creamy cake has a caffeine kick.

THE CRUST

1¼ cups (310 mL) graham cracker or chocolate cookie crumbs

⅓ cup (80 mL) melted butter

¼ cup (60 mL) sugar

2 Tbsp (30 mL) cocoa

THE FILLING

1½ lb (750 g) brick cream cheese, softened

1 cup (250 mL) sugar

3 large eggs

1 Tbsp (15 mL) instant coffee granules

2 Tbsp (30 mL) boiling water

1 tsp (5 mL) vanilla extract

preparation time	•	20 minutes
cooking time	•	60 minutes
makes	•	8 servings

ERIC'S OPTIONS
If desired, garnish wedges of the cake with a dollop or piped spiral of whipped cream. Top the whipped cream with a little shaved dark chocolate or a few chocolate-coated espresso beans.

To make the crust, preheat the oven to 300°F (150°C). Combine the crust ingredients and press into the bottom and partially up the sides of a 10-inch (25 cm) springform cake pan.

To make the filling, beat the cream cheese until smooth. Gradually beat in the sugar. Beat in the eggs one at a time, scraping the sides of the bowl after each addition. Combine the coffee with the boiling water and mix to dissolve. Beat it and the vanilla into the cream cheese mixture. Pour the batter into the crust.

To help prevent the cheesecake from cracking, place a pan of water in the bottom of the oven during baking. Bake for 60 minutes, or until the center of the cake barely jiggles when the pan is tapped. Place the cake on a rack and cool to room temperature. To prevent cracking after baking, run a sharp, wet knife around the edge of the cake to a depth of 1 inch (2.5 cm) before refrigerating. Refrigerate for at least 3 hours before unmolding and serving.

MANDARIN CRANBERRY TARTS with GANACHE

Take ganache, a dreamy mixture of melted chocolate and whipping cream, add sweet segments of fresh mandarin orange and tangy cranberries, and you have a dessert that's irresistible and also beautiful to present.

12 frozen 3-inch (8 cm) tart shells

⅓ cup (80 mL) whipping cream

4 oz (125 g) semisweet chocolate, chopped

1 Tbsp (15 mL) orange liqueur

4 mandarin oranges, peeled and separated into segments

¼ cup (60 mL) dried cranberries

icing sugar for dusting

12 small mint sprigs, for garnish (optional)

preparation time • 30 minutes plus chilling time
cooking time • 15 minutes
makes • 12 tarts

ERIC'S OPTIONS

The tarts can be filled with the ganache and refrigerated up to a day in advance of serving. Top with the oranges, cranberries, icing sugar and mint, if using, just before serving. For an even more exotic-looking tart, substitute small slices of fresh fig for half the mandarin orange segments. In summer, omit the oranges and cranberries and top the tarts with summer berries, such as blackberries, blueberries and raspberries.

Preheat the oven to 350°F (175°C). Place the tart shells on a baking sheet and prick each one several times with a fork. Bake until golden brown, about 15 minutes. Cool to room temperature. Remove the foil liners and set the tart shells on a serving tray.

Place the whipping cream in a small pot and bring to a boil. Add the chocolate and orange liqueur and stir until the chocolate is melted and well incorporated. Spoon the ganache into the tart shells, cool to room temperature and then refrigerate until the ganache is set, about 1 hour.

Decorate the tarts with orange segments and dried cranberries. To serve, dust the tarts lightly with icing sugar. Garnish with a mint sprig, if desired.

LEMON LOVER'S CUPCAKES

Lemon zest, lemon juice, lemon glaze and a lemon candy—this is definitely the cupcake for lemon lovers!

THE CUPCAKES

½ cup (125 mL) butter, softened

1½ cups (375 mL) sugar

1 Tbsp (15 mL) grated lemon zest

1 tsp (5 mL) pure vanilla extract

4 large eggs

½ cup (125 mL) fresh lemon juice

⅓ cup (80 mL) milk

2 cups (500 mL) all-purpose flour

1 Tbsp (15 mL) baking powder

½ tsp (2 mL) salt

THE GLAZE

2 Tbsp (30 mL) fresh lemon juice

⅓ cup (80 mL) icing sugar

18 jelly lemon candy slices

18 small mint sprigs (optional)

preparation time • 30 minutes
cooking time • 20–25 minute
makes • 18 cupcakes

ERIC'S OPTIONS
Make orange-flavored cupcakes by replacing the lemon juice, lemon zest and lemon candies with orange juice, orange zest and orange candies.

THE CUPCAKES

Preheat the oven to 350°F (175°C). Line one 12-cup muffin pan, and 6 cups of another muffin pan with paper liners. Place the butter, sugar, lemon zest and vanilla in a bowl and beat until well combined and lightened, about 3 to 4 minutes. Beat in the eggs one at a time. Mix in the lemon juice and milk. Whisk the flour, baking powder and salt together in a second bowl. Gradually mix the flour mixture into the egg mixture until just combined.

Spoon the batter into the baking cups. Bake for 20 to 25 minutes, or until puffed and golden and the top of a cupcake springs back when gently touched in the center. Cool the cupcakes on a baking rack to room temperature before removing them from the pan.

THE GLAZE

Place the lemon juice in a bowl. Whisk in the icing sugar very gradually, stirring constantly to form a smooth mixture. Spread on the tops of the cupcakes. Decorate the top of each cupcake with a lemon candy slice. Let the glaze set. Tent the cupcakes with plastic wrap until ready to serve; can be made up to a day before serving. When ready to serve, arrange the cupcakes on a serving tray and, if desired, garnish each with a small sprig of mint.

ESPRESSO SHORTBREAD

These espresso bean–shaped cookies have a pleasing coffee flavor and a caffeine kick. It's important to chill the cookies before baking. If you don't, the cookies won't hold their bean shape during baking.

preparation time • 20 minutes
cooking time • 15–18 minutes
makes • 20 shortbread

¾ cup (185 mL) all-purpose flour

¼ cup (60 mL) cocoa

½ cup (125 mL) butter, at room temperature

½ cup (125 mL) icing sugar

½ tsp (2 mL) pure vanilla extract

2 tsp (10 mL) finely ground espresso beans

ERIC'S OPTIONS

Make chocolate-dipped espresso shortbread by dipping each baked cookie halfway into a bowl of melted white or dark chocolate. Let the excess chocolate drip away, and then place the cookie on a parchment paper–lined baking sheet. Refrigerate until the chocolate is set.

Line a large baking sheet with parchment paper. In a medium bowl, whisk together the flour and cocoa until well combined. In another bowl, beat the butter, sugar, vanilla and ground coffee beans until lightened and well combined. Mix in the flour and cocoa until a soft dough forms.

With your hands, roll the dough into ¾-inch (2 cm) round balls. Flatten and shape each dough ball into a ½-inch (1 cm) thick oblong and place on the baking sheet, leaving a 2-inch (5 cm) space between each cookie. Using the dull side of a dinner knife, score a deep line lengthwise down the center of each cookie. Chill the cookies in the refrigerator for 20 minutes. Preheat the oven to 300°F (150°C). Bake for 15 to 18 minutes, or until the cookies are slightly firm to the touch and just cooked through.

WHIPPED SHORTBREAD

Unlike traditional shortbread recipes, this dough is pliable, making it easy to shape and use in a variety of ways.

3 cups (750 mL) all-purpose flour

½ cup (125 mL) cornstarch

½ tsp (2 mL) salt

1 lb (500 g) butter, at room temperature

1 cup (250 mL) icing sugar

1 tsp (5 mL) vanilla extract

preparation time • 20–30 minutes
cooking time • 15–18 minutes
makes • 48–60 cookies depending on the size

ERIC'S OPTIONS
You can make an assortment of shortbread from one batch of dough by dividing it in two or three pieces and following the suggestions in Shaping and Flavoring Shortbread Dough (see page 396).

Preheat the oven to 325°F (160°C). Sift the flour, cornstarch and salt together in a bowl. In a separate bowl, cream the butter and sugar until quite light. Mix in the vanilla. Gradually add the flour mixture and beat until smooth. Pipe or shape the cookies as suggested on page 396. Place on nonstick or parchment paper–lined cookie sheets, spacing them about 1 inch (2.5 cm) apart. Bake until very pale golden in color, about 15 to 18 minutes depending on the thickness. Place the sheets on a rack and allow the cookies to completely cool before removing and storing in a tightly sealed jar or tin.

SHAPING and FLAVORING SHORTBREAD DOUGH

ROLLED AND DECORATED
Chill the dough for 30 minutes. Roll out on a lightly floured surface to ¼ inch (6 mm) thick. Use cookie cutters to create various shapes. Before baking decorate, if desired, with whole or half nuts, silver balls, colored sugar, chocolate chips, candies or candied fruit.

PIPED
Place the dough in a piping bag fitted with a large star tip. Pipe into small rounds or fingers. Chill for 20 minutes before baking. If desired, make a small indentation in the center of the rounds before baking and fill with jam or jelly after baking. Or dip one end of each finger in melted chocolate after baking.

RUM AND CURRANT
Soak ½ cup (125 mL) currants in rum overnight. Drain well. (Reserve the rum for another use, such as Rum-Glazed Fresh Pineapple Rings on page 412). Mix the currants into half the dough. Roll into small balls and bake. If desired, coat in icing sugar, cocoa or cinnamon sugar when cool.

CHOCOLATE CHIP
Mix ½ cup (125 mL) semisweet chocolate chips into half the dough. Proceed as for rum and currant shortbread.

NUT CRESCENTS
Mix ½ cup (125 mL) finely chopped nuts, such as pecans, walnuts or hazelnuts, into half the dough. Lightly flour your hands and form the dough into small crescent shapes. When baked and cooled, dust with icing sugar or cocoa.

COCOA BROWNIE SQUARES

The sweetness of these dense, chocolatey brownies is balanced by a light dusting of bitter-tasting cocoa powder.

1½ cups (375 mL) all-purpose flour

¾ cup (185 mL) cocoa powder, plus some for dusting

½ tsp (2 mL) baking powder

1 cup (250 mL) pecan pieces

1¾ cups (435 mL) sugar

1 cup (250 mL) butter, melted

2 tsp (10 mL) pure vanilla extract

2 large eggs

preparation time • 15 minutes
cooking time • 18–20 minutes
makes • 48 pieces

ERIC'S OPTIONS
Use chopped walnuts instead of pecan pieces. For a sweeter brownie, dust the top with icing sugar instead of cocoa. Bake and cut these brownies in advance and freeze in a single layer in an airtight container for up to 1 month. When ready to eat, take the brownies out, thaw, dust with cocoa and serve.

Preheat the oven to 350°F (175°C). Cut a 13- × 13-inch (33 × 33 cm) piece of parchment paper to fit the bottom and up 2 of the 4 sides of a 9- × 13-inch (3.5-L) baking pan. (The parchment paper extending up the sides of the pan will later be used as handles to lift the brownie out of the pan once baked.) Sift the flour, cocoa and baking powder into a bowl. Mix in the pecans and set aside. In another bowl, beat the sugar, butter and vanilla until well combined. Beat in the eggs, 1 at a time. Mix the dry ingredients into the wet until just combined. Spoon and spread the batter into the prepared pan. Bake for 18 to 20 minutes or until a toothpick inserted into the center of the brownie comes out clean. Cool the brownie on a baking rack to room temperature; cover and refrigerate for at least 2 hours. When fully chilled, run a paring knife around the outer edges of the brownie to separate from the pan. Hold on to the parchment paper above the brownie and carefully lift it out of the pan and onto a cutting board. Dust the top of the brownie square lightly with sifted cocoa powder. Cut into 48 squares, arrange on a platter and serve.

ALMOND CRANBERRY BISCOTTI

These crunchy cookies are great for dunking in coffee or tea.

⅓ cup (80 mL) butter

¾ cup (185 mL) sugar

2 eggs

½ tsp (2 mL) almond extract

½ tsp (2 mL) vanilla extract

1 tsp (5 mL) grated orange zest

2¼ cups (560 mL) all-purpose flour

2 tsp (10 mL) baking powder

¼ tsp (1 mL) salt

½ cup (125 mL) whole almonds, lightly toasted
(see Note) and coarsely chopped

¼ cup (60 mL) dried cranberries

1 large egg white, beaten

sugar for sprinkling on top

preparation time • 40 minutes
cooking time • 40 minutes
makes • 24–30 cookie

NOTE
To toast the almonds, place them in a single layer in a small baking pan. Bake in a 350°F (175°C) oven for 10 minutes, or until lightly toasted.

ERIC'S OPTIONS
Substitute unsalted, shelled pistachios for the almonds. Coarsely chop them before adding them to the dough. Use dried blueberries, raisins or currants instead of dried cranberries.

Preheat the oven to 350°F (175°C). Beat the butter and sugar until light. Beat in the eggs, extracts and orange zest. Sift the flour with the baking powder and salt. Beat the dry mixture into the butter mixture. Mix in the almonds and cranberries. Divide the dough in half and place on a lightly floured work surface. Shape and knead each half into a smooth, oval-shaped log about 12 inches (30 cm) long and 2½ inches (6 cm) wide. Place the logs on a large, nonstick or parchment paper–lined baking sheet. Brush the tops with beaten egg white and sprinkle with a little sugar. Bake for 20 minutes, or until a light golden brown.

Carefully lift from the baking sheet and cool on a rack for 5 minutes. Carefully lift from the rack and place on a cutting board. With a serrated knife, slice the logs on a slight diagonal into ½-inch (1 cm) slices. Lay the slices flat on the baking sheet. Return to the oven and bake for 10 minutes. Turn and bake for 10 minutes more. Cool the cookies completely on a baking rack. Store in a tightly covered container for up to 3 weeks.

EASY-ROLL GINGER COOKIES

The key to these cookies is the soft and pliable dough, which makes them quick and easy to roll. It's difficult to eat just one of these pleasingly spicy and moist-in-the-middle cookies. It's best to have a stand mixer to make them (see Note).

1¾ cups (435 mL) all-purpose flour

¾ tsp (4 mL) baking soda

2 tsp (10 mL) ground ginger

pinch ground cloves

⅓ cup (80 mL) butter, at room temperature

1 cup (250 mL) sugar

1 large egg

1 tsp (5 mL) white vinegar

¼ cup (60 mL) molasses

Place an oven rack in the middle position. Preheat the oven to 325°F (160°C). Line 2 large baking sheets with parchment paper.

Place the flour, baking soda, ginger and cloves in a bowl and whisk to combine. Place the butter and sugar in the bowl of your stand mixer and beat until light and well combined, about 3 to 4 minutes. Beat in the egg, vinegar and molasses. Add the flour mixture and beat until just combined. Roll the dough into 1-inch (2.5 cm) balls and place on the baking sheets, spacing them about 2 inches (5 cm) apart. Bake, 1 sheet at a time, for 15 minutes. Cool on a rack, then store in an airtight container at room temperature for up to 2 weeks.

preparation time	•	20 minutes
cooking time	•	15 minutes per cookie sheet
makes	•	30 cookies

NOTE
If you don't have a stand mixer, you could vigorously beat the cookie dough with a large wooden spoon. Hand-held electric mixers don't work well with this batter; the beaters are too closely spaced and don't do a good job of pulling the dough together into a soft and pliable form.

ERIC'S OPTIONS
These make delicious ice cream sandwiches: simply put a scoop of vanilla ice cream between 2 ginger cookies, press together and freeze until the ice cream is solid again. To store, wrap the sandwich in plastic wrap and keep frozen until you're ready to serve them.

TIPS FOR MAKING COOKIES

Invest in good-quality baking sheets that promote even baking. Baking sheets—also called cookie sheets—come in a variety of sizes, but buy larger ones so your cookies will have ample room to spread as they bake. The ones used when creating the recipes for this book were 13 × 18 inches (33 × 45 cm). For easy cleanup, line the sheets with parchment paper.

Read the recipe and make sure you have everything required. You don't want to be driving to the store for a missing ingredient while the unbaked batter languishes on your countertop.

Measure the ingredients carefully, using standard measuring spoons and cups and making sure your measurements are level, not heaped or almost full. Baking recipes are formulas, and if you're too far off the mark when measuring, you could end up with cookies that are flat and thin instead of puffed and plump, for instance.

Chill butter-rich cookies in the refrigerator for 20 to 30 minutes before baking. If you bake them right after rolling, the room-temperature butter, warmed even more during shaping, can melt and seep out of the cookies before the flour and other ingredients get a chance to set.

Bake cookies in the middle of the oven. If the rack is in the lower part of the oven they may burn on the bottom before they're baked. If it's in the upper half, the tops of the cookies may become overly brown before the cookie is baked through.

OATMEAL COOKIES with MIXED FRUIT and PECANS

The oats, fruit and nuts in these cookies provide ample energy for tossing the Frisbee several hundred times or making countless dives into the lake.

1 cup (250 mL) butter, softened

1 cup (250 mL) packed golden brown sugar

2 large eggs

1 tsp (5 mL) pure vanilla extract

1 tsp (5 mL) ground cinnamon

pinch ground nutmeg and cloves

½ tsp (2 mL) salt

½ tsp (2 mL) baking soda

3 cups (750 mL) quick-cooking oats

1 cup (250 mL) all-purpose flour

½ cup (125 mL) dried cranberries

½ cup (125 mL) golden raisins

½ cup (125 mL) pecan pieces

¼ cup (60 mL) currants

¼ cup (60 mL) unsweetened coconut flakes

preparation time	•	20 minutes
cooking time	•	15 minutes per cookie sheet
makes	•	30 cookies

ERIC'S OPTIONS
These cookies freeze well in a tightly sealed container. If time allows, make a double batch and freeze the extras. If you're taking them to a picnic, they should thaw by the time you're ready to serve them.

Preheat the oven to 350°F (175°C). Line two 13- × 18-inch (33 × 45 cm) baking sheets with parchment paper. Beat the butter and brown sugar in a bowl until well combined and lightened. Beat in the eggs. Mix in the vanilla, cinnamon, nutmeg, cloves, salt and baking soda. Add the oats, flour, cranberries, raisins, pecans, currants and coconut and mix until well combined. Roll the dough into 1½-inch (4 cm) balls and place on the baking sheets, spacing the cookies about 2 to 3 inches (5 to 8 cm) apart. Press the balls into ½-inch-thick (1 cm) disks. Bake the cookies, one sheet at a time, for 15 minutes, or until light golden and cooked through.

PEANUT BUTTER COOKIES

Classic cookies—moist, melt-in-your-mouth treats great for dunking into milk.

1¼ cups (310 mL) all-purpose flour

¾ tsp (4 mL) baking soda

½ tsp (2 mL) baking powder

¼ tsp (1 mL) salt

½ cup (125 mL) sugar

½ cup (125 mL) packed golden brown sugar

½ cup (125 mL) peanut butter

¼ cup (60 mL) vegetable shortening

¼ cup (60 mL) butter, at room temperature

1 large egg

preparation time	•	20 minutes
cooking time	•	13–15 minutes per cookie sheet
makes	•	24 cookies

ERIC'S OPTIONS
Make peanut butter chocolate chip cookies by mixing ¾ cup (185 mL) of chocolate chips into the batter before rolling.

Line 2 large baking sheets with parchment paper. Whisk the flour, baking soda, baking powder and salt together in a bowl. Place the sugar, brown sugar, peanut butter, shortening, butter and egg in a large bowl and beat until well combined. Add the flour mixture to the peanut butter mixture and beat until well combined.

Lightly flour your hands and roll the dough into 1½-inch (4 cm) balls. Place on the baking sheets, spacing them about 3 inches (8 cm) apart. Slightly flatten the cookies with a floured fork. Chill the cookies in the refrigerator for 30 minutes.

Place an oven rack in the middle position. Preheat the oven to 375°F (190°C). Bake the cookies, 1 tray at a time, for 13 to 15 minutes, until light golden brown. Cool on a rack, then store in an airtight container at room temperature for up to 2 weeks.

WHOLE WHEAT CHOCOLATE CHIP COOKIES

Whole wheat flour adds fiber to this version of one of the world's favorite cookies.

1¼ cups (310 mL) whole wheat flour

½ tsp (2 mL) baking soda

1½ cups (375 mL) chocolate chips

½ cup (125 mL) butter, at room temperature

¾ cup (185 mL) packed golden brown sugar

1 tsp (5 mL) pure vanilla extract

2 large eggs

preparation time	•	20 minutes
cooking time	•	15 minutes per cookie sheet
makes	•	20–24 servings

ERIC'S OPTIONS
If you like nuts, replace ½ cup (125 mL) of the chocolate chips with ½ cup (125 mL) of chopped walnuts or pecans.

Place an oven rack in the middle position. Preheat the oven to 325°F (160°C). Line 2 large baking sheets with parchment paper.

Place the flour and baking soda in a bowl and whisk to combine; stir in the chocolate chips. In another bowl, beat the butter, brown sugar and vanilla until well combined and lightened, about 3 to 4 minutes. Beat in the eggs, one at a time. Add the flour mixture and mix until just combined.

Drop 2 Tbsp (30 mL) amounts of the dough on the baking sheets, spacing them about 3 inches (8 cm) apart. Bake the cookies, 1 sheet at a time, for 15 minutes, or until golden brown. Cool on a rack, then store in an airtight container at room temperature for up to 2 weeks.

CHOCOLATE GUINNESS CAKE

Guinness, the famous Irish beer, adds a rich color to this moist and chocolatey cake.

1 cup (250 mL) butter, cubed

1 cup (250 mL) Guinness beer

2/3 cup (150 mL) cocoa powder

2 cups (500 mL) all-purpose flour

2 cups (500 mL) sugar

1¼ tsp (6 mL) baking soda

1 tsp (5 mL) salt

2 large eggs

½ cup (125 mL) sour cream

cocoa powder or icing sugar for dusting

vanilla ice cream or whipped cream

preparation time • 20 minutes
cooking time • 70–75 minutes
makes • 12 servings

ERIC'S OPTIONS
If serving the cake with whipped cream, make it extra rich by flavoring the whipping cream with a splash or two of Irish cream liqueur.

Place the butter, Guinness and 2/3 cup (150 mL) cocoa powder in a medium pot over medium heat. Cook just until the butter melts, whisking to combine it with the Guinness and cocoa. Remove from the heat. Cool the mixture to room temperature.

Preheat the oven to 350°F (175°C). Lightly grease a 10-inch (3 L) springform cake pan. Cut a circle of parchment paper to fit the bottom of the pan and place in the pan. Whisk the flour, sugar, baking soda and salt in a bowl until combined. Add the beer mixture and beat thoroughly. Add the eggs and sour cream and beat until well combined. Spoon and spread the batter into the prepared pan. Bake 70 to 75 minutes, or until the cake springs back when gently touched in the center. Cool the cake on a baking rack to room temperature.

Unmold the cake and place on a cake plate. Dust the top lightly with cocoa or icing sugar. Serve wedges of cake with a scoop of vanilla ice cream or a dollop of whipped cream.

LEMON BLUEBERRY TARTS

The old favorite, lemon tarts, is taken to new heights with the addition of sweet blueberries. If you enjoy making pastry, by all means use your own (see Flaky Pie Dough on page 375), but the tart shells available in the frozen foods aisle of most supermarkets are a boon to busy cooks.

twelve 3-inch (8 cm) frozen tart shells, thawed

3 large eggs

½ cup (125 mL) fresh lemon juice

½ cup (125 mL) sugar

2 Tbsp (30 mL) melted butter

2 cups (500 mL) fresh blueberries

icing sugar for dusting

preparation time • 25 minutes
cooking time • 25 minutes
makes • 12 tarts

ERIC'S OPTIONS
Instead of blueberries, top the tarts with fresh raspberries, blackberries or a mix of fresh berries.

Preheat the oven to 375°F (190°C) and place a rack in the middle position. Place the tart shells on a parchment paper–lined baking sheet. Poke the bottom of each tart with a fork a few times to prevent the pastry from puffing as it bakes. Bake for 10 minutes. Remove from the oven and cool to room temperature. Leave the oven on.

Place the eggs in a medium bowl and beat until the whites and yolks are well blended. Mix in the lemon juice, sugar and butter until well combined. Pour the mixture evenly into the tart shells, filling them as close to the top as possible. Return the tarts to the oven and bake for 15 minutes, or until the filling is set. Cool to room temperature and then chill in the refrigerator for at least an hour.

Carefully remove the foil liners and place the tarts on a platter. Top each tart with 9 to 12 blueberries, depending on their size. Cover and refrigerate until serving time. (Can be prepared several hours in advance.) Just before serving, lightly dust each tart with icing sugar.

BANANAS FLAMBÉ with BOURBON and PECANS

This classic dessert is given a southern-US style by flambéing the bananas with bourbon instead of rum or brandy, and accenting them with pecans, the only nut tree native to the United States.

preparation time	•	10 minutes
cooking time	•	about 5–6 minutes
makes	•	2 servings

ERIC'S OPTIONS
Sprinkle the bananas with toasted, sliced almonds instead of pecans.

1½ Tbsp (22 mL) butter

2 Tbsp (30 mL) packed golden brown sugar

1 Tbsp (15 mL) orange juice

1 Tbsp (15 mL) fresh lime juice

pinch ground cinnamon

pinch ground nutmeg

2 large bananas, peeled and quartered

1 oz (30 mL) bourbon, warmed

2 Tbsp (30 mL) pecan pieces

vanilla ice cream

Melt the butter in a small skillet over medium-high heat. Stir in the brown sugar and cook until the sugar melts. Add the orange and lime juice and cook, whisking, until a smooth, caramel-like sauce forms, about 1 minute. Mix in the cinnamon and nutmeg. Add the bananas and turn to coat. Add the bourbon, tilt the pan slightly away from you, and very carefully ignite with a long match. Cook until the flames die out, about 1 to 2 minutes. Sprinkle in the pecans. Serve the bananas warm over ice cream.

COCOA PAVLOVA with ORANGE-SCENTED STRAWBERRIES

Light, chocolatey, fruity and very impressive—and the meringue can be made ahead of time!

4 large egg whites, at room temperature

½ tsp (2 mL) cream of tartar

1 cup (250 mL) extra fine (berry) sugar (see Note)

2 Tbsp (30 mL) cocoa powder

1 Tbsp (15 mL) cornstarch

1 tsp (5 mL) pure vanilla extract

1 lb (500 g) fresh strawberries, hulled and sliced

2–3 tsp (10–15 mL) finely grated orange zest

2 Tbsp (30 mL) orange liqueur or fresh orange juice

4 Tbsp (60 mL) icing sugar

1 cup (250 mL) whipping cream

preparation time	•	30 minutes
cooking time	•	90 minutes plus oven cooling time
makes	•	8 servings

NOTE
The finely granulated texture of extra fine (berry) sugar means it dissolves easily, which is why it's great for meringues. It's sold in small bags at most supermarkets.

ERIC'S OPTIONS
Instead of just strawberries, top the meringue with a mix of sliced and whole fresh fruit, such as kiwi, mango, blueberries, raspberries and passion fruit.

Preheat the oven to 250°F (120°C). Line a baking sheet with parchment paper. Draw a 9-inch-diameter (23 cm) circle on the parchment paper. I use a 9-inch (23 cm) round cake pan as a guide.

Beat the egg whites and cream of tartar in a large stainless bowl with an electric beater, or in the bowl of your stand mixer, until very soft peaks form. Gradually add the extra fine sugar, whipping constantly, until all is incorporated. Keep whipping until the mixture is thick and glossy and stiff peaks form. Whip in the cocoa, cornstarch and vanilla until well combined.

Spoon the meringue to fit inside the circle drawn on the paper; build up the sides and make a shallow depression in the middle. Bake for 1½ hours. Turn off the heat and let the meringue cool in the oven for 3 hours. (The meringue can be made up to a day in advance. Store it in an airtight container at room temperature.)

Place the strawberries, orange zest, orange liqueur or juice and 2 Tbsp (30 mL) of the icing sugar in a bowl and gently toss to combine. Cover and let the strawberries macerate at room temperature for 20 minutes.

Whip the cream until soft peaks form. Sweeten with the remaining 2 Tbsp (30 mL) icing sugar and beat until stiff peaks form. Spread the whipped cream in the center of the meringue, leaving a 1-inch (2.5 cm) border at the outer edge. Artfully arrange the strawberries on top of the whipped cream. Drizzle with any juices left in the bowl. Serve immediately.

RUM-GLAZED FRESH PINEAPPLE RINGS

Rum, butter and spice combine to make fresh pineapple more splendid than it already is.

4 slices peeled and cored fresh pineapple, cut 1½ inches (4 cm) thick

2 Tbsp (30 mL) melted butter

1 lime, juice of

2 oz (60 mL) dark rum

½ cup (125 mL) lightly packed brown sugar

¼ tsp (1 mL) ground nutmeg

½ tsp (2 mL) ground cinnamon

4 scoops vanilla ice cream

4 fresh mint sprigs

preparation time • 10 minutes
cooking time • 15–20 minutes
makes • 4 servings

ERIC'S OPTIONS
To enhance the tropical taste, try ginger or macadamia nut ice cream.

Preheat the oven to 450°F (230°C). Place the pineapple rings in a single layer in a shallow baking dish just large enough to hold them. Combine the butter, lime juice and rum in a small bowl. Spoon over the pineapple. Combine the brown sugar, nutmeg and cinnamon in a small bowl, then sprinkle over the pineapple. Bake for 15 to 20 minutes, until the pineapple is glazed and just tender. Place the pineapple rings on dessert plates and spoon the pan juices overtop. Place a scoop of vanilla ice cream in the middle of each ring. Garnish with fresh mint sprigs and serve immediately.

COOKING WITH ALCOHOL

Cooking does not evaporate or burn off all the alcohol you add to a dish. Cooking time and the strength of the alcohol determine how much of it is retained. For example, when alcohol is added at the end of cooking, even if it's ignited and then removed from the heat, much of it will remain. If it's simmered for hours, only a trace will be left. The higher the alcohol content of the beverage you add, the more alcohol is left after cooking.

CHAMPAGNE SABAYON

This classic French dessert will bring a light, sweet ending to a romantic meal for two.

2 large egg yolks, at room temperature

¼ cup (60 mL) sugar

¼ cup (60 mL) champagne or other sparkling wine

2 mint sprigs (optional)

ladyfingers or other cookie and strawberries

preparation time • 5 minutes
cooking time • 10 minutes
makes • 2 servings

ERIC'S OPTIONS
For an orange-scented sabayon, replace ¼ of the champagne with orange liqueur, such as Grand Marnier.

Place the egg yolks, sugar and wine in a medium-sized heatproof bowl. Beat with a thin wire whisk until very light and foamy. Place the bowl over, not in, simmering water. Continue beating until the mixture becomes almost as thick as whipped cream, greatly increases in volume, and begins to feel warm. (It should not feel hot.) You may need to remove it from the heat occasionally to reach the correct thickness and temperature. Do not overcook it or you will curdle the eggs. Spoon the sabayon into two martini or other decorative glasses. Garnish each with a sprig of mint, if using. Serve with ladyfingers or other cookie and strawberries for dipping.

PINOT NOIR–POACHED PEARS

Pears poached in wine are an elegant way to close a special dinner. The pears and sauce can be made a day or two in advance and stored in the refrigerator until needed.

preparation time • 30 minutes
cooking time • 25–30 minutes
makes • 4 servings

2 cups (500 mL) Pinot Noir

2 cups (500 mL) water

1 cup (250 mL) sugar

1 cinnamon stick

2 whole cloves

1 tsp (5 mL) vanilla extract

4 slightly underripe medium-sized pears

whipped cream to taste

4 mint sprigs

ERIC'S OPTIONS

Leftover poaching liquid can be saved and refrigerated for another use. I use it to moisten cake pieces when making trifle or to poach other fruits, such as peaches or apricots.

For Italian-style poached pears, substitute Chianti for the Pinot Noir. Replace the whipped cream with a small dollop of mascarpone cheese.

Combine the Pinot Noir, water, sugar, cinnamon, cloves and vanilla in a pot large enough to hold the pears. Place over medium-high heat and bring to a boil, stirring to dissolve the sugar. Peel and core the pears. (A melon baller works well to core the pear from its blossom end.) Trim a little from the bottom of each pear so it will stand up when served. Add the pears to the syrup. Cover the pan, reduce the heat to medium-low and gently simmer, turning them from time to time. Cook until the pears are just tender, about 15 to 20 minutes. Remove from the heat and allow to cool in the syrup, turning them over occasionally. Use a slotted spoon to transfer the pears to a plate, standing them up. Store the pears in the refrigerator until needed.

To make the sauce, boil 1½ cups (375 mL) of the poaching liquid until it is reduced to ½ cup (125 mL). Cool to room temperature and refrigerate until needed. To serve, spoon a little sauce on a dessert plate. Place a pear in the center and spoon or pipe some whipped cream alongside. Garnish with mint and enjoy.

STRAWBERRIES in SPARKLING WINE with HONEY WHIPPED CREAM

Here's a simple dessert that's at its best when local strawberries are in season.

4 cups (1 L) sliced strawberries

1 cup (250 mL) sparkling wine

½ cup (125 mL) whipping cream

liquid honey to taste

4 mint sprigs

preparation time • 15 minutes
cooking time • none
makes • 4 servings

ERIC'S OPTIONS
Replace half the sliced strawberries with a mix of whole berries, such as raspberries, blueberries and blackberries.

Place the strawberries in a bowl. Add the sparkling wine. Cover with plastic wrap and let stand for 30 minutes. Whip the whipping cream until soft peaks form. Flavor with honey, then beat until stiff peaks form. Spoon the strawberries into serving glasses (champagne flutes are ideal). Top with whipped cream and garnish with mint sprigs.

WHITE CHOCOLATE, CRANBERRY and PECAN CLUSTERS

Sweet, festive treats for your family or to package up and give as a gift.

preparation time • 20 minutes
cooking time • 3–4 minutes
makes • 20 clusters

²/₃ lb (350 g) white chocolate, coarsely chopped

1 cup (250 mL) dried cranberries

¾ cup (185 mL) pecan halves

ERIC'S OPTIONS
Instead of white chocolate, use dark or milk chocolate. Replace the pecans with roasted unsalted cashews.

Line a baking sheet with parchment paper and set aside. Melt the chocolate in a heatproof bowl over simmering water. Remove from the heat. Mix in the cranberries and pecans. Drop heaping tablespoonfuls (15+ mL) of the mixture onto the prepared baking sheet. Refrigerate until the clusters are set. Store in a tightly sealed container at cool room temperature. If stacking the clusters, be sure to place a sheet of parchment paper between each layer.

INDEX

ABOUT THE AUTHOR

Eric Akis has been a food writer for the Victoria *Times Colonist* since 1997. His biweekly, recipe-rich columns are published in newspapers across Canada. Prior to becoming a journalist, Akis trained as a professional chef and pastry chef. He worked for 15 years in a variety of operations in Ontario and British Columbia, from fine hotels to restaurants to catering companies.

In 2003, his experiences as a chef and food writer inspired him to create the bestselling *Everyone Can Cook* series of cookbooks, which includes *Everyone Can Cook*, *Everyone Can Cook Seafood*, *Everyone Can Cook Appetizers*, *Everyone Can Cook Midweek Meals*, *Everyone Can Cook for Celebrations*, *Everyone Can Cook Slow Cooker Meals* and now *Everyone Can Cook Everything*.

Eric Akis was born into a military family in Chicoutimi, Quebec, and has lived in six provinces. Victoria, BC, where he moved to in 1992, is now officially home. He lives there with his wife, Cheryl Warwick, also a chef, and their son, Tyler.

To learn more about Eric Akis and his books, visit www.everyonecancook.com.